The Business Behind a Bottle:

An Insider's Guide to Wholesale Alcohol Distribution in the USA

Brand Building Trends, Traditions, and Mechanics to
Leverage Market Growth

By

Ian Pfeffer

This is the first printing of an original work by Ian Pfeffer.

ISBN: 979-8-218-43072-6

Published in the United States of America.

For updates and more content, visit Substack or Graeworks.com.

grae.substack.com

Dedication

To Tanya and Riley.

This book is as much yours as it is mine. The countless nights and weekends spent writing were only possible because of your unwavering support, love, and understanding.

Tanya, your encouragement and belief in me are the foundation for everything I do.

Riley, you are an inspiration and my greatest hope for the future.

Everything I do is for you both.

Acknowledgements

I have had the privilege of learning from many incredible mentors, bosses, colleagues, and friends over the years. Your guidance and the opportunities you provided have shaped the knowledge and insights contained in this book. While I cannot list each of you by name, please know that your contributions have been invaluable.

To the companies and organizations that have been part of my journey, thank you for the experiences and the environment to grow and learn.

Contents

Introduction

What's up?! My name is Ian Pfeffer and I wrote this book about wholesale spirits distribution because for a brief time, I was a terrible wine and spirits supplier. I sold a few cases but the brand manager at my distributor must have wanted to pull his hair out. Often, I emailed multiple times per day, and asked pricing questions without understanding the math. I requested meetings with VP's of sales without a plan to discuss; just because my boss told me to get a meeting. It was dreadful. Back then I couldn't tell you what a depletion allowance was.

Since that time, I became a supplier liaison for a wholesale wine and spirits distributor. I've been in that role for over 6 years at the time of publishing this book. I have learned more about business acumen than I knew there was to learn, and transparently, I had no idea how much work it took just to get the product I was selling from the maker to the drinker.

Whatever penance I owed, has certainly been paid. If you work for a wholesale distributor, regardless of your role, be it portfolio, supply chain, or sales, you'll find something in this book helpful. And if you're on the producer, importer, supplier, distiller, brewer, or winemaker side of this business you will probably find a great number of things helpful here.

For any Malcom Gladwell fans, these pages are my ten thousand hours. I probably captured those 10k in the first 3 years, but either way you slice it, I've learned enough to be able to put these words down with confidence.

So consider this a backstage pass to the world of wholesale alcohol distribution in the USA.

The alcohol industry in the United States is as complex as it is captivating. Behind every bottle sold, there's a saga of logistics, branding, compliance, and market adaptation. Whether it's understanding the nuances of state laws, unraveling the intricacies of the three-tier distribution system, or leveraging the latest consumer trends, this book dives deep into the elements that shape this vibrant sector.

But why should you care? Because in these pages lies more than just information; here, you'll find the heartbeat of an industry. You'll uncover strategies that have propelled brands from obscurity to ubiquity, and you'll explore how tradition and innovation can coexist to create something truly exceptional.

From crafting compelling brand stories to navigating the digital revolution in alcohol sales, "From Barrel to Business" is your guide to prosperity in the competitive landscape of alcohol distribution. You'll get insider insights into collaborations that transformed the industry, case studies of market triumphs, and a peek into the future of alcohol retail.

This book isn't just for industry veterans. It's for the curious, and ambitious. It's for the entrepreneurs looking to carve their niche in a billion-dollar industry, for the retailers seeking to elevate their game, and for anyone fascinated by this beautiful ballet of commerce and culture.

Chapter 1: Choosing a Distributor

This isn't exactly the beginning but let's start here. Choosing a distributor isn't just about who has the shiniest brochure or the most charismatic sales pitch. It's about aligning with a partner who understands your brand's soul, quirks, and aspirations. It's about matching the size and scope of your business. In brand building there are steps, and often you will outgrow your place more than once. In this chapter, we'll explore the key factors to consider when choosing a distributor, ensuring that you find the perfect match for your brand's unique needs.

Overview: The Dance of Distributor Selection

When you're on the hunt for the right distributor, it's essential to have a checklist. Not the kind you hastily scribble on a napkin, but a comprehensive one that covers all the bases. Let's break it down:

Size and Scale: How big is the distributor? Can they provide access to the markets you're eyeing? Their size and reach can determine how effectively they can introduce your brand to new territories.

Marketing Muscle: It's not just about distributing; it's about promoting. What marketing resources can the distributor flex to elevate your brand?

Retailer Relationships: A distributor's rapport with retailers is the bedrock of your market presence. It's like the secret handshake that gets you into the exclusive club.

Financial Fitness: Money talks, and in this case, it speaks volumes about the distributor's ability to support and sustain a partnership with your brand.

Performance Metrics and Accountability: How does the distributor measure success? And more importantly, how will they help you track your brand's progress?

Compatibility and Cultural Vibes: Beyond the numbers and strategies, it's about the vibe. Does your brand's ethos resonate with the distributor's culture?

Reputation: Last but not least, what's the word on the street about the distributor? A solid reputation can be the cherry on top, assuring you of their dedication and professionalism.

In the upcoming articles, we'll take a magnifying glass to each of these factors, giving you a 360-degree view of what to look for in a distributor.

Article Breakdown:

Scale, Scope, and Marketing Resources: Dive into the world of distributor size, reach, and the marketing firepower they bring to the table.

Relationships with Retailers and Services: Unravel the intricacies of distributor-retailer relationships and the bouquet of services that can supercharge your brand's growth.

Distributor's Financial Health and Performance Metrics: A deep dive into the financial robustness of distributors and the metrics that matter.

Compatibility, Cultural Fit, and Turnover: Explore the harmony between your brand and the distributor, and the significance of diversity in their ranks.

Reputation of the Distributor: A look into the importance of a distributor's standing in the market and the role of open communication in nurturing a thriving partnership.

Article 1: Evaluating Distributor's Size, Reach, and Promotional Capabilities

Selecting the right distributor for your brand hinges on comprehending their overall size, reach, and promotional prowess. These elements are pivotal in determining how far your products can go and their potential success trajectory in the marketplace.

Understanding Size and Reach The magnitude and expanse of a distributor you're eyeing are contingent on where your brand currently stands and where you envision it heading. Let's say you're a budding brand, still in its infancy, with a large staff and aspirations of aggressive growth. In such a scenario, a smaller distributor with tentacles spread across various markets might just be your golden ticket. They can serve as a springboard, simplifying your foray into diverse territories. You'll need the personnel thought to support those wider markets. Typically speaking you're going to want to start out with a smaller distributor with far fewer brands than the medium size ones in multiple states. Grab the focused attention in one market and build there first before moving outward.

Once your brand has made it's mark in that first market or region, then will be the time to start eyeing new market conquests. It's worth noting that while behemoth distributors might boast of an extensive account list, they're also juggling a plethora of vendors. This could mean your brand might not always be in the limelight or be their top priority.

By gauging where your brand currently stands and its envisioned trajectory, you can zero in on a distributor that aligns perfectly with your brand's scale and reach aspirations. Think of the number of markets your brand is able to facilitate immediately, and then look at how many states your desired distributor is in. Do they match?

Promotional Capabilities Another linchpin in this equation is the promotional arsenal a distributor brings to the table. In the wholesale distribution landscape, this often boils down to how well you can mesh with their sales brigade. The deeper your engagement with the sales squad, the higher the chances of your brand being the toast of bars, eateries, and retail outlets.

The key to success for any brand is to make it the easiest product to sell. Often this means starting out by making sales for the sales team to demonstrate value and credibility. While a distributor can amplify your brand's market presence, it's imperative you're not solely reliant on them. Your marketing blueprint should ideally dovetail with the distributor's promotional endeavors, forging a synergy that catapults brand recognition and adoption.

Moreover, in today's digital-driven epoch, having a robust online footprint is non-negotiable. Harness the power of social media and other digital avenues to bolster your brand's market presence. Remember, this isn't a solo journey; it's a joint venture where both you and the distributor pool in resources and efforts to achieve the best outcomes.

In essence, zeroing in on a distributor is a monumental decision with far-reaching implications for your brand's journey. By meticulously evaluating their size, reach, and promotional capabilities, you ensure they're in sync with your brand's aspirations. The ultimate aim? To craft a symbiotic alliance that sets your brand on an upward trajectory, maximizing visibility and growth avenues.

Review Questions:

1. Why is understanding a distributor's size and reach crucial when choosing one for your brand?
2. How can a brand's engagement with a distributor's sales team influence its market presence?
3. Why is it essential for brands to have their own marketing strategies in addition to relying on a distributor's promotional efforts?
4. How can a brand's online presence in today's digital age impact its market visibility and acceptance?

Article 2: Strengthening Bonds and Harnessing Additional Services

As a brand owner, understanding the depth of a distributor's ties with retailers and their knack for offering extra services is key to forging a successful alliance. Let's dive into these elements, see how they shape your brand's trajectory, and grasp the extent of duty resting on your plate.

Cultivating Robust Retailer Ties The strength of a distributor's bond with retailers can be the wind beneath your brand's wings or the anchor that drags it down. These ties often act as the doorway to placing your brand on the spotlighted shelves. A distributor with solid connections can champion your brand effectively, amplifying its chances of being the retailer's top pick.

However, it's essential to note that these ties aren't set in stone; they're fluid, changing as salespeople and buyers transition. While a distributor can lay down the red carpet for your brand's debut to retailers, the onus of deepening and preserving these ties falls on you.

In the booze business, thriving relationships aren't just a byproduct of a distributor's clout. As the brand's captain, you're in the driver's seat, ensuring you're in tune with the retailer's pulse. This harmonious dance sets the stage for your brand's flourishing presence in the marketplace.

Tapping into Extra Services When on the hunt for a distributor, it's impossible to turn a blind eye to the bonus services they bring to the table. A distributor isn't merely a conduit connecting your brand to retailers; they can also be your guiding star, navigating you through the maze of market fluctuations, promotional tactics, and sales figures.

Usually, a portfolio manager at the distributor's end takes the reins of these services. A skilled manager can be a goldmine, offering a deep dive into your sales figures, bridging the gap between you and pivotal sales team members, and dishing out wisdom on riding the waves of market trends and tactics.

Some distributors might also roll out the red carpet with educational hubs, category specialists, and key account managers. These perks can be a game-changer, especially for budding brands aiming to carve their niche in an ever changing and competitive market.

External firms (brokers, data collection agencies, etc.) can be your eyes and ears, keeping tabs on your sales and logging detailed notes of your account visits—a crucial toolkit for gauging performance and charting future game plans.

To wrap it up, the strength of a distributor's ties with retailers and the bonus services they dish out are the pillars of your brand's triumph. While the distributor lays the groundwork, remember, the ball's in your court to build and nurture these ties.

Review Questions:

1. True or False: A distributor's bond with retailers can be the determining factor in a brand's success.
2. Which role does a portfolio manager typically play within a distributor's organization?

   a. Handling the financial books of the distributor.
   b. Overseeing the bonus services, offering insights into sales figures, and guiding on market trends.
   c. Building relationships with retailers.
   d. Managing the distributor's online advertising.

3. True or False: The sole responsibility of nurturing and maintaining ties with retailers lies with the distributor.
4. What can third-party firms offer brands in terms of value-added services?

   a. Manufacturing the products.
   b. Designing the product packaging.
   c. Tracking sales and maintaining records of account visits.
   d. Handling customer complaints.

Article 3: Assessing a Distributor's Financial Stability and Performance Metrics

Navigating the landscape of brand-distributor partnerships, two elements stand out as cornerstones: the distributor's financial stability and the performance metrics used to gauge success. Grasping these components can profoundly shape your decision-making and play a pivotal role in the partnership's duration.

Diving into Distributor's Financial Stability While scouting for a distributor, their financial health is sometimes pushed to the backburner, but it's undeniably vital. It mirrors their capacity to champion your brand and hints at their staying power in the industry.

Distributors come in various financial shades—some rooted in family traditions, others buoyed by private funds, and a few backed by global investments. No matter the origin, a distributor's financial steadiness acts as a beacon of trust for your brand's upward journey.

To get a pulse on a distributor's financial footing, it's a good idea to connect with their current partners. Dive into their experiences, uncover any hurdles they've navigated, and unearth the golden moments of their collaboration. If you end up with that distributor, you'll be selling along side these other brands so make friends early and often.

Deciphering Performance Metrics and Holding Accountable Metrics and accountability tools serve as the barometers of a distributor's prowess. The crux, though, is pinpointing the metrics that resonate with where your brand currently stands.

Familiar yardsticks encompass shipment case volumes, the tally of accounts won, or distribution points (PODs). Brands with a more refined approach might keep tabs on distributor earnings or their gross sales, aiming for a sweet spot between escalating case volumes for budget-friendly items and momentary sales surges for limited-edition products.

In the early days, the spotlight should be on accounts secured—how many consumers have been introduced to your brand's universe? How many of them have at least one of your products in their arsenal? As your brand flourishes, the objective should morph towards persuading accounts to adopt a wider range of your products, culminating in pinpointing high-volume accounts.

The goal is to strike a harmony between a handful of high-volume accounts and a vast expanse of individual placements. This approach not only boosts brand visibility but also lays a robust groundwork for brand evolution.

Review Questions:

1. True or False: The financial health of a distributor is often the primary factor considered by brands.
2. Which of the following is NOT a common performance metric for evaluating a distributor?

> a. Shipment case volumes
> b. Number of social media followers
> c. Points of distribution (PODs)
> d. Accounts sold

3. True or False: In the early stages of a brand's development, the primary focus should be on the number of high-volume accounts secured.
4. Why is it beneficial to strike a balance between high-volume accounts and individual placements?

> a. It ensures maximum profit.

    b. It facilitates brand visibility and lays a foundation for brand growth.
    c. It reduces the workload for the distributor.
    d. It guarantees product exclusivity in the market.

Article 4: Compatibility, Cultural Fit, and Embracing Diversity: Crafting Equitable Partnerships

In this segment, we delve into compatibility and cultural alignment between brands and distributors. We'll also shine a spotlight on the pivotal role of diversity, equity, and inclusion (DEI) in shaping these relationships. These elements transcend mere business strategies, touching the very core of shared values, mutual respect, and a commitment to fairness.

Harmony in Compatibility and Cultural Alignment When we talk about compatibility between a brand and its distributor, it's not just about aligning business objectives. It's about resonating visions, parallel work values, and a mutual language of interaction and communication. A distributor in tune with your brand's rhythm comprehends more than just your product; they grasp the essence, the ethos, and the narrative behind it.

So, what does it mean when we say 'cultural fit' in the distributor's context? It's the tone they use when discussing your brand, their sales methodology, and the alignment of their team's values with yours. It's also their commitment to nurturing a diverse and inclusive workspace.

Championing Diversity, Equity, and Inclusion (DEI) The conversation around DEI isn't just trending; it's essential. Whether it's the beverage sector or any other industry, DEI initiatives are the building blocks of a resilient, innovative, and harmonious work environment. A distributor championing these values offers a richer, more diverse perspective, enhancing the way they present and sell your product.

Diversity isn't just a headcount of varied backgrounds. It's the distributor's pledge to inclusivity and fairness. Does their sales approach cater to a diverse clientele? Is their team equipped to engage with a spectrum of accounts, cultures, and backgrounds? Are they inquisitive, continuously learning about their customers and the end consumers? With every passing generation, the beverage industry landscape shifts. The question is, are both you and your distributor evolving with it?

Before you seal the deal with a distributor, it's imperative to ensure their DEI actions speak louder than words. This might mean doing some homework, engaging with their other brand partners, or candidly discussing their DEI strategies and initiatives.

Review Questions:

1.   True or False: Cultural fit with a distributor is solely about having aligned business objectives.
2.   What does a distributor's commitment to DEI indicate?

   a.   Their marketing strategies
   b.   Their approach to sales and understanding of diverse markets
   c.   Their product range
   d.   Their pricing strategies

3.   True or False: A distributor's team diversity is solely about the varied backgrounds of its members.
4.   Which of the following is NOT a way to gauge a distributor's commitment to DEI?

    a. Speaking to their other brand partners
    b. Checking their social media follower count
    c. Discussing their DEI strategies directly
    d. Conducting background research on their initiatives

Article 5: Trustworthiness and Consistency: Navigating Distributor Reputation and Sales Team Continuity

In this concluding chapter lets discuss trustworthiness and consistency, two pillars that should stand tall in the ideal distributor for your brand. We'll shed light on the distributor's standing in the industry and the steadfastness of their sales brigade—factors that can profoundly shape the efficacy of your partnership and the path your brand treads.

Deciphering Distributor's Standing A distributor's reputation is the distilled essence of their past endeavors, ethical compass, dependability, and trustworthiness. So, how does one decode this intangible asset?

A hands-on approach often works best. Engage with the very audience you aim to captivate—your consumers. Frequent the bars, eateries, and liquor stores where you envision your brand. Identify the trendsetters in the business. A casual chat with a bartender about their favorite haunts or a bar manager about their go-to sales reps can offer a goldmine of information about a distributor's professional conduct, service caliber, and market position.

Push the envelope; don't just skim the surface. Probe deeper: How do top-tier distributors nurture their ties? How adept are they at championing their brands? Are they swift problem solvers? The insights gleaned will paint a vivid picture of your potential collaboration.

Assessing Sales Team Continuity The heart and soul of any commendable distributor lies within the sales force. The tenure of its sales personnel often mirrors the distributor's organizational culture and stability.

It's not a mere numbers game; the essence of service often outweighs its duration. A dynamic blend of seasoned sales veterans, with their treasure trove of established connections, and the zest of young Turks, eager to challenge conventions, can be a formidable force. Bear in mind, your rapport with the sales team and your accessibility to them often outweigh their organizational tenure. The onus is on you. Foster those connections. Be approachable. Exude warmth. Be their pillar of support.

A word to the wise—skyrocketing attrition rates can signal underlying organizational turbulence. Yet, in today's fluid job landscape, a certain churn rate is par for the course and not always a cause for alarm.

Charting the Path to a Fruitful Alliance Zeroing in on a distributor is akin to picking a dance partner for a marathon jig; you're on the lookout for someone in sync with your moves, that matches your tempo.

To be clear, this odyssey of acquainting yourself with your distributor isn't a sprint; it's a marathon. From sizing up their reach and offerings, to gauging their commitment to DEI, to finally getting a handle on their reputation and steadiness—each milestone steers you closer to an informed choice.

As we wrap up this series, here's a parting thought: the quintessential distributor for your brand will resonate not just with your product but with your narrative, ethos, and dreams. They'll champion your brand, amplifying its voice in a bustling marketplace. When this symphony of collaboration hits the right notes, your brand will not only sparkle but will also strike a chord with your audience, leaving them yearning for an encore.

Review Questions:

1. Why is understanding a distributor's reputation crucial when choosing a partner for your brand?
2. True or False: The longevity of a distributor's sales team is the sole indicator of its stability.
3. What are some effective ways to gauge a distributor's reputation in the market?
4. How can a brand owner actively contribute to building and maintaining relationships with retailers?
5. Why is it essential for a brand owner to be accessible and supportive to the distributor's sales team?
6. In the context of the article, what does the metaphor "dance partner for a marathon performance" signify?

Chapter 2: Compliance and Regulatory Considerations

In the creative world of the alcohol industry, there's a foundational pillar that keeps everything in check—compliance. For all the suppliers, distributors, and retailers out there, it's clear that adhering to the legalities and industry norms is not just a necessity but a responsibility. It ensures the safe, ethical, and responsible journey of alcoholic beverages from production to the consumer's glass.

This chapter is dedicated to unraveling many of the compliance and regulatory measures that shape our industry. Compliance is more than just a set of rules; it's a commitment to public safety, ethical business practices, and the preservation of the industry's integrity.

Central to our discussion is the complex network of federal and state regulations that dictate our operations. To successfully navigate this maze, one must grasp the nuances of the three-tier system, where suppliers, distributors, and retailers collaboratively ensure that products reach consumers while adhering to regulations. The federal Alcohol and Tobacco Tax and Trade Bureau (TTB) is a key player in this arena, and understanding its directives is paramount for every industry stakeholder.

In this chapter, we'll demystify federal and state regulations, offering insights to streamline compliance. From the nitty-gritty of licensing to the specifics of labeling and packaging, we'll touch upon every facet that requires our diligent attention.

However, remember, while this chapter provides a comprehensive overview, it's not a substitute for legal counsel. With ever-evolving state laws and frequent legislative updates, staying informed and seeking expert advice is crucial.

Article 1 sets the stage discussing federal and state regulations. It's your roadmap to the legal landscape, highlighting the implications of these regulations on daily operations and emphasizing the need for state-specific compliance insights.

Article 2 illuminates the path of licensing and permits. It's not just about getting a license; it's about getting the right one. Every alcohol-related business has its set of requirements, and understanding these is the first step towards impeccable compliance.

Article 3 ventures into the realm of labeling and packaging. Labels are more than brand ambassadors; they're information carriers. By aligning with federal labeling norms and packaging guidelines, we ensure our consumers get accurate and transparent product details.

In Article 4, we shift gears to discuss alcohol taxation and excise duties. It's a topic that directly impacts the financial pulse of our businesses. Here, we'll dissect federal excise tax structures and emphasize the significance of meticulous record-keeping for compliance.

Finally, Article 5 wraps up our journey with a focus on trade practices and advertising norms. While promotions and marketing fuel our industry's growth, it's essential to operate within the boundaries of fairness and transparency, ensuring an even playing field for all.

To reiterate, in our industry, compliance isn't a destination but an ongoing journey. As we navigate the regulatory waters, it's essential to remember that each state has its own set of rules, and this chapter provides a broad overview. However, when in doubt, always turn to legal experts; these laws update and adjust all the time.

Article 1: Navigating Federal and State Regulations in the Adult Beverage Industry

Understanding the Three-Tier System The three-tier system is the foundational structure of the U.S. alcohol distribution industry. It consists of suppliers who create the beverages, distributors who ensure these products are delivered throughout the market, and retailers, including bars and restaurants, who sell these drinks to consumers.

Role of the Federal Alcohol and Tobacco Tax and Trade Bureau (TTB) The TTB is the primary federal regulatory body overseeing the alcohol industry. They establish and enforce rules encompassing aspects such as labeling, advertising, and record-keeping. Compliance with these regulations is crucial for all industry players. Obtaining the appropriate permits, depending on your role in the industry – whether it's brewing, distributing, or selling – is a fundamental requirement.

Navigating State Regulations In addition to federal regulations, each state in the U.S. imposes its own set of laws governing alcohol distribution and sales. These state regulations can vary significantly, making the compliance landscape complex. Understanding and adhering to these state-specific regulations is essential for operating legally and successfully in different markets.

Seeking Expert Guidance Navigating the intricacies of both federal and state regulations can be challenging. Fortunately, there are experts and consultants who specialize in compliance within the alcohol industry. These professionals can provide guidance and support to ensure that your business remains compliant with all relevant regulations.

First lean on your wholesale distributor for answers but of course there are third party companies that specifically handle the compliance pieces here. If you work with companies like Park Street or MHW they have their own divisions dedicated to this task.

Conclusion Compliance in the adult beverage industry is critical to maintaining the integrity and smooth operation of the market. By thoroughly understanding the three-tier system, adhering to TTB guidelines, obtaining the necessary permits, and staying informed about state-specific regulations, businesses can ensure they operate effectively and legally. Navigating these regulatory waters with diligence and precision ensures a stable and compliant business environment.

Disclaimer: This article offers insights based on available resources and industry knowledge. However, for the most accurate and up-to-date information, always consult relevant authorities like the TTB and state Departments of Revenue (DOR).

Review Questions

1. What system is described as the backbone of alcohol distribution?

> a. Two-tier system
> b. Four-tier system

    c. Three-tier system
    d. Single-tier system

2.   Which federal agency is responsible for crafting and enforcing regulations that govern the alcohol industry?

    a. FDA (Food and Drug Administration)
    b. ATF (Bureau of Alcohol, Tobacco, Firearms, and Explosives)
    c. TTB (Alcohol and Tobacco Tax and Trade Bureau)
    d. DOR (Department of Revenue)

3.   State regulations in the alcohol industry are described as:

    a. Being uniform across all states.
    b. Adding a unique flair or variation to the federal regulations.
    c. Being less important than federal regulations.
    d. Being optional for businesses to follow.

Article 2: Licensing and Permit Requirements

Alright, it's time for licensing and permits, the cornerstone of legality in the alcohol industry.

The Alcohol and Tobacco Tax and Trade Bureau (TTB) is the federal authority overseeing this domain. To partake in the alcohol industry, you'll need federal licenses. The alcohol producer permit is essential for those wishing to produce brews, wines, or spirits. For those importing unique flavors from abroad, the importer permit is what you'll need.

Alcohol Producer Permit

- **First Step**: Apply for a Permit: Qualifying with TTB
- **TTBGov** - Qualify with TTB
- **Three-Step Process** – 1. Determine your business. 2. Gather your documents. 3. Apply.
  - TTBGov - Applications[1]
  - TTBGov - What to Gather Before You Apply[2]
  - TTBGov - Permits Online - Customer Support[3]

Importer Permit The TTB's online portal and tutorials are designed for user convenience. For a comprehensive guide on becoming an importer, refer to:

- TTBGov - Permits Online - Customer Support[4]

The regulatory process doesn't end at the federal level. Each state has its unique regulations. It's essential to familiarize yourself with state-specific licensing requirements. This landscape is ever-evolving, so staying updated with local laws, typically available on the department of revenue sites for each state.

Several third-party companies, such as Park Street, MHW, and American Spirits Exchange can assist in this process for a fee. They offer services like TTB label approvals, federal and state licensing, and warehousing arrangements.

Different alcohol-related businesses, like breweries, wineries, or distilleries, have distinct permit requirements. It's vital to understand the specific permits tailored to your business needs.

Navigating the permit acquisition process can seem daunting, but with expert guidance, it becomes manageable. Consult with industry veterans or specialized companies to streamline the process.

While the administrative aspect of the alcohol industry might not be the most glamorous, it's undeniably vital. Federal licenses from the TTB are your foundation but remember to delve into the nuances of state-specific requirements.

Embarking on this journey requires diligence and attention to detail. With the right permits and licenses, you're set to make a significant impact in the alcohol industry. Here's to navigating the complexities of legality and achieving success!

Disclaimer: The information in this article is derived from publicly available sources and industry insights. While accuracy is prioritized, readers should consult relevant authorities like the TTB and state Departments of Revenue (DOR) for the most recent regulations and compliance requirements.

Footnotes

1. TTBGov - Applications
a. https://www.ttb.gov/applications
2. TTBGov - What to Gather Before You Apply
a. https://www.ttb.gov/business-tools/qualify-with-ttb
3. TTBGov - Permits Online - Customer Support
a. https://www.ttb.gov/ponl/customer-support

Review Questions:

1. Which federal agency oversees the licensing and permits for the alcohol industry?

    a. FDA
    b. ATF
    c. TTB
    d. DOR

2. Why is it essential to be familiar with state-specific licensing requirements in the alcohol industry?

> a. Each state has the same regulations.
> b. State regulations are optional.
> c. Each state has its unique set of rules and regulations.
> d. Federal regulations cover all state requirements.

3. What is the primary purpose of the alcohol producer permit?

> a. For importing unique flavors from abroad.
> b. For producing brews, wines, or spirits.
> c. For selling alcohol directly to consumers.
> d. For warehousing and storage of alcohol.

Article 3: Labeling and Packaging Compliance: Unveiling the Art of Transparency

Labels, in this context, are more than just identifiers; they are storytellers, bridging the gap between producers and consumers.

Central to this narrative are the federal regulations that dictate label content. As consumers, people seek transparency in their choices, and labels provide just that. They detail the alcohol content, serving size, health warnings, and even include responsible drinking messages. Beyond these essentials, labels also embody a brand's identity, offering a first impression of the drink within.

Packaging, too, is an art. It's not just about aesthetics; it's about ensuring accuracy and preventing misbranding. The choice of materials, colors, and the bottle's shape all contribute to the consumer's experience.

State-specific regulations add another layer to this narrative. While the federal framework provides the foundation, each state might have its nuances, akin to regional variations in a global brand.

For a deeper dive into alcohol labeling:

- The TTB's **Labeling Resources** offers comprehensive insights[1].
- The **Certificate of Label Approval (COLA)** system, Colas Online, is the portal for label approvals and tracking[2].
- The TTB's **Labeling FAQs** page addresses common queries[3].
- The **Health Warning Statement for Alcohol Beverages** page details mandatory health warnings[4].

In essence, labeling and packaging compliance is about transparency and connection. By adhering to regulations and embracing state-specific requirements, brands can foster trust and ensure their beverages resonate with consumers. Here's to a future where every bottle tells its authentic story, bridging the gap between producers and consumers in the vibrant world of alcoholic beverages.

Disclaimer: This article is based on publicly available data and insights. Readers should consult relevant authorities like the TTB and state DORs for the latest regulations and requirements.

Footnotes

1. TTB's Labeling Resources

a. www.ttb.gov/labeling-resources
2. Certificate of Label Approval (COLA) system, Colas Online
a. www.ttb.gov/colas-online
3. TTB's Labeling FAQs
a. www.ttb.gov/labeling-faqs
4. Health Warning Statement for Alcohol Beverages
a. www.ttb.gov/health-warning-statement

Review Questions:

1. Why are labels considered essential storytellers in the alcoholic beverages sector?
2. How do packaging and labeling together contribute to a consumer's experience?
3. What role do state-specific regulations play in the context of labeling and packaging compliance?

Article 4: Compliance with Alcohol Taxation and Excise Duties

Welcome to alcohol taxation and excise duties. It's riveting! As we delve into this aspect of the alcohol industry, we'll balance the approachability of our discussion with the gravitas that compliance demands.

Understanding Alcohol Taxation In the vast landscape of the alcohol industry, taxation plays a pivotal role. Picture the federal government, represented by the colloquial "Uncle Sam," ensuring that every producer pays their due share in excise taxes. This tax is akin to a ticket—granting producers the privilege to introduce their beverages to the eager market. It's essential to note that different beverages—whether spirits, beer, or wine—have distinct tax rates, each tailored to its category[1,2].

State-Specific Twists and Turns As we traverse the diverse states of the U.S., it becomes evident that each state has its unique take on excise taxes[3]. This state-specific approach adds layers of complexity to the already intricate world of alcohol taxation. It's akin to each state having its distinct dance in the grand ballet of compliance.

The Art of Record-Keeping Record-keeping, while seemingly mundane, is the linchpin of effective compliance. It's not merely about documenting transactions but ensuring they can be retrieved and reviewed when necessary. This meticulous approach ensures transparency, accuracy, and fosters trust between producers and regulatory bodies. Proper organization and diligence make this task less daunting, much like a well-practiced dance routine.

Cheers to Compliance! Navigating the world of alcohol taxation and excise duties, while intricate, is a testament to the industry's commitment to fairness, transparency, and responsibility. With the right knowledge and a proactive approach, this journey becomes less of a challenge and more of an enlightening experience.

Disclaimer: The information provided here is grounded in publicly available sources and industry insights. While every effort is made to ensure its accuracy and reliability, readers are urged to verify the specifics with pertinent authorities such as the Alcohol and Tobacco Tax and Trade Bureau (TTB) and state Departments of Revenue (DOR) for the most current regulations and compliance prerequisites.

Footnotes

1.   TTBGov - Forms Helpful Hints and Tips
1.   https://www.ttb.gov/business-tools/forms-helpful-hints-and-tips
2.   TTBGov - Excise Tax and Export Due Dates

1.   https://www.ttb.gov/tax-audit/excise-tax-and-export-due-dates
3.   Distilled Spirits Taxes by State | Liquor Taxes | Alcohol Taxes
1.   https://taxfoundation.org/data/all/state/state-distilled-spirits-taxes-2023/#:~:text=Across%20states%2C%20Washington%20levies%20the%20greatest%20excise%20tax,taxed%20the%20least%20in%20Wyoming%20and%20New%20Hampshire.

Review Questions:

1.   Why is understanding different tax rates for spirits, beer, and wine crucial for producers?
2.   How do state-specific regulations add complexity to alcohol taxation?
3.   Why is meticulous record-keeping essential in ensuring compliance with alcohol taxation?

Article 5: Understanding Trade Practices, Advertising, and Social Media Compliance in the World of Alcohol Beverages

Next up is an important one. Let's discuss trade practices, advertising regulations, and the vibrant realm of social media in the alcohol industry.

Navigating Trade Practices Trade practice regulations maintain harmony and fairness in the industry. Like tightrope walkers, suppliers, distributors, and retailers navigate with precision, ensuring integrity from pricing to promotions. For a comprehensive understanding, refer to the guide on national alcohol Trade Practices[1]. For specific inquiries, contact TradePractices@TTB.gov.

Permissible Promotions Trade promotions and marketing activities balance creativity with restraint. While suppliers can offer discounts, they must adhere to federal and state regulations. The potential for tastings varies by state, so consult local agencies and wholesale partners for guidelines.

The State-by-State Showcase Each state showcases its unique advertising and trade practice rules. Performers adjust their routines to local laws, with more restrictions in control or franchise markets and fewer in open markets.

Labeling and Packaging Compliance: Unveiling the Art of Transparency Labels tell tales of craftsmanship and quality. Federal regulations ensure clear and accurate information, spotlighting alcohol content, packaging sizes, health warnings, and responsible drinking messages.

Social Media Magic: A New Era of Advertising The TTB's Industry Circular 2022-2 highlights social media advertising guidelines for alcohol beverages. Whether on Facebook, Instagram, or YouTube, compliance with the FAA Act and TTB regulations is essential. Advertisements must include mandatory information, and regulations against misleading statements apply universally, regardless of the platform[2].

The Oath of Transparency As we conclude this journey, let's embrace transparency as a source of strength and excellence, ensuring that our practices reflect knowledge and wisdom.

Disclaimer: The information provided is based on publicly available sources and industry insights. Readers are encouraged to verify details with relevant authorities such as the TTB and state Departments of Revenue (DOR) for up-to-date regulations and compliance requirements.

Footnotes

1. Federal Trade Practices: What Every Industry Member Should Know
    a. https://www.ttb.gov/images/pdfs/faa-trade-practice-master.pdf#:~:text=Keep%20criminal%20element%20out%20of%20alcohol%20industry%20and,lead%20to%20corruption%20or%20excessive%20consumption%20%28section%20205%29
2. TTB's Industry Circular 2022-2
    a. https://www.ttb.gov/industry-circulars/ttb-industry-circular-2022-2

Review Questions:

1. Which entity is described as the "tax collector extraordinaire" in the alcohol industry?

    a. Uncle Brian
    b. Uncle Sam
    c. Uncle Dave
    d. Uncle Ian

2. True or False: All states have uniform advertising and trade practice rules.
3. In the context of the article, what is the primary role of labels in alcoholic beverages?

    a. To provide colorful designs
    b. To tell tales of craftsmanship and quality
    c. To display the price of the product
    d. To show the manufacturer's address

4. Which platform is NOT mentioned as a realm for advertising regulations in the alcohol industry?

    a. Facebook
    b. Snapchat
    c. YouTube
    d. Instagram

5. Fill in the blank: "_____ and packaging compliance is an art of transparency."

Conclusion: Understanding Compliance in the Alcohol Industry As we wrap up this topic, please take a moment to recognize the critical balance between responsibility and innovation. This section has covered the essentials of federal and state regulations, licensing, and permit requirements, labeling and packaging compliance, alcohol taxation and excise duties, and the guidelines for trade practices, advertising, and the ever evolving social media compliance.

The Three-Tier System Our exploration began with the three-tier system, a crucial structure that manages the roles of suppliers, distributors, and retailers in the alcohol industry. Federal regulations, overseen by the Alcohol and Tobacco Tax and Trade Bureau (TTB), govern this system. Additionally, state-specific regulations add layers of complexity, underscoring the importance of understanding local compliance requirements.

Licensing and Permits Licensing and permits are fundamental for legally operating in the alcohol industry. Federal licenses are required for production, distribution, and sales of alcoholic beverages, while state-specific licenses vary. It's essential to seek guidance to navigate these requirements effectively.

Labeling and Packaging Labeling and packaging compliance is vital for transparency and consumer safety. This area of compliance ensures that all products accurately convey essential information, including alcohol content and health warnings, thereby maintaining product integrity and preventing misbranding.

Taxation and Excise Duties Understanding and correctly applying alcohol taxation and excise duties is crucial for financial compliance. This involves being aware of federal tax rates and state-specific regulations and maintaining accurate records to ensure compliance with financial obligations.

Trade Practices, Advertising, and Social Media Navigating the regulations around trade practices and advertising is crucial for ethical consumer engagement. These rules ensure fair market practices and ethical promotion of products. Additionally, with the rise of social media as an advertising tool, it's important to adhere to TTB guidelines to maintain transparency and honesty in digital marketing.

Moving Forward with Compliance Compliance in the alcohol industry is an ongoing process that requires staying informed about regulatory changes, seeking expert advice, and committing to ethical practices. By embracing transparency and responsibility, businesses can navigate the complexities of the industry, ensuring its growth, success, and safety.

This chapter has highlighted the importance of diligent adherence to regulations, ethical conduct, and staying informed. Upholding these principles is key to building a responsible and enduring presence in the alcohol industry.

Disclaimer: This information is based on publicly available sources and industry insights. For the most current regulations and compliance requirements, consult the Alcohol and Tobacco

Tax and Trade Bureau (TTB) and state Departments of Revenue (DOR).

Chapter 3: Branding and Marketing Strategies

An endless amount of time and often "billable hours" get spent on marketing. This chapter is your guide, offering insights into crafting a compelling brand identity, weaving engaging content, harnessing the power of social media and digital marketing, and fine-tuning strategies for diverse market segments. These are the tools that carve out a niche, resonate with consumers, and drive the narrative of success. By grasping the essence of branding and mastering the art of marketing, businesses in the alcohol beverage industry can ascend to prominence and foster enduring bonds with their audience.

Article 1: Importance of Branding in the Adult Beverage Industry. Branding is a pillar of the adult beverage industry. Dive deep into its core significance, understanding that branding is not merely a visual emblem but the heartbeat of differentiation, trust, and emotional resonance. Discover how a potent brand can sway choices, anchor loyalty, and become a consumer's trusted companion.

Article 2: Defining Your Brand Identity. A distinct brand identity is your compass. Navigate the journey of sculpting a brand's identity, encompassing its ethos, character, stance, and the audience it serenades. Unravel the magic of consistent messaging and visuals that paint a vivid picture of the brand, leaving an indelible mark on consumers.

Article 3: Developing a Marketing Strategy. Charting a course in the adult beverage industry requires a robust marketing strategy. Embark on a voyage to craft a strategy that mirrors business aspirations and resonates with target demographics. Delve into the realms of market analysis, competitive reconnaissance, goal setting, channel selection, and the art of gauging campaign triumphs.

Article 4: Leveraging Social Media and Digital Marketing. In the digital age, the alcohol beverage industry finds its stage on social media and digital platforms. Explore the nuances of harnessing these platforms, from content creation to influencer collaborations, community stewardship, paid promotions, and the alchemy of analytics.

Article 5: Creating Engaging Content and Storytelling. More than ever, quality content comes at a premium. Immerse in the craft of curating content and narratives that captivate, using tales, visuals, and experiences that etch memorable brand sagas. Understand how to weave stories that spark curiosity, loyalty, and a deep-rooted bond with the brand.

Insights and Summary of Each Article
As the chapter culminates, we present a treasure trove of insights and a concise summary of each article's essence. Reiterating the pivotal role of branding and marketing in the adult beverage industry, we underscore the importance of brand identity, strategic marketing, digital prowess, content alchemy, and market-specific endeavors. This finale is designed to equip you with actionable wisdom, guiding you to orchestrate triumphant branding and marketing symphonies in the adult beverage realm.

Article 1: The Importance of Branding in the Adult Beverage Industry

I'm sure you're aware but I feel the need to state it anyway; branding isn't about a catchy logo or a memorable slogan. It's the essence of identity. It's your promise to consumers, and the emotional connection fostered. As we get into this article, we'll uncover different layers of branding in the adult beverage industry and its profound impact on differentiation, trust-building, and long-term success.

Consider your own personal brand at the same time. If someone said "If I had two more <insert your name here> I could take over the world!" what would that mean? What part of you are you leaving people with after you walk out of the room? And better, what have you done today to make that "brand" be what you want it to be?

Why Branding Matters in the Adult Beverage Industry
Branding is the heartbeat of the adult beverage industry, serving as the bridge between businesses and consumers.

Here's why it's indispensable:

Differentiation: Amidst a sea of choices, branding is the lighthouse guiding consumers. It's the unique signature that sets a product apart, ensuring it's not just another bottle on the shelf.

Building Trust: Trust isn't given; it's earned. And in the world of adult beverages, a strong brand is the trust certificate. It's the assurance that every sip is worth it.

Emotional Connection: Beyond the taste and aesthetics, it's the stories and values that resonate. A brand that strikes the right emotional chords creates loyalists, not just consumers. Be sincere. Even if you could lie about your story and get away with it, please don't. There's already too much BS out there.

The Role of Branding in Influencing Consumer Behavior
Branding is the silent influencer, subtly shaping choices and preferences.

Here's how:

Perception and Recognition: A powerful brand isn't just recognized; it's remembered. It's the difference between being a choice and being the choice.

Product Differentiation: In the spectrum of flavors and spirits, branding carves out a niche, spotlighting what's unique and why it matters.

Emotional Appeal: The best brands evoke feelings, memories, and a sense of belonging.

Building a Strong Brand in the Adult Beverage Industry
Crafting a brand is a little bit art and a little bit science.

Here's a blueprint:

Brand Identity: It's the soul-searching phase. What does the brand stand for? Who does it speak to? What's its story? Introspection before projection.

Consistency and Coherence: A brand is a promise, and consistency ensures it's kept. Whether it's the color palette, messaging, or customer experience, consistency is the thread that weaves it all together.

Authenticity and Transparency: Today's consumers are discerning. Many have already made up their mind on what they like. The challenge is not just exposure, it's the ability to convert people to your product. Most value authenticity and transparency. It's about being genuine, open, and accountable.

Engaging Experiences: Brands come alive through experiences. It's the pop-up events, the tasting sessions, and the interactive campaigns that make a brand tangible and relatable. You cannot do this from home.

Remember that branding isn't a one-time effort. It's a continuous journey of discovery, innovation, and connection. In the business of adult beverages, it's not always about what's in the bottle; it's often about the people that put the liquid in there.

Review Questions

1. Which of the following is NOT a primary purpose of branding in the adult beverage industry?

    a. Differentiation
    b. Building Trust
    c. Emotional Connection
    d. Increasing Production

2. True or False: Branding is solely about the visual elements, such as logos and packaging.
3. In your own words, describe the role of branding in influencing consumer behavior.
4. Branding in the adult beverage industry serves as a bridge between _____ and _____.
5. **Matching**: Match the following branding elements with their descriptions:

    a. Brand Identity
    b. Consistency and Coherence
    c. Authenticity and Transparency

d. Engaging Experiences

1) Ensures a brand's promise is kept across all touchpoints.
2) The soul-searching phase of introspection before projection.
3) Being real, open, and accountable to consumers.
4) Making a brand tangible and relatable through events and campaigns.

6. Discuss the importance of emotional appeal in branding within the adult beverage industry. How does it influence consumer loyalty and decision-making?
7. Which of the following is a key aspect to consider when understanding the role of branding in influencing consumer behavior? a. Perception and Recognition b. Price Reduction c. Production Techniques d. Packaging Materials
8. True or False: All brands in the adult beverage industry should have the same values and target audience for maximum success.
9. Imagine you are launching a new craft beer. How would you utilize the principles of branding discussed in the article to ensure its success in the market?
10. Which of the following are essential components for building a strong brand in the adult beverage industry? (Choose all that apply)

a. Brand Identity
b. Consistency and Coherence
c. Authenticity and Transparency
d. Production Speed

Article 2: Defining Your Brand Identity in the Adult Beverage Industry

Establishing a strong brand identity is crucial for differentiation, consumer connection, and long-term success. Lets explore the process of defining your brand identity. Identify your key elements such as brand values, personality, target audience, and unique selling propositions. By understanding and strategically shaping your brand identity, you can create a distinct and compelling presence in the market.

Identifying Your Brand Values and Mission

Core Values: Start by identifying the fundamental principles and values that guide your brand. These values should align with your overall vision and resonate with your target audience. Remember the advice given in the previous article regarding the free site, personalvalu.es.

Mission Statement: Craft a clear and concise mission statement that encapsulates the purpose and direction of your brand. It should reflect your values and communicate the value proposition you offer to consumers. I have always appreciated approaching these types of difficult tasks with one word in mind: "intentionality." Always ask yourself "why?"

Determining Your Brand Personality

Personality Traits: Define the personality traits that best represent your brand. Consider whether your brand is adventurous, sophisticated, playful, or something entirely different. These traits will guide your brand's tone of voice, messaging, and overall communication style. Would you want to hang out with your brand after work? Would you have wanted to sit at the same lunch table as your brand?

Brand Archetype (original pattern): Explore different archetypes that align with your brand's personality, such as the hero, the rebel, the creator, or the jester. Understanding your brand archetype helps create consistency and coherence across all brand touchpoints. Is your brand socially driven? Freedom focused? Ego (structurally) driven? Or is it designed for order, to leave a mark? For more information on this subject, look up Carl Jung's 12 Archetypes.

Understanding Your Target Audience

Consumer Demographics: It's time for something measurable. Conduct market research to gain insights into your target audience's demographics, including age, gender, location, and income level. This information will help tailor your brand messaging and communication channels. You can google, or you can walk into the accounts you want to work with and ask about who drinks which products. Micro and macro research are both valuable. I suggest a combination.

Psychographics: Don't be intimidated by this big word. It just means to look at the actions of your intended consumers. Dive deeper into your target audience's psychographics, such as their lifestyle, values, interests, and preferences. Understanding their motivations and aspirations will enable you to connect with them on a deeper level. Do you sell your product downtown at high-end cocktail bars, or should it be on retail shelves in the suburbs? I've lived in both places. Don't judge either way.

Defining Your Unique Selling Propositions

Product Attributes: Identify the distinctive qualities and features of your adult beverage products. Whether it's the sourcing of premium ingredients, unique flavor profiles, or innovative production techniques, pinpoint what sets your products apart. Also, consider what sets YOU apart. It's always nice if your brand can share in your story as well.

Brand Story: Craft a compelling brand story that captures the essence of your product, its heritage, and the inspiration. Authentic storytelling helps build emotional connections with consumers and reinforces your unique selling propositions. Authenticity means sharing something about yourself. If this makes you uncomfortable, it's time to look up Ted Talks on vulnerability. Shout out to Gina Parenti for making me do that a few years back.

Creating Brand Guidelines

Visual Identity: Develop a cohesive visual identity that includes your brand logo, typography, color palette, and imagery. Consistency in visual elements enhances brand recognition and reinforces your brand identity. That said, don't be afraid to sneak some easter eggs into your labels. Everyone wants to feel a part of the inner circle, and nothing gives them that experience more than learning a new fact about something they thought they knew everything about. St. George Spirits does this with many of their labels. A year or two ago I learned new pieces of their story through their Gin labels. That's after having bought and sold their brand for over a decade in bar programs.

Tone of Voice: Define a consistent tone of voice that reflects your brand's personality. Whether it's conversational, authoritative, or humorous, your tone of voice should align with your target audience and support your brand values. Again, intentionality.

Defining your brand identity is a vital step in establishing a strong presence in the adult beverage industry. By identifying your brand values, determining your brand personality, understanding your target audience, and defining your unique selling propositions, you can create a distinct and compelling brand identity. This identity serves as a foundation for effective marketing strategies, consumer connections, and long-term success in the competitive beverage market.

And as always, do not be afraid to evolve and have your brand evolve as time goes on.

Review Questions

1.   Which of the following best describes the role of branding in the adult beverage industry?

   a.   Solely focused on logo design.
   b.   Primarily about product packaging.
   c.   Encompasses the overall perception and personality of a brand.
   d.   Only about differentiating from competitors.

2.   True or False: A brand's mission statement should reflect its values and communicate its value proposition to consumers.

3.   When determining a brand's personality, which question might be helpful to consider?

   a.   How much does the product cost?
   b.   Would you want to hang out with your brand after work?
   c.   How many competitors are in the market?
   d.   What is the primary ingredient in the product?

4. On a scale of 1 to 5, where 1 is "Not Important" and 5 is "Extremely Important", how crucial is consistency in visual elements (like logo, typography, and color palette) for enhancing brand recognition?

5. Which of the following is NOT a key aspect to consider when understanding the influence of branding on consumer behavior?

    a. Perception and Recognition
    b. Product Differentiation
    c. The number of sales in the last quarter
    d. Emotional Appeal

Article 3: Crafting a Killer Marketing Strategy for the Boozy World

Alright, folks, let's dive into the intoxicating world of adult beverages. But instead of sipping on a cocktail, we're going to mix up a killer marketing strategy. Ready to shake things up? Let's go!

Know Thy Drinker

Buyer Personas: Picture your ideal customer. Is it Donna who loves a good wine after work? Or maybe it's Dave who's all about craft beers. Dive deep into their world. What do they like? Where do they hang out? Get to know them.

Market Research: I'm not saying you should hit every bar in town, but... actually, that's not a bad idea! You absolutely should be visiting the types of establishments you want to see your product featured in. This isn't just bars and restaurants. You should be personally visiting retailers and every possible avenue your products could flow through. Keep an eye on industry trends. If you're feeling fancy, check out sources like

SipSource or Nielsen. Knowledge is power, and what a luxury that our knowledge may involve tequila!

Set Goals Like a Pro

SMART Goals: This shouldn't be anything new but just in case. Specific, Measurable, Attainable, Relevant, and Time-bound. Want to be the next big thing in the wine world? Set clear goals to get there.

KPIs: (Key performance indicators) Think of these as the heartbeat of your marketing strategy. They'll tell you what's working and what's not.

Pick Your Battlefields

Digital Marketing: From tweeting about tequila to Instagramming your Irish whiskey, know where your audience hangs out online. You can hire someone for SEO marketing but if you don't understand it, you're bound to spend too much money on it.

Traditional Marketing: Good old-fashioned print ads and radio spots still have their charm. But always ask: is it right for your brand? Or possibly, how can you share the cost on these with other brands like yours?

Serve Up Some Stellar Content

USP: This is an old school term but indispensable. Unique Selling Proposition. Always ask why someone would want your product over the next competitors?

Content Strategy: Whether it's a hilarious video or a heartwarming story about your distillery dog, make sure your content resonates. Social media should be about "why." Don't show product photos. Publish the feeling your product evokes. Show the community your product creates or belongs in. Show the energy of your product and its consumers. Connect!

Roll Out the Red Carpet

Campaign Execution: Launch your campaigns with flair and finesse. But always, <u>always</u> keep an eye on how they're doing. *AB testing*. Run two separate ads and keep everything the same save for 1 thing. Then see which one gets more attention. Then do THAT thing in your future ads. Test everything and keep learning always!

Marketing Automation: Embrace the future! Let AI and automation tools do the heavy lifting. They're like having a robot bartender on your team. Don't read this book on advice for AI. There's something new every hour. You need to be using, watching, playing, and learning. On-going curiosity will be your friend here. And if in doubt watch my Substack newsletter. I'm learning more every day.

Did It Work? Check the Receipts!

Analytics and Reporting: Dive into the data. What's working? What's flopping? Adjust accordingly.

A/B Testing: Remember this from 2 minutes ago? Think of this as a taste test for your marketing. Try out different flavors and see what your audience loves.

A top-notch marketing strategy is indispensable. Know your audience, set clear goals, pick the right channels, serve up engaging content, roll out your campaigns, and always measure your results.

Review Questions

1. Which of the following is NOT a component of SMART goals?

    a. Specific
    b. Sensational
    c. Measurable
    d. Time-bound

2. True/False: Traditional marketing channels, such as print advertising, are outdated and no longer effective.

3. On a scale of 1-5, how important is it to understand your target audience when crafting a marketing strategy? (1 being not important, 5 being extremely important)

4. Which tool can help streamline and automate certain marketing tasks?

    a. A magic wand
    b. Marketing Automation tools
    c. A crystal ball
    d. A time machine

5. A/B testing is a data-driven approach that helps optimize your _____ efforts.

Article 4: My Digital Adventure - Navigating Social Media and Digital Marketing in the Boozy World

In this digital era, a tweet can make waves and a well-timed meme can be more impactful than a billboard. Lets talk about how to activate social media platforms for engaged marketing. Step 1, stop filling your feed with product photos. People don't want to be sold to.

Understanding the Social Media Landscape Firstly, it's essential to know where the action is happening.

Facebook: Think of Facebook as the town square. It's where everyone gathers, making it a prime spot to engage with a broad audience. Facebook has a vast user base and it shares specific data on it's users. Targeted ads are available and can be impactful if you have links that can connect people to impulse buying opportunities.

Instagram: This platform is the digital equivalent of a glossy magazine. It's visually driven, and I learned quickly that it's not just about posting pretty pictures. The algorithm is ever-evolving. I do my best to stay up to date using relevant keywords and prioritizing quality content over hashtags. The key is to be authentic and visually compelling. Show your story, community, impact. Tell with words in videos and in the details. Gathering engagement with users right at the time of posting should be impactful for the media getting spread to wider audiences.

Twitter: The bustling marketplace of ideas and opinions. Engaged in real-time conversations. Here more than others it's important to comment and discuss. Reply to people and keep the dialog going. Using hashtags effectively and participating in relevant Twitter chats can boost your brand visibility.

LinkedIn: The boardroom of the digital world. This platform blew up in 2023 with more ways to engage. It expanded into learning platforms, networking, and tons of consulting business models. It's not just an online yearbook and resume. In the early days of my Substack newsletter, this platform garnered more engagement and direct contact than any other social media outlet.

Crafting Your Digital Blueprint

Pay-per-Click (PPC) Advertising: Utilize PPC platforms like Google Ads to reach potential customers actively searching for adult beverage-related keywords. If you're not in the business of creating creative copy, use ChatGPT to help you create compelling ad copy, target specific geographic locations, and use ad extensions to maximize visibility.

Display Advertising: Leverage display advertising networks to showcase your brand on relevant websites and apps. Utilize eye-catching visuals, compelling messaging, and precise targeting to drive brand awareness and website traffic. Look for the opportunities to measure your results and continue to modify and adjust as quickly as possible.

Influencer Marketing: Collaborate with influencers in the adult beverage industry to promote your brand to their engaged audiences. Identify influencers with a genuine connection to your target market, establish authentic partnerships, and leverage their reach and credibility.

There is a gigantic market for affiliate marketing. Look for those that can provide a higher click and sell through rate. Be prepared to have a landing page to sell your product through an online retailer before venturing through advertising. All the visibility in the world won't help you, if there's nowhere for people to buy your product.

Creating Compelling Content

Engaging Videos: Produce high-quality videos showcasing your products, brand story, cocktail recipes, or behind-the-scenes footage. Optimize videos for different platforms and engage viewers with captivating storytelling. Be candid and authentic.

Captivating Blog Posts: Share informative and engaging blog posts that educate and entertain your audience. Cover topics such as cocktail recipes, industry trends, mixology tips, and brand updates to establish yourself as a trusted resource. Volunteer your time and expertise to help drive positive conversations for the industry. Provide value.

User-Generated Content: Encourage customers to create and share content featuring your products. Repost user-generated content, run contests, and engage with your audience to foster a sense of community and brand advocacy. It's a running theme in my writing I hope, but please provide value. Offer services, knowledge, and use what you're promoting to build or grow a community.

Analyzing Performance and Adjusting Strategies

Social Media Analytics: Utilize built-in analytics tools on social media platforms to track engagement, reach, and audience demographics. Monitor key metrics, identify top-performing content, and optimize your strategy based on data-driven insights.

Conversion Tracking: Implement conversion tracking tools to measure the effectiveness of your digital advertising campaigns. Track website visits, online purchases, lead generation, and other desired actions to assess campaign ROI.

A/B Testing: Experiment with different ad formats, visuals, headlines, and targeting options through A/B testing. Test various elements to optimize campaign performance and refine your targeting strategy.

Leveraging social media and digital marketing strategies is essential for effectively promoting your alcoholic beverage brand and connecting with your target audience. By understanding the strengths of each social media platform, implementing targeted digital advertising, creating compelling content, and analyzing performance metrics, you can enhance brand awareness, drive engagement, and ultimately boost sales. As always though, revisit the compliance piece of this book and research online. The same advertising laws apply to advertising on social media as the ones for T.V.

Review Questions

1. **Multiple Choice**: Which social media platform is described as the "town square" where everyone gathers?

    a. Instagram
    b. LinkedIn
    c. Twitter
    d. Facebook

2. **True/False**: On Instagram, it's only about posting visually appealing pictures without considering the ever-evolving algorithm.

3. Which digital marketing tool is described as the "digital spotlight" highlighting the brand to those actively searching for related keywords?

    a. a) Display Advertising
    b. b) Influencer Marketing
    c. c) Pay-per-Click (PPC) Advertising
    d. d) User-Generated Content

4. **True/False**: A/B testing is used to experiment with different marketing elements to optimize campaign performance.

Article 5: Effective Branding and Marketing across different market segments

Understanding the tides of different consumer segments is the compass to success. This article is about how to tailor your branding and marketing strategies to resonate with each unique sector. By recognizing distinct tastes, behaviors, and backgrounds, you can craft campaigns that not only catch attention but also anchor brand loyalty and carry sales.

Identifying Target Market Segments

Millennials: Understand the preferences of millennials, who are known for their adventurous and experiential consumption habits. Craft marketing messages that emphasize authenticity, sustainability, and innovation to appeal to this tech-savvy and socially conscious demographic. As this demographic ages the spending habits are seeming to become more conservative but recent data (2023) could be reflective of immediate economic circumstance.

Gen X: Connect with the Gen X audience through nostalgia, quality, and convenience. Emphasize the craftsmanship and heritage of your products and leverage digital platforms to engage with this demographic.

Baby Boomers: Recognize the purchasing power of baby boomers and their preference for established and trusted brands. Develop marketing strategies that focus on tradition, quality, and timeless appeal.

Gen Z: Cater to the youngest consumer segment by leveraging social media, influencer collaborations, and interactive experiences. Highlight customization options, authenticity, and unique product offerings to capture their attention. Keep in mind, each generation tends to be slightly healthier than the previous. No and Low ABV products are getting more popular year by year.

Tailoring Branding Messages

Storytelling: Develop a compelling brand story that resonates with the values and aspirations of each target segment. Emphasize the origin, craftsmanship, and unique aspects of your brand to create an emotional connection with consumers.

Brand Personality: Define the personality traits that align with each market segment. Whether it's sophisticated, adventurous, eco-conscious, or fun-loving, infuse your branding with these characteristics to attract and engage the desired audience.

Visual Identity: Create a visually appealing and cohesive brand identity that aligns with the preferences of each market segment. Consider color schemes, typography, and design elements that evoke the desired emotions and perceptions.

Customizing Marketing Channels

Digital Channels: Utilize social media platforms, targeted online ads, and email marketing to reach and engage with your target segments. Tailor your content and messaging based on the specific platform preferences and behaviors of each segment.

Traditional Marketing: Don't overlook traditional marketing channels like print media, radio, and events, particularly when targeting specific segments that have a preference for offline engagement.

Influencer Marketing: Collaborate with influencers who resonate with your target segments. Their credibility and influence can help you reach and connect with a wider audience and build trust among consumers. Remember that this is about visibility. Have a landing page for those influencers to introduce your brand to their network. That landing page needs to provide a true and authentic introduction to your brand with links for end consumers to find the product.

Engaging Experiences and Events

Tasting Events: Organize tasting events that allow consumers to experience your brand and products firsthand. Create memorable and immersive experiences that cater to the preferences of each segment.

Virtual Events: Adapt to the digital landscape by hosting virtual events such as webinars, live tastings, or interactive workshops. Ensure these events offer valuable and engaging content to capture the attention of your target segments. This is the opportunity to introduce producers and owners to the end consumer on a large but approachable scale.

Partnerships: Form strategic partnerships with complementary brands or venues to host joint events that attract your target segments. This allows you to tap into an existing customer base and create mutually beneficial experiences. The brands in your category should be seen as allies, not competition.

Effective branding and marketing in the adult beverage industry require a deep understanding of different market segments and their preferences. By tailoring branding messages, customizing marketing channels, and creating engaging experiences, you can establish a strong connection with your target audience. Remember, the key is to constantly adapt and evolve your strategies as consumer preferences and market dynamics change.

Review Questions

1.   Which generation is known for their adventurous and experiential consumption habits?

      a.   Baby Boomers
      b.   Gen X
      c.   Millennials
      d.   Generation Z

2.   **True/False**: Gen X values nostalgia, quality, and convenience in their beverage choices.
3.   On a scale of 1 (Not Important) to 5 (Very Important), how crucial is it to tailor branding messages and marketing channels based on the specific preferences of each market segment?
4.   **Fill in the Blank**: Partnering with _____ can help brands reach and connect with a wider audience and build trust among consumers in the adult beverage industry.
5.   Which of the following is NOT a recommended strategy for engaging with the Generation Z market segment in the adult beverage industry?

a. Leveraging social media
b. Highlighting customization options
c. Focusing solely on traditional marketing channels
d. Collaborating with influencers

Conclusion: The Art and Science of Branding in the Beverage World

In this chapter on branding and marketing strategies in the adult beverage industry, we have explored the importance of understanding and catering to different market segments. Here are the key takeaways.

Identifying Target Market Segments:

Millennials seek authentic, sustainable, and innovative experiences. Some of us are older than cell phones, but we know how they work. Let us live.

Gen X values nostalgia, quality, and convenience. Use the current 90's trend to win their hearts.

Baby Boomers prioritize established and trusted brands.

Generation Z craves customization, authenticity, and unique offerings. More than anything though, they continue to surprise. Think of healthier and more conscientious products.

Tailoring Branding Messages:

Develop a compelling brand story that connects emotionally with each segment.

Define and infuse brand personality traits that align with the preferences of each segment.

Create a visually appealing and cohesive brand identity.

Customizing Marketing Channels:

Utilize digital channels like social media, targeted online ads, and email marketing.

Don't overlook traditional marketing channels, particularly when targeting specific segments.

Collaborate with influencers who resonate with your target segments.

Engaging Experiences and Events:

Organize tasting events and create immersive experiences that cater to each segment.

Adapt to the digital landscape with virtual events such as webinars and live tastings.

Form strategic partnerships to host joint events that attract your target segments.

If you want to take this One step further:

Craft a marketing campaign targeting millennials that highlights sustainable sourcing practices, innovative product offerings, and immersive experiences that connect them with nature and community.

Develop a brand personality for Gen X that emphasizes authenticity, quality craftsmanship, and the convenience of online purchasing options.

Create visually stunning packaging and design elements that evoke nostalgia and appeal to baby boomers' preference for traditional and trusted brands.

Engage Generation Z through social media platforms with interactive content, user-generated campaigns, and collaborations with influencers they admire.

To successfully implement effective branding and marketing strategies for different market segments:

Conduct thorough market research and consumer analysis to understand the preferences and behaviors of your target segments.

Continuously monitor and adapt your strategies to align with evolving consumer trends and market dynamics.

Collaborate with marketing professionals and agencies specializing in the adult beverage industry to leverage their expertise and insights.

Remember, building strong connections with your target audience through tailored branding and marketing strategies will lead to increased brand loyalty, sales growth, and a competitive advantage in the adult beverage industry.

Chapter 4: Building Successful Partnerships and Collaborations

The most transformative moments arise from collaborations, partnerships, and shared aspirations. As the industry's landscape continually evolves, one element remains timeless: the power of connection. These aren't just fleeting interactions but deep, impactful partnerships that propel brands to new heights. Over the course of this chapter we'll discuss strategic alliances, influencer partnerships, event sponsorships, and successful co-branding initiatives.

Strategic Alliances and Their Impact: Embracing the strategy of 'all your eggs in one basket' can be a game-changer. While national alignments promise rewards, they're not without challenges. Yet, when orchestrated with precision, they can revolutionize how businesses etch their presence across diverse markets.

Influencer Collaborations: Today a single post can echo across continents. Influencers have emerged as the modern-day heralds of brands. But how does one discern the voice that truly harmonizes with their brand's essence? And once that voice is found, how can we craft a collaboration that's authentic and mutually enriching?

Event Sponsorships: From grand international festivals to intimate local tastings, events are the stages where brands come to life. Together, we'll explore strategies that ensure brands don't merely participate but captivate and leave a lasting impression.

Joint Marketing and Co-branding: When two brands unite effectively, it can be more than a partnership. We'll delve into stories of brands that, by joining forces, didn't just market products but actually crafted something uniquely memorable.

Industry Associations and Trade Shows: The alcohol industry is a close-knit community. Associations and trade shows pulse at its core, offering golden opportunities for those ready to seize them. We'll journey through these avenues, ensuring you're equipped to not just attend but truly immerse and leave a mark.

As we work through this chapter I hope I deliver the message effectively that it's not merely about the liquid but the stories and connections it fosters. Partnerships and collaborations epitomize this sentiment.

Article 1: Forging Strategic Alliances and Partnerships in the Alcohol Industry

In the alcohol industry like all others, the adage "two heads are better than one" rings particularly true. Strategic alliances and partnerships emerge as pivotal tools for businesses aiming to expand their reach, enhance their offerings, and adeptly navigate the market's complexities. When executed with precision, these collaborations can lead to mutual growth, efficient resource allocation, and a strengthened position in multiple industries.

The Power of Collaboration Strategic alliances in the alcohol sector often involve collaborations between producers, distributors, and retailers. These partnerships can take various forms, from joint marketing efforts to shared distribution channels. The primary objective is to leverage each participant's unique strengths to achieve mutual goals. Examples include private label wines or spirits produced for large on-premise groups. Many brands collaborate across industries, such as the partnership between Huckberry and High West Whiskey[1], or artist collaborations like the one between Devin B. Johnson and Ten to One Rum for their 2023 Black History Month Limited Edition bottling[2].

Benefits of Strategic Alliances

Shared Resources and Expertise

Collaborations allow businesses to pool resources, be it financial, technological, or human. This collective approach can lead to cost savings, increased efficiency, and access to specialized expertise.

Risk Mitigation: Entering new markets or launching new products comes with inherent risks. Collaborations can distribute this risk, ensuring that no single entity bears the brunt of potential challenges.

Increased Market Access: Collaborative efforts can unlock new markets or consumer segments. The right partnerships can also signal alignment with specific demographics.

Innovative Solutions: The amalgamation of diverse entities can lead to a fusion of ideas, resulting in innovative solutions to industry challenges.

Key Considerations for Successful Alliances

While the benefits of strategic alliances are evident, it's crucial to approach these collaborations with a clear strategy:

Alignment of Goals: Ensure all parties have a clear understanding of the partnership's objectives.

Clear Communication: Open dialogue is essential for any successful partnership.

Legal and Contractual Clarity: Clearly defined roles, responsibilities, and terms can prevent future conflicts. Some items cannot be sold in the same stores. Some sponsorships are restricted at the federal level[3].

Flexibility: The alcohol industry is dynamic. Collaborations should be adaptable to changing market trends.

Real-world Examples of Successful Alliances

Celebrity and brand collaborations in the alcohol industry have become a strategic tool for expansion:

Lady Gaga x Dom Pérignon: This collaboration led to a limited edition of the Dom Pérignon Rosé Vintage 2005 and a custom sculpture by Lady Gaga. Proceeds went to The Born This Way Foundation[4].

Liu Wei x Hennessy: For the 2021 Lunar New Year, Hennessy introduced limited-edition packaging designed by artist Liu Wei[4].

W Aspen's Spring & Dean Single Barrel Club: This club offers exclusive access to single barrel bottles, partnering with brands like Last Drop Distillers for early access to new releases[5].

In the competitive landscape of the alcohol industry, strategic alliances and partnerships offer a pathway to growth and dominance. By combining resources, expertise, and market insights, businesses can overcome challenges, capitalize on opportunities, and ensure lasting success in the industry.

Footnotes:

1. Huckberry and High West Whiskey Collaboration
    1. https://www.youtube.com/watch?v=M6s03pjjhw8
2. Devin B. Johnson and Ten to One Rum's 2022 Black History Month Limited Edition
    1. https://www.tentoonerum.com/black-history-month-artist-edition/
3. Federal and State Compliance in the Alcohol Industry
    1. https://www.ttb.gov/
4. Alcohol Collaborations You Need to Know About in 2021
    1. https://wandereater.com/alcohol-collaborations-to-know-about-2021/
5. W Aspen's New Whiskey Club Gives Guests Access to Rare Single Barrel Whiskeys
    1. https://www.forbes.com/sites/kevingray/2023/09/01/w-aspens-new-whiskey-club-gives-guests-access-to-rare-single-barrel-whiskeys/?sh=7466a5722ba3

Review Questions:

1. Which of the following is NOT a benefit of strategic alliances in the alcohol industry?

    a. Shared Resources and Expertise
    b. Increased Market Access
    c. Limited Product Offerings
    d. Risk Mitigation

2. True or False: Collaborations in the alcohol sector only involve producers.
3. Which factor is essential for the success of a strategic alliance?

> a. Limited Communication
> b. Ambiguous Goals
> c. Legal and Contractual Clarity
> d. Rigidity

4. What was the primary objective of the collaboration between Lady Gaga and Dom Pérignon?

> a. Increase sales
> b. Philanthropic efforts
> c. Introduce a new flavor
> d. Expand to new markets

5. Which of the following collaborations emphasized the importance of exclusive offerings in forging strong partnerships in the industry?

> a. Lady Gaga x Dom Pérignon
> b. Liu Wei x Hennessy
> c. W Aspen's Spring & Dean Single Barrel Club
> d. Huckberry and High West Whiskey

Article 2: Navigating the Alcohol Industry: Identifying and Approaching Potential Partners

The alcohol industry is a vast and intricate tapestry of brands, flavors, and marketing tactics. For businesses aspiring to carve a niche or expand their footprint in this sector, pinpointing and engaging potential partners can seem like navigating a labyrinth. Yet, armed with astute strategy and insights, one can adeptly chart this intricate terrain.

Understanding the Landscape Before contemplating potential collaborations, it's paramount to thoroughly comprehend the alcohol industry. This entails recognizing dominant entities, nascent trends, and consumer inclinations. For instance, Coca-Cola's venture into the alcohol domain underscored the escalating allure of flavored alcoholic beverages. Their strategy zeroed in on three segments: hard seltzers, hard alternatives, and pre-mixed cocktails[1]. Such discernments can steer businesses toward market segments brimming with collaborative potential.

Identifying Potential Partners With a firm grasp on the industry's contours, the subsequent phase is pinpointing potential collaborators. This encompasses:

Researching Market Leaders: Seek brands or entities boasting robust market visibility that resonate with your business ethos and aspirations. Venturing outside the industry for collaboration partners can expose your brand to an expansive customer demographic.

Exploring Niche Brands: Occasionally, promising or smaller brands proffer distinctive partnership prospects, especially if they cater to a particular demographic or trend.

Attending Industry Events: Conferences, seminars, and networking congregations can be treasure troves for unearthing potential partners.

Approaching Potential Partners Post identification, the approach becomes pivotal. Here are some tactics:

Build Genuine Relationships: Eschew overt sales pitches in favor of nurturing a rapport. Grasp their objectives, hurdles, and how a collaboration can yield mutual dividends. Listen twice as much as you talk.

Showcase Your Value Proposition: Lucidly convey your unique offerings. Whether it's an avant-garde marketing ploy, an expansive distribution nexus, or a groundbreaking product, ensure your prospective collaborator discerns the merits of allying with you.

Leverage Existing Connections: Harness mutual business acquaintances to orchestrate introductions. A warm overture often trumps a cold outreach.

Ensuring Responsible Collaborations The alcohol domain is imbued with inherent responsibilities. Echoing Coca-Cola's sentiments, any entity venturing into the alcohol category must shoulder its responsibilities with gravitas[1]. This encompasses championing responsible consumption and collaborating with industry peers to advocate moderation and curtail harm. For an in-depth dive into compliance, refer to previous discussions on labeling and packaging[2].

Evolving with the Market The alcohol sector, akin to others, is in perpetual flux. As consumer predilections metamorphose, novel trends surface, and regulatory frameworks oscillate. Flourishing alliances are those agile enough to adapt and evolve in tandem with the market. Periodically scrutinize the partnership's goals, tactics, and outcomes to ensure sustained alignment and triumph.

While the alcohol domain teems with collaborative prospects, triumph hinges on a tactical, enlightened, and conscientious approach. By fathoming the landscape, pinpointing apt partners, and cultivating authentic relationships, businesses can adeptly and ethically steer through this sector.

Footnotes:

I.   Coca-Cola's venture into the alcohol market
   a) https://www.coca-colacompany.com/media-center/deeper-look-at-coca-colas-emerging-business-in-alcohol

II.   Chapter 2, Article 3: Labeling and Packaging Compliance: Unveiling the Art of Transparency

Review Questions:

1.   Which of the following is NOT a segment Coca-Cola focused on in their alcohol venture?

   a. Hard seltzers
   b. Hard alternatives
   c. Hard ciders
   d. Pre-mixed cocktails

2.   True or False: Attending industry events is not a recommended method for finding potential partners in the alcohol industry.

3.   Which of the following is crucial when approaching potential partners?

   a. Making a direct sales pitch
   b. Keeping your value proposition a secret
   c. Building genuine relationships
   d. Avoiding mutual business acquaintances

4. What is one of the primary responsibilities for businesses entering the alcohol category?

    a. Ignoring consumer preferences
    b. Avoiding collaborations
    c. Ensuring responsible consumption
    d. Focusing solely on profit

5. True or False: The alcohol industry remains static and does not evolve over time.

Article 3: Collaborating with Influencers and Industry Experts in the Alcohol Sector

In the contemporary digital epoch, influencers have ascended as formidable entities capable of molding consumer inclinations and amplifying product cognizance. The alcohol sector, characterized by its burgeoning array of brands and culture, is rife with avenues for influencers and brands to synergize. By allying with apt influencers, alcohol manufacturers can penetrate novel consumer segments, augment their brand persona, and catalyze sales. They have the ability to adjust your voice to deliver your message to a new audience. Similarly to what I did with the fancy words in this paragraph.

The Ascendancy of Influencer Marketing in the Alcohol Realm Influencer marketing, underscored by Open Influence[1], has entrenched itself as an indispensable facet across myriad sectors, with the alcohol domain being no outlier. Ranging from delightful beverage concoctions to immersive brand experiences, influencers infuse a rejuvenating and bona fide dimension to alcohol endorsements. They act as conduits linking brands and consumers, proffering candid commendations that reverberate with their audience. Furthermore, as postulated by Common Ground PR[2], harnessing influencer marketing emerges as a sagacious maneuver for spirits brands, facilitating a more tailored and resonant connection with audiences.

Rationale Behind Influencer Collaborations

Genuine Engagement: Influencers have engendered trust amidst their audience. Their product endorsements exude an aura of authenticity, transcending the veneer of paid promotions. A pivotal aspect is aligning with genuine individuals, eschewing mere promotional social media presences. Delve into your target consumer demographic and your brand's ethos before opting for this marketing trajectory.

Focused Outreach: Brands can synergize with influencers whose audience mirrors their target demographic, ensuring marketing endeavors resonate with the intended audience.

Content Genesis: As highlighted by The Brand Guild[3], influencers epitomize content creators. They craft premium photos, videos, and articles, which brands can incorporate into their promotional campaigns.

Selecting Apt Influencers The art of influencer selection, as revealed by GRIN[4], is intricate. Brands must gravitate towards influencers whose principles resonate with theirs and who genuinely endorse the product. Key considerations include:

Relevance: Does the influencer's content harmonize with your brand's persona and principles?

Outreach: While an expansive follower base is advantageous, engagement metrics are paramount.

Engagement: How does the influencer's audience engage with their content? Elevated engagement rates signify a devoted and proactive audience.

Engaging with Industry Connoisseurs Beyond influencers, industry savants proffer a reservoir of expertise and credibility. These individuals, having dedicated years to the alcohol sector, possess profound insights into its intricacies. Collaborating with such luminaries can bestow a brand with credibility and invaluable perspectives on market trends and consumer predilections.

Blueprint for Fruitful Collaborations

Explicit Communication: Isolate the objectives and anticipations of the collaboration at the outset.

Artistic Autonomy: While brands should delineate guidelines, bestowing influencers with creative latitude can culminate in more genuine and captivating content.

Transparency: Ascertain that all sponsored content is transparently labeled to preserve audience trust. Even if you're not the content architect, revisit those advertising responsibility guidelines by the TTB as discussed in Chapter 6, Article 5[5].

To maintain a vanguard position necessitates avant-garde marketing stratagems. Collaborating with influencers and industry mavens extends brands a distinctive avenue to meaningfully engage with consumers. By nurturing authentic alliances and accentuating authenticity, alcohol brands can amplify their marketing endeavors and secure enduring triumph.

Footnotes

1. **Open Influence on Influencer Marketing**
   1. **https://www.openinfluence.com/**
2. **Common Ground PR's Insights**
   1. **https://www.commongroundpr.com/**
3. **The Brand Guild on Content Creation**
   1. **https://www.thebrandguild.com/**
4. **GRIN's Guide on Influencer Selection**
   1. **https://www.grin.co/**
5. **TTB Advertising Responsibility Guidelines**
   1. **https://www.ttb.gov/advertising/alcohol-beverage-advertising**

Review Questions:

1. Which of the following is NOT a reason for collaborating with influencers in the alcohol industry?

   a. Boosting sales
   b. Enhancing brand image
   c. Reducing production costs
   d. Tapping into new audiences

2. True or False: Influencers with a large following are always the best choice for collaboration.
3. Which of the following is NOT a factor to consider when selecting influencers for collaboration?

   a. Relevance
   b. Engagement rates
   c. Number of posts per day
   d. Outreach

4. Why is transparency important in influencer collaborations?

    a. To increase sales
    b. To maintain trust with the audience
    c. To reduce production costs
    d. To increase the number of followers

5. True or False: Industry experts in the alcohol sector can provide valuable insights into market trends and consumer preferences.

Article 4: Unlocking Growth: Sponsorships and Event Partnerships in the Alcohol Industry

The alcohol sector is replete with avenues for brands to resonate with their audience. A strategy to realize this is through sponsorships and event alliances. Such synergies not only amplify brand prominence but also cultivate profound affiliations with consumers, stakeholders, and industry contemporaries.

The Potency of Sponsorship in the Alcohol Realm When smartly orchestrated, sponsorships can morph brands within the alcohol domain. They proffer a distinctive theatre to exhibit products, narrate brand tales, and captivate a specific audience.

Brand Congruence: Opting for events or endeavors that resonate with a brand's principles and ethos is pivotal. For instance, a distillery such as Cathead, which champions the credo "Support Live Music," might find merit in endorsing a local music festivity[1]. Conversely, an opulent champagne marque might find affinity with upscale fashion galas.

Augmented Prominence: Sponsorships bestow brands with a stage to distinguish themselves. This could manifest through exclusive branding prospects, product placements, or interactive pavilions, with the resultant exposure being invaluable.

Cultivating Brand Allegiance: Engaging with consumers in an informal, event-centric milieu can engender brand allegiance. It empowers brands to craft indelible experiences that linger with participants post-event.

Event Alliances: Transcending Conventional Sponsorships While sponsorships typically entail monetary patronage in reciprocation for brand prominence, event alliances can be more symbiotic. They might span from jointly orchestrating events to initiating combined marketing endeavors.

Co-branded Galas: Allying with another brand or entity to curate an event can be mutually beneficial. It facilitates resource amalgamation, audience sharing, and the genesis of singular experiences. For instance, a whiskey label might collaborate with a cigar enterprise for an elite tasting soirée[2].

Interactive Encounters: Contemporary consumers prioritize experiences over mere commodities. Establishing interactive kiosks, virtual reality escapades, or mixology sessions can render your brand the cynosure of an event.

Harnessing Influencers: Allying with influencers for events can magnify outreach. An influencer's vouching can bestow credibility and allure their ardent followers to the occasion.

Quantifying the ROI of Sponsorships and Alliances
Channeling resources into sponsorships and alliances necessitates substantial investment. Consequently, quantifying the return on investment (ROI) emerges as imperative. With many of these events being "non-selling" events, this can be subjective. Here are some suggestions on how to track returns and types of channels that enable solid tracking.

> **Digital Engagement Metrics:** Monitor online traffic, social media interactions, and digital mentions during and post-event. A surge in these metrics can signify a triumphant event alliance. Delve into geofencing advertisements. Collaborate with retailers to juxtapose sales augmentations against targeted promotions, ensuring digital transparency to steer ROI analysis[3].

> **Sales and Conversion:** Scrutinize sales trajectories during and post-event. A sales escalation, especially in locales hosting the event, can be a direct success indicator. Of course, work with sales teams locally ahead of events to ensure awareness and enable selling returns.

> **Feedback and Surveys:** Engage post-event with attendees. Their insights can shed light on successful facets and potential enhancement areas.

Sponsorships and event alliances, when astutely strategized, can catapult a brand to unparalleled echelons within the alcohol sector. However, if mismanaged, they can deplete resources. They amalgamate visibility, engagement, and brand augmentation opportunities. Brands must be vigilant in tracking and capitalizing on ensuing opportunities. As the sector perpetually metamorphoses, brands that innovatively harness these collaborations will indubitably maintain a vanguard position.

Footnotes

1. Cathead Distillery's Support Live Music Initiative
   1. https://www.catheaddistillery.com/
2. Whiskey and Cigar Tasting Events
   1. https://www.whiskeyandcigarclub.com/
3. Geofencing Advertisements and Digital Transparency
   1. https://www.geofencing.com/

Review Questions:

1. Which of the following is NOT a benefit of sponsorships in the alcohol industry?

   a. Enhanced brand visibility
   b. Reduced production costs
   c. Building brand loyalty
   d. Brand alignment with events

2. True or False: Event partnerships are solely about financial support in exchange for brand visibility.
3. What is a primary advantage of co-branded events?

   a. Reducing competition
   b. Sharing audiences and pooling resources
   c. Increasing production
   d. Reducing marketing costs

4. Why is it important to measure the ROI of sponsorships and partnerships?

   a. To ensure brand loyalty

    b. To validate the effectiveness of the collaboration
    c. To increase brand visibility
    d. To reduce production costs

5. True or False: Modern consumers value experiences over mere products.

Article 5: Joint Marketing Initiatives and Co-Branding Opportunities in the Alcohol Industry

Joint marketing and co-branding, while not novel concepts, hold immense potential in the adult beverage industry. By synergizing their efforts, brands can magnify their outreach, pool resources, and craft unforgettable experiences for their audience.

The Power of Joint Marketing Initiatives Joint marketing initiatives entail a collaborative effort by two or more brands to collectively champion their products or services. For instance, a liqueur brand might team up with a gourmet chocolate company for a curated tasting event, or a winery might join hands with a luxury hotel to orchestrate an exclusive wine weekend.

    Shared Resources and Costs: Such collaborations allow brands to consolidate their resources, both monetary and expertise-wise. This often results in expansive and influential campaigns without a proportional surge in individual brand expenses. A case in point is Heineken's alliance with Coachella, which exemplifies how brands can capitalize on events to present their products to a pertinent audience[1].

    Amplified Reach: Collaborative ventures enable brands to access each other's clientele, leading to heightened visibility and the acquisition of potential new patrons.

This is especially advantageous for emerging or niche brands aspiring to broaden their audience.

Unique Consumer Experiences: Joint marketing endeavors can culminate in distinctive events or experiences that a single brand might find challenging to curate. Such initiatives not only allure consumers but also etch lasting brand-associated memories.

Co-Branding Opportunities in the Alcohol Sector Co-branding is the confluence of two or more brands to conceive a novel product or service. This could manifest as two breweries concocting a limited-edition brew or a spirits brand amalgamating with a non-alcoholic counterpart to introduce a distinctive mixer.

Innovative Products: Co-branding is synonymous with innovation. By amalgamating the expertise of collaborating brands, pioneering products can be birthed, catering to the ever-evolving palate of consumers. For instance, certain brands have ventured into partnerships with coffee enterprises to unveil barrel-aged coffee[2].

Shared Brand Values: Successful co-branding often stems from a convergence of brand values or philosophies. When brands resonate in terms of quality, sustainability, or other foundational values, the resultant products deeply connect with their target demographic.

Increased Brand Loyalty: Observing favored brands in collaboration can bolster consumer loyalty, evoking a sense of pride in endorsing brands that are at the forefront of innovation.

Navigating the Challenges Despite the myriad advantages of joint marketing and co-branding, challenges are inevitable. It's paramount for brands to ensure that their collaborations resonate with their brand ethos and image. Equally challenging is the equitable distribution of costs, profits, and responsibilities. Transparent communication, well-defined contracts, and a unified vision are the cornerstones of triumphant collaborations.

Real-world Examples of Successful Collaborations

Jameson and Craft Breweries: Jameson's Caskmates series is a testament to the brand's collaboration prowess, partnering with craft breweries. This symbiotic relationship sees breweries aging their beer in Jameson barrels, introducing unique flavor profiles, and reciprocally, Jameson matures their whiskey in these beer-infused barrels[3].

Red Bull and GoPro: In 2016, Red Bull and GoPro embarked on a strategic partnership. This alliance, albeit between products of divergent natures, targeted similar demographic facets. Red Bull unlocked a plethora of video marketing avenues, while GoPro became a staple feature in numerous Red Bull events. This partnership epitomizes one of the most inventive, large-scale collaborations in the beverage domain[4].

The Future of Collaborations in the Alcohol Industry The alcohol industry's trajectory suggests an increasing emphasis on collaborations. With the ascent of craft brands and a focus on bespoke consumer experiences, brands adept at collaboration will undoubtedly distinguish themselves in a saturated market.

The realm of joint marketing initiatives and co-branding in the alcohol industry is replete with possibilities. Through effective collaboration, brands can introduce pioneering products, captivate new demographics, and cement their industry stature.

Footnotes

1. **Heineken's collaboration with Coachella**
   1. **https://info.6connex.com/blog/about-alcohol-sponsorship-heineken-coachella-style**
2. **Cobranded barrel aged coffee**
   1. **https://comfyliving.net/barrel-aged-coffee/**
3. **Jameson's Caskmates - collaboration with Craft Breweries**
   1. **https://www.jamesonwhiskey.com/en-us/our-whiskey/jameson-stout-edition/**
4. **Infosys Consulting – Red Bull and Go Pro**
   1. **https://www.linkedin.com/pulse/red-bull-go-pro-smart-alliance-pranali-lokhande/**

Review Questions:

1. Multiple Choice: What is a primary benefit of joint marketing initiatives in the alcohol industry?

   a. a) Limited product range
   b. b) Amplified reach and visibility
   c. c) Reduced brand loyalty
   d. d) Isolation from industry trends

2. True/False: Co-branding in the alcohol industry always involves two alcohol brands collaborating.
3. Which of the following is NOT a challenge associated with joint marketing and co-branding?

a. a) Ensuring brand alignment
b. b) Equitable distribution of profits
c. c) Transparent communication
d. d) Limited consumer engagement

4. True/False: Jameson's Caskmates series involves the whiskey brand collaborating with craft breweries.
5. What was the primary benefit of the Red Bull and GoPro partnership?

   a. a) GoPro's entry into the beverage industry
   b. b) Red Bull's introduction of a new camera line
   c. c) Access to video marketing opportunities for Red Bull
   d. d) GoPro's exclusive sponsorship of Red Bull events

6. Opinion Question: Reflect on the importance of brand alignment in joint marketing initiatives. How do you think it impacts consumer perception and brand loyalty?

Article 6: Harnessing the Power of Industry Associations and Trade Shows in the Alcohol Sector

Staying updated and connected is vital. Industry associations and trade shows serve as crucial platforms for gaining insights, fostering collaborations, and enhancing brand visibility. Moreover, in the post-COVID era, the approach to local wholesale holiday-style trade shows has become more targeted, yielding a higher return on investment (ROI).

Industry Associations are not mere membership bodies

Key Players: Notable industry associations in the U.S. alcohol sector include WSWA, The Distilled Spirits Council,

American Distilling Institute, American Craft Spirits Association, and for insights into bars and restaurants, the USBG.

Advocacy and Voice: In a landscape with evolving regulations, these associations champion the industry's concerns, influence policymaking, and ensure the sector's interests remain a priority.

Tailored Education: Beyond standard seminars, these associations offer training tailored to the unique challenges of the industry, from understanding the three-tier system to state-specific regulations.

Purposeful Networking: It's more than just a handshake. These platforms offer curated networking opportunities, ensuring meaningful connections between suppliers and distributors.

The Essence of Trade Shows – trendsetting in the alcohol industry

Identifying Trends: Emerging trends often debut at trade shows, providing suppliers an opportunity to align their strategies with market demands.

Forge Collaborations: Beyond product displays, trade shows are arenas for strategic alliances, co-branding ventures, and potential mergers or acquisitions.

Direct Feedback: These events offer a direct channel for feedback, allowing suppliers to refine their products based on real-time insights.

Maximizing Trade Show Participation - standing out

Data-Driven Approach: The era of generic booths is over. Employ data analytics to tailor your booth experience to attendee preferences.

Beyond the Booth Engagement: Host auxiliary events, workshops, or tasting sessions to attract and engage attendees more deeply with your brand.

Post-Event Strategy: The journey doesn't end when the show does. Implement a robust post-show strategy, from personalized follow-ups to scheduling meetings with potential leads.

Success in the alcohol industry hinges on strategic insights and collaborations. By effectively leveraging industry associations and trade shows, brands can not only navigate the market's intricacies but also influence its trajectory.

Review Questions:

1. Which of the following is NOT a benefit of industry associations in the alcohol sector?

    a. a) Tailored education
    b. b) Generic seminars
    c. c) Advocacy and representation
    d. d) Purposeful networking

2. True or False: Trade shows are only beneficial for showcasing products.
3. What is the primary advantage of a data-driven approach at trade show booths?

    a. a) Increased costs
    b. b) Tailored attendee experience

c. c) Generic presentations
d. d) Reduced brand visibility

4. In the context of the article, what does the term "Purposeful Networking" imply?

   a. a) Exchanging business cards randomly
   b. b) Curated networking opportunities with meaningful connections
   c. c) Attending all events without a strategy
   d. d) Networking without any specific goal

5. Post-event strategies after trade shows are essential for:

   a. a) Immediate brand discontinuation
   b. b) Ignoring potential leads
   c. c) Strengthening connections and following up with potential leads
   d. d) Reducing brand visibility

Reflective Question: How do you think the role of trade shows and industry associations will evolve in the next decade, especially considering the rise of digital platforms and virtual events?

Chapter 4 Recap: Mastering Collaborative Strategies in the Alcohol Industry

The alcohol industry presents both challenges and opportunities. As we've delved into this chapter, it's evident that the key to thriving in this sector hinges on forging meaningful partnerships and collaborations. Let's encapsulate the core insights we've gathered.

1. Embracing Strategic Alliances Our exploration commenced with the profound impact of strategic alliances. More than just business engagements, these alliances lay the groundwork for sustained growth. By synergizing with partners that resonate with a brand's vision, there's potential for enhanced market visibility and pioneering innovation.

2. Navigating the Digital Wave with Influencers The digital revolution has catapulted influencers to the forefront. Aligning with these digital mavens and industry connoisseurs offers brands a gateway to specialized audiences. Yet, it's the authenticity and trustworthiness influencers embody that can truly elevate a brand's stature.

3. The Spotlight of Events Events, through sponsorships and partnerships, present brands with a tangible interface to engage their audience. Be it unveiling a new product or curating tasting escapades, events craft immersive brand narratives, etching lasting memories and bolstering brand allegiance.

4. The Synergy of Co-Branding Venturing into joint marketing and co-branding, we discerned the immense potential of amalgamating brand strengths. It's not merely about pooling resources; it's about sculpting a distinctive value narrative that captivates consumers.

5. The Epicenters of Insight: Associations & Trade Shows Concluding our journey, we immersed ourselves in the realm of industry associations and trade shows. Far from mere networking arenas, these hubs pulsate with industry lifeblood, dispensing invaluable insights, emerging trends, and golden opportunities to refine brand strategies.

Fresh Perspectives & The Path Forward

While the essence of partnerships is undeniable, it's paramount to embark on them with lucidity and intent. Here are some pivotal takeaways for the road ahead:

Data-Infused Collaborations: In today's data-centric era, it's imperative for brands to harness analytics, pinpointing potential collaborators, gauging collaboration efficacy, and perpetually fine-tuning their alliance blueprints.

Eco-Conscious Collaborations: With the global shift towards sustainability, it's crucial for brands to champion collaborations echoing eco-friendly ethos, spanning from production to promotional endeavors.

Broadening the Collaboration Horizon: The horizon beckons brands to diversify their collaborative ventures, from allying with tech giants for Augmented Reality-infused campaigns to synergizing with culinary maestros for unparalleled beverage-culinary fusions.

As we stand at the precipice of an industry metamorphosis, steered by groundbreaking partnerships and collaborations, it's evident that brands championing thoughtful, strategic alliances will spearhead the industry's future. Here's to collaborations that inspire, revolutionize, and etch an everlasting legacy!

Chapter 5: Pricing Strategies for Your Products

There is both art and science behind the pricing of any product or service. Whether you're a supplier, producer, vendor, or importer, understanding the nuances of pricing can be the difference between thriving, surviving, or neither. This chapter offers a deep dive into the realm of pricing, focusing on three essential strategies: FOB (Freight on Board), DAs (Depletion Allowances), and SPAs (Special Purchase Agreements). By mastering these techniques, you'll be better equipped to position your products, ensure profitability, and foster enduring relationships with wholesalers.

Sub-chapter 5.1: FOB - Freight on Board: Positioning Your Products for Success

The journey begins with an exploration of FOB pricing. At its core, FOB pricing represents the cost at which you offer your products to wholesalers. But why is it so crucial? This sub-chapter unravels the significance of FOB pricing, shedding light on the associated freight options and the art of calculating the FOB price to align with retail expectations. Grasping the intricacies of FOB is more than just understanding numbers; it's about strategically positioning your products to achieve your envisioned retail and cocktail pricing objectives. Remember, this foundational pricing element can be the determining factor in your business's success or failure during its initial years.

Sub-chapter 5.2: DAs - Depletion Allowances: Optimizing Pricing and Inventory Management

Venturing further, we delve into the concept of Depletion Allowances (DAs). These are not mere pricing tools but mechanisms that can significantly influence your pricing strategy to support specific price points, monitor targeted sales performance, and uphold desirable profit margins. This sub-chapter offers a comprehensive look at DAs, from their inherent benefits to the methodology behind their calculation and application. By the end, you'll appreciate the symbiotic relationship DAs foster between you, your enterprise, wholesalers, and their dedicated sales teams.

Sub-chapter 5.3: SPAs - Special Purchase Agreements: Enhancing Pricing Flexibility

Concluding our pricing trilogy, we focus on Special Purchase Agreements (SPAs). Often referred to as free goods provided to wholesalers, SPAs are instrumental in offering a more flexible pricing structure. They present an avenue to reduce the cost of goods for wholesalers while safeguarding your profitability. This sub-chapter demystifies SPAs, from understanding their primary applications to the mathematical computations and considerations integral to their effective implementation. Additionally, we'll highlight the myriad benefits SPAs extend to wholesalers, suppliers, and sales teams alike.

In the alcohol industry, staying ahead requires not just knowledge but the ability to apply it effectively. This chapter promises to equip you with the insights and tools needed to master pricing, ensuring your products are not only competitively priced but also resonate with market demands. So, let's embark on this enlightening journey, unraveling the complexities of FOB, DAs, and SPAs, and unlocking the secrets to optimal pricing strategies in a fiercely competitive market.

Sub-chapter 5.1 Introduction: FOB: Pricing Your Products to Position at the Wholesaler

In the intricate dance of pricing within the alcohol industry, FOB, or "freight on board," emerges as a pivotal player. As a producer or importer, understanding FOB pricing isn't just about numbers; it's about positioning. It's about ensuring that your products are not only priced competitively but also resonate with wholesalers, ultimately influencing retail and cocktail pricing. This sub-chapter promises a deep dive into the world of FOB pricing, offering insights and strategies to navigate its complexities.

Article 1: Why FOB Pricing Matters: Positioning at the Wholesaler The foundation of any pricing strategy lies in understanding its significance. Here, we'll unravel the importance of FOB pricing, emphasizing its role in product positioning at the wholesaler level. Dive into the nuances of aligning with wholesaler margin expectations and the broader retail pricing landscape. By the end, you'll appreciate how a well-calibrated FOB pricing strategy can be a game-changer in market positioning.

Article 2: Decoding FOB Pricing: Exploring Types of Freight and Freight Options Beyond the product price, FOB pricing encompasses the intricate world of freight costs. This article promises a detailed exploration of the different freight types and options integral to FOB pricing. While wholesalers often bring a plethora of freight options to the table, understanding what each entails is crucial. We'll guide you through the maze, offering insights and recommendations to align your pricing objectives seamlessly.

Article 3: Calculating FOB Pricing: Meeting Retail Expectations Setting the right FOB price is an art, balancing various factors from margin expectations to regional cost of living variations. This article delves into the methodology behind calculating an FOB price that not only meets retail expectations but also ensures competitiveness. By understanding the multifaceted factors at play, you'll be better equipped to set a price that resonates with both retailers and consumers.

Article 4: FOB Pricing and Channel Differentiation: On-Premise vs. Off-Premise The world of FOB pricing isn't one-dimensional. Different channels, namely on-premise and off-premise sales, bring their unique dynamics. This article offers a deep dive into the distinctions between these channels and their implications for FOB pricing. By tailoring your strategy to these diverse channels, you can ensure that your product reaches its intended audience effectively.

Article 5: Ensuring Profitability: Margins and Cost Considerations in FOB Pricing At the heart of any business strategy lies profitability. In this article, we'll explore the critical margins and cost considerations that underpin FOB pricing. From understanding the cost of goods to factoring in carrying costs, we'll provide a comprehensive overview to ensure that your FOB pricing not only positions your product effectively but also safeguards your business's bottom line.

As we journey through this sub-chapter, you'll gain a holistic understanding of FOB pricing. From its significance to the intricate calculations and strategies, you'll be equipped to position your products effectively at the wholesaler level. And as we progress, stay tuned for deeper dives into other pivotal pricing strategies, ensuring that you're always a step ahead.

Article 1: Why FOB Pricing Matters: Positioning at the Wholesaler

Understanding the intricacies of pricing is paramount. At the heart of this is FOB (Freight on Board) pricing. Lets dig in.

Understanding FOB Pricing FOB pricing isn't just a term; it's a strategy. It encapsulates the price at which products are sold to the wholesaler, potentially inclusive of freight costs if the supplier handles logistics. While FOB often denotes the product's price, the logistics aspect can't be overlooked. Wholesalers, with their freight arrangements, factor in transportation costs, emphasizing the advantage of bulk purchases. As we progress, we'll touch upon the concept of carrying cost, shedding light on the benefits of frequent, smaller quantity purchases. In essence, FOB is the price tag you put on your product for your wholesale partner.

Positioning Your Products FOB pricing is instrumental in product positioning. The right FOB price ensures market competitiveness, aligning with the wholesaler's margin expectations. Given the diverse margin expectations across wholesalers, especially when dealing with multiple products at varied price points, understanding these nuances is crucial. A blended margin approach, factoring in different products and pricing tiers, can be complex and beneficial if able to be maintained but simplicity is key, especially for newcomers.

Price to Maintain Operations FOB pricing isn't just about market positioning; it's the lifeblood of your operations. This price, your primary revenue source, should encompass all production-related costs, from raw materials to compliance. It's not just about profit; it's about sustaining growth and ensuring operational continuity.

Retail Expectations and Margins Retail expectations, influenced by regional cost of living variations, play a pivotal role in FOB pricing. Retailers in high-cost areas might sell at higher margins compared to their counterparts in more affordable regions. Recognizing these disparities and calibrating your FOB price ensures market-appropriate product pricing. Selling a product at the same price in rural Ohio, vs. downtown NYC will result in widely varied pricing in bars or retailers.

On-Premises vs. Off-Premises Sales FOB pricing considerations also extend to the distinction between on-premises and off-premises sales. On-premise sales refer to products consumed at bars or restaurants, where the focus is on a cost per ounce calculation or pour cost. In contrast, off-premises sales involve selling the product to retail locations where customers purchase it to consume elsewhere. These two types of sales have different pricing dynamics, with on-premises locations often working on wider mark-up/margins due to additional services offered. Off-premises locations focus on selling full bottles to customers with a similar cost plus model as your wholesaler.

In the realm of the alcohol industry, FOB pricing stands tall as a critical determinant of product positioning at the wholesaler. A deep understanding of its nuances, from retail expectations to sales dynamics, ensures a robust FOB pricing strategy. As you venture further into this domain, remember to factor in market dynamics and wholesaler margin expectations, setting the stage for a successful pricing journey. Stay connected as we delve deeper into freight, pricing options, and the mathematical underpinnings of FOB pricing.

Review Questions

1. What does FOB stand for in the context of pricing in the alcohol industry?
2. Why is understanding the distinction between on-premises and off-premises sales important for FOB pricing?
3. How does FOB pricing play a role in maintaining business operations for a producer or importer?
4. How can regional variations in the cost of living influence FOB pricing?
5. What is the primary purpose of FOB pricing in the alcohol industry?

Article 2: Decoding FOB Pricing: Exploring Types of Freight and Freight Options

FOB (Freight on Board) pricing stands as a pivotal component. Central to this is the understanding of various freight types and options. This article aims to demystify the complexities surrounding freight, offering insights to aid in informed decision-making and strategic pricing.

Types of Freight

Domestic: Over the Road (OTR) Freight: Over the road freight, akin to the Uber Black of transportation, involves truck or trailer-based transportation. Predominantly used for domestic shipments, it offers flexibility in pick-up and delivery. However, it's worth noting the distinction between limited truck load (LTL) shipping, which, though faster, is costlier than full truckload shipments. Of course there's always a dedicated truck, which has a fixed cost and depending on the amount of product you put on the truck, will then have a still higher cost per case likely than partial or consolidated shipments.

Rail Freight: Rail freight, as the name suggests, involves train-based transportation. Ideal for long-distance and bulk shipments, it's a cost-effective method. However, the involvement of trucks in transporting goods to and from railways and warehouses is inevitable. Despite potentially extended shipping timelines domestically, it offers cost benefits for larger consignments.

Direct Import (DI) Freight: Direct import freight (shipping containers on boats) is the go-to for international importers, especially for large quantities. It demands meticulous coordination, ensuring timely delivery and adherence to customs regulations. Typically, direct import orders to the USA span between two to four months. Partial containers can be air freighted into the USA also. Like dedicated trucks with partial shipments, you get the product fast, but run up against some very high costs respective to the alternatives. Planning and time = profit. Lack of planning and forecasting = expensive shipping, and wasted money.

Choosing the Right Freight Option

Cost: Cost considerations encompass transportation fees, handling charges, and additional services, such as the choice between refrigerated and non-refrigerated trucks. It's essential to juxtapose these costs with your budget and pricing strategy. Often, relying on the wholesaler for domestic shipping is advantageous due to their contractual rates with logistics entities.

Timeliness: Transit times can vary based on carriers, shipping lanes, and even seasons. The urgency of shipments and customer expectations should guide the choice of freight. Opt for an option that aligns with market demands and desired delivery timelines.

Reliability: The track record of carriers in terms of punctuality and condition of delivery is paramount. The significance of packaging cannot be overstated, as it directly impacts transportation. This goes back to the product design and structure. Thin bottles or poorly wrapped cases get broken in transit. My advice is to make your product sturdy enough to travel in a truck that moves the way you would drive your rental car.

Volume and Size: The volume and size of shipments play a decisive role in freight choice. While some options cater to bulk shipments, others are tailored for smaller quantities. It's advisable to seek estimates for different pallet quantities when consulting a domestic carrier, providing a cost spectrum for FOB pricing considerations. If you forecast for higher freight, then you and your wholesale partner get advantages in pricing and margins as your product grows in distribution. At the same time you avoid out of stock situations due to requirements of larger orders.

Deciphering the nuances of freight types and options is instrumental in understanding FOB pricing. By weighing factors like cost, delivery speed, reliability, and shipment dimensions, one can make enlightened choices in freight selection. This not only optimizes pricing strategies but also ensures seamless logistics and supply chain efficiency. A grasp of these elements, even if the wholesaler manages logistics, enriches one's understanding of the underlying processes and challenges. I'm not going to tell you the best freight company to use because that answer varies based on where you live. But now you know what to look for when getting cost estimates and factoring that into your models.

Review Questions

1. What does FOB stand for in the context of pricing?

    a. Freight on Business
    b. Free on Board
    c. Freight on Board
    d. Free on Business

2. Which freight method involves transportation by trucks or trailers, typically for domestic shipments?

    a. Rail Freight
    b. Direct Import Freight
    c. Over the Road (OTR) Freight
    d. Air Freight

3. True or False: Direct Import (DI) Freight is commonly used for domestic shipments within the USA.
4. Why is it recommended to defer to the wholesaler for domestic shipping?

    a. Wholesalers have a wider range of products.
    b. Wholesalers often have contract rates with logistics companies.
    c. Wholesalers prefer handling their own shipments.
    d. Wholesalers have larger storage facilities.

5. True or False: Packaging does not play a significant role in the transportation of products.

Article 3: Calculating FOB Pricing: Meeting Retail Expectations

Mindfully setting the right FOB price to the wholesaler is essential to meet retail expectations of your product. This involves understanding the margin expectations of both wholesalers and retailers and applying the right formulas. In this article, we'll delve into the calculations and considerations involved in setting the FOB price.

Understanding the Margin Expectation Before diving into the calculations, it's essential to grasp the margin expectation. Wholesalers typically operate on a cost-plus business model, marking up products based on their costs. The margin expectations can vary based on factors such as market conditions, location, and competition. By understanding these expectations, you can target a shelf price that aligns with both the wholesaler's and retailer's goals.

Calculating the FOB Price To determine the FOB price that meets retail expectations, consider the following formula:

$$\text{FOB Price} + \text{State Tax} = \frac{\text{Desired Price to Retail}}{1 + \text{Wholesaler Margin Percentage}}$$

FOB Price + state tax = Desired Price to retail / (1 + Wholesaler Margin Percentage)

$$\text{SRP (Suggested Retail Price)} = \frac{\text{Price to Retail}}{1 + \text{Retailer Margin Percentage}}$$

SRP (Suggested Retail price) = Price to retail / (1 + Retailer Margin Percentage)

Let's break down the formulas

Desired Retail Price This is the price at which you want your product to be sold at the retail level. (Shelf price to end consumers) It's important to consider factors such as market demand, competition, and target customer segment when determining the desired retail price.

Margin Percentage This is the percentage markup that the retailer aims to achieve. It represents the difference between the retail price and the cost of the product. This will be different from place to place and will require some local research to pin down.

By dividing the desired price to retail by 1 plus the wholesaler's expected margin percentage, you can calculate the FOB price that will enable the wholesaler to achieve their desired margin when selling your product. The SRP formula helps you determine the retail shelf price based on the price to retail and the retailer's margin percentage. Using these formulas, you can reverse engineer the FOB price that allows the wholesaler to achieve their desired margin. The SRP formula helps determine the retail shelf price based on the price to retail and the retailer's margin percentage.

Factors to Consider

When applying the formula to determine the FOB price, consider:

Market Factors Assess market conditions such as consumer demand, competition, and price sensitivity. These factors can influence the margin expectation and, consequently, the FOB price. Stay informed by utilizing industry analytics and resources like IRI, Sip Source, Nielsen ratings, and newsletters from industry experts.

Retailer's Business Model Understand the retailer's business model and their approach to pricing. Different retailers may have varying strategies, such as higher volume sales with lower margins or higher margins with lower sales volumes. Tailor your FOB price calculation to align with the business models of retailers you want to work with. Research retailers and engage in conversations to understand their preferences and ideal product partners.

Negotiation and Flexibility Pricing is often subject to negotiation, especially in non-price posting or state-controlled markets. Be prepared to have discussions with retailers and be flexible in adjusting the FOB price based on mutual agreement.

Setting the right FOB price requires understanding margin expectations and applying the appropriate formulas. By considering various factors and being flexible, you can ensure your FOB price aligns with retail expectations. Effective pricing is an ongoing process, so continuous assessment and adjustments are crucial.

Review Questions

1. What does FOB stand for in the context of pricing?

    a. Free on Business
    b. Freight on Business
    c. Freight on Board
    d. Free on Board

2. Which of the following is NOT a factor to consider when calculating FOB pricing?

    a. Market Factors
    b. Retailer's shoe size
    c. Retailer's Business Model
    d. Negotiation and Flexibility

3.   True or False: The SRP formula helps determine the retail shelf price based on the price to retail and the retailer's margin percentage.

4.   Which resource is NOT mentioned as a tool for assessing market conditions?

    a. IRI
    b. Sip Source
    c. Netflix ratings
    d. Nielsen ratings

5.   True or False: Wholesalers typically operate on a cost-plus business model.

Article 4: FOB Pricing and Channel Differentiation: On-Premise vs. Off-Premise

When determining FOB prices for products, it's imperative to discern the distinction between on-premise and off-premise channels. This section outlines the significance of channel differentiation, its influence on FOB pricing, and considerations for markets with pricing constraints.

Recognizing the Value of On-Premise and Off-Premise Channels

Both on-premise and off-premise channels are integral to a brand's triumph. Understanding their inherent value and the prospects they present is vital.

On-Premise: Establishments like bars and restaurants fall under this category. Their strength lies in directly selling products to patrons, crafting distinctive experiences, concocting signature cocktails, and enlightening customers about a brand. These venues serve as potent marketers, presenting your product to an expansive audience.

Off-Premise: Retailers such as liquor stores typify this channel. Their primary aim is to vend products intended for consumption elsewhere. While direct marketing opportunities might be scantier here, it remains an indispensable conduit for accessing a vast customer demographic. Depletion volume is driven by this channel long term.

Considerations for Control States and Price-Posted Markets

Certain markets function as "control states" or adhere to price-posting regulations. In such territories, differential pricing for on-premise and off-premise channels might be impracticable. The emphasis should be on forging a pricing model echoing the national shelf pricing average.

National Shelf Pricing: This denotes the uniform price at which a product retails nationwide, regardless of the channel. Upholding pricing uniformity across markets fortifies brand identity and precludes pricing inconsistencies. This is difficult but wholesaler alignments often make this more manageable.

Collaboration with Wholesalers: Engage wholesaler partners to craft a pricing model resonating with national shelf pricing. By grasping market dynamics and wholesalers' margin anticipations, a win-win pricing structure can be established, fostering brand growth and ensuring pricing consistency.

Flexibility and Adaptability

Notwithstanding the importance of channel differentiation, pricing strategies should embody flexibility and adaptability. As market conditions and regulations transform, pricing strategies might necessitate revisions. It's paramount to stay abreast of pricing regulation shifts and be poised to recalibrate strategies in alignment with market requisites.

Discriminating between on-premise and off-premise channels is a cornerstone in setting FOB prices. Acknowledging the distinct advantages each channel offers, especially the promotional potential of on-premise venues, is foundational for a prosperous pricing strategy. In regulated markets, the emphasis should be on preserving a harmonized national shelf pricing average and synergizing with wholesalers for aligned pricing. A malleable and adaptable stance ensures that a brand's pricing approach is conducive to both growth and profitability.

Review Questions

1.   True or False: On-premise establishments, like bars, primarily focus on selling products for consumption outside their premises.
2.   In which type of markets is it challenging to have different pricing for on-premise and off-premise channels?

   a.   Free markets

   b. Control states
   c. Competitive markets
   d. Open markets

3. What does the term "National Shelf Pricing" refer to?

   a. The price of products on the top shelf
   b. The average price of a product in a specific state
   c. The consistent price at which a product is sold nationwide
   d. The discounted price offered during sales

4. Why is it essential to collaborate closely with wholesalers when determining pricing in regulated markets?

   a. To ensure bulk purchases
   b. To align with national shelf pricing
   c. To get feedback on product quality
   d. To understand customer preferences

5. Written Response: Explain the primary difference between on-premise and off-premise channels and their significance in FOB pricing.

Article 5: Ensuring Profitability: Margins and Cost Considerations in FOB Pricing

Ensuring profitability is a fundamental aspect of setting your FOB prices. A comprehensive understanding of margins and cost considerations is pivotal to devising a successful pricing model. This article delves into the intricacies of how margins and cost considerations influence FOB pricing, highlighting the importance of offering flexibility to wholesalers to foster mutual success.

Margins: A Balancing Act for Profitability

Blended margins are instrumental in determining the profitability of a product. Achieving the right equilibrium between your margins and the wholesaler's margin expectations is vital for continuous business growth.

Supplier Margins: Ascertain the cost associated with producing, packaging, and storing your product. This encompasses costs like materials, labor, and storage. It's imperative that your margins adequately cover these expenses and facilitate future production and expansion. Don't forget to give yourself a buffer for marketing and support.

Wholesaler Margins: Familiarize yourself with the margin expectations of your wholesaler. Engage closely with them to discern the margins they require to uphold their business model. By being flexible with margins, you equip the wholesaler to make informed pricing decisions promptly, enhancing efficiency.

Cost Considerations: Building a Sustainable Pricing Model

Various cost factors should be taken into account when formulating your pricing model:

Product Costs: Determine the cost of goods, factoring in raw materials, production, and packaging. Recognizing the cost linked with bulk production and sales can help set a baseline pricing.

Carrying/Storage Costs: Evaluate the expenses related to inventory storage. This includes storage fees at importer warehouses and the financial implications of unsold stock.

Depreciation, often calculated as 9% of the cost, can influence your product expenses. Aligning production with market demand can enhance cost efficiency.

Marketing and Promotional Expenses: Dedicate a segment of your pricing to support marketing and promotional endeavors, ensuring you have the necessary funds to bolster brand visibility.

Achieving profitability in FOB pricing necessitates a meticulous assessment of margins and costs. A proficient supplier can set a reasonable FOB price while granting wholesalers flexibility. This adaptability enables wholesalers to devise a pricing model congruent with suggested retail prices (SRPs). By comprehending your cost structure and collaborating with your wholesaler, a sustainable pricing model that benefits both parties can be established.

Review Questions:

1.   True or False: Supplier margins primarily consider the cost of marketing and promotional activities.
2.   Which of the following is NOT a factor considered under cost considerations for FOB pricing?

   a.   Product Costs
   b.   Marketing and Promotional Expenses
   c.   Wholesaler Margins
   d.   Carrying/Storage Costs

3.   True or False: Depreciation associated with carrying/storage costs is typically calculated as 5% of the cost.
4.   Why is it essential to provide flexibility in margins to wholesalers?

a. To ensure bulk purchases
b. To allow them to make quick pricing decisions
c. To get feedback on product quality
d. To understand customer preferences

5. Written Response: Explain the significance of blended margins in determining the profitability of a product.

Sub-chapter 5.2: Depletion Allowances (DAs): Optimizing Pricing and Margin Control

Understanding the nuances of pricing strategies is paramount. Having previously delved into the realm of FOBs (Freight on Board) and their significance in product positioning at the wholesaler level, this chapter shifts focus to another pivotal pricing mechanism: Depletion Allowances (DAs). Through this chapter, readers will gain insights into the influence of DAs on pricing strategies and margin control.

Article 1: The Power of Depletion Allowances: Enhancing Pricing Strategies

Depletion Allowances, commonly referred to as DAs, serve as a strategic instrument enabling producers and suppliers to refine their pricing approaches. This segment will illuminate the advantages and importance of harnessing DAs to bolster profitability, offering a pathway to achieving a competitive market stance and structuring pricing for enduring success.

Article 2: Demystifying Depletion Allowances: Definition, Mechanisms, and Calculations

This offers a comprehensive definition of DAs, shedding light on their operational role within the pricing framework. Additionally, the mechanisms and calculations integral to the effective deployment of DAs will be explored, facilitating a robust comprehension of their integration into pricing tactics.

Article 3: Beneficiaries of Depletion Allowances: Maximizing Profits for Wholesalers, Suppliers, and Sales Teams

Beyond suppliers and producers, DAs extend their benefits to wholesalers and sales teams. This article delves into the multifaceted advantages of DAs, emphasizing their role in amplifying profits across the supply chain. Recognizing the collective benefits of DAs can pave the way for nurturing synergistic relationships with wholesalers and sales teams, propelling sales and enhancing profitability.

Article 4: Strategic Implementation of Depletion Allowances: Making Informed Decisions for Pricing Success

The incorporation of DAs into a pricing strategy demands astute decision-making and a thorough evaluation of diverse elements. This segment offers a deep dive into the strategic assimilation of DAs, presenting insights to guide informed decision-making. Factors such as pricing models, market dynamics, and consumer inclinations will be discussed, underscoring the importance of a strategic DA implementation for maintaining a market advantage.

Article 5: Margin Control with Depletion Allowances: Maintaining Desired Margins for Long-Term Profitability

DAs stand out for their capacity to uphold targeted margins, fostering sustained profitability. This article centers on the theme of margin control, exposing how DAs can be leveraged to meet pricing objectives. Practical strategies and methodologies for the adept use of DAs will be presented, emphasizing their role in safeguarding profitability and fostering business expansion.

This chapter's journey into Depletion Allowances aims to arm readers with the expertise to fine-tune pricing strategies and adeptly manage margins. Grasping the potency of DAs and their repercussions on pricing equips industry professionals to adeptly traverse the intricate terrain of the alcohol sector. The subsequent articles promise a deeper exploration of DAs, offering actionable insights for their effective application.

Article 1: The Power of Depletion Allowances: Enhancing Pricing Strategies

Depletion Allowances (DAs) emerge as a potent strategic instrument, pivotal in refining pricing strategies. Their inherent capability to modulate pricing structures bestows businesses with a competitive advantage, paving the way for heightened profitability. This section digs into the multifaceted influence of Depletion Allowances and their role in augmenting pricing strategies.

Harnessing Pricing Flexibility

Depletion Allowances usher in an unmatched pricing adaptability, facilitating alignment with market exigencies and refining product offerings. Through judicious DA application, businesses can adeptly respond to evolving customer inclinations, market trajectories, and actions of competitors. Such nimbleness positions businesses at the forefront, primed to harness emerging growth avenues. It's imperative to remain cognizant of the legal contours and disparities inherent to each state, especially in contexts where price postings or state-controlled agencies are prevalent. Rigorous due diligence in comprehending the legal and state compliance stipulations for each operational market is paramount.

Gaining Competitive Advantage

Apt pricing emerges as the linchpin for securing a competitive edge. DAs empower businesses to adeptly position their products, enhancing their allure for wholesalers and retailers. By proffering competitive pricing, all the while safeguarding coveted profit margins, DAs pave the way for business expansion, customer base augmentation, and outpacing competitors.

Building Strong Relationships

Beyond mere pricing strategy enhancement, DAs play a pivotal role in nurturing robust, mutually advantageous relationships with wholesalers, retailers, and sales teams. By proffering enticing pricing incentives via DAs, partners are galvanized to champion and vend your products with heightened efficacy. Such synergies bolster brand visibility, amplify market share, and foster enduring alliances anchored in trust and collective triumph.

Optimizing Margins

A salient advantage of DAs lies in their capacity to fine-tune margins. With meticulous control over pricing modulations, businesses can synchronize their margins with aspired profitability objectives. Strategic DA deployment ensures the preservation of robust margins, even while accommodating market flux and customer requisites, thereby guaranteeing enduring profitability and fiscal robustness.

Supporting Growth and Expansion

DAs are instrumental in bolstering business growth and territorial expansion. Effective DA harnessing can catalyze sales volume augmentation, facilitate entry into novel markets, and broaden distribution networks. The adaptability inherent to DAs empowers businesses to customize pricing strategies tailored to distinct markets, channels, or customer demographics, thereby unlocking growth prospects and amplifying market presence. Crucially, DAs facilitate these endeavors without necessitating FOB recalibrations to align with market and wholesaler transformations.

Translation: The ability to navigate depletion allowances makes your pricing model agile. Depletion Allowances stand out as transformative agents, capable of quickly adjusting pricing strategies and propelling businesses forward. Their multifaceted benefits, spanning pricing adaptability, competitive positioning, relationship fortification, margin optimization, and growth support, collectively enhance the overarching pricing framework, ensuring sustained profitability.

Review Questions:

1. True or False: Depletion Allowances primarily focus on building relationships with wholesalers and have minimal impact on pricing strategies.
2. Which of the following best describes the primary advantage of Depletion Allowances?
   a. Enhancing product quality
   b. Facilitating market research
   c. Offering pricing flexibility and competitive advantage
   d. Expanding production capabilities

3. In the context of the alcohol industry, why is it essential to be aware of legal parameters and state variances when using DAs?
   a. To ensure product quality
   b. To align with state compliance regulations and legal stipulations
   c. To enhance marketing strategies
   d. To collaborate with competitors
4. **Written Response:** Explain how Depletion Allowances can support the growth and expansion of a business in the alcohol industry.
5. Which of the following is NOT a benefit of Depletion Allowances?
   a. Gaining a competitive advantage
   b. Building strong relationships with wholesalers
   c. Reducing production costs
   d. Optimizing margins

Article 2: Demystifying Depletion Allowances: Definition, Mechanisms, and Calculations

Depletion Allowances (DAs) can seem complex, but understanding their definition, mechanisms, and calculations is crucial for effectively leveraging their power in your pricing strategies. In this section, we will demystify DAs, breaking down the concepts into simple terms and providing clear explanations of the mechanics and calculations involved.

Defining Depletion Allowances

At its core, a Depletion Allowance is a mechanism that allows suppliers or producers to support specific price points for their products while still maintaining healthy margins for themselves and their wholesale partners. It serves as a financial tool to bridge the gap between desired pricing and required margins, ensuring profitability for all parties involved.

Understanding the Mechanisms

The mechanisms of DAs involve a billback system from the wholesaler to the supplier. When the wholesaler sells the product to a retailer or bar at a price that does not align with the margin they need to make, they can generate a chargeback to the supplier. This chargeback reflects the difference between the actual cost of the product to the wholesaler (including freight and taxes) and the desired pricing point. By using this mechanism, suppliers can support specific price points without lowering the overall FOB. With this model, a supplier has the opportunity to price their product at an FOB that makes sense primarily for their operating costs, while offering some competitive price points for key targets that the wholesaler will need to be able to meet for selling success.

Calculating Depletion Allowances

Calculating the value of a Depletion Allowance requires a deeper dive into the formulas and calculations involved. Let's break it down step by step:

Step 1: Determine the desired pricing point

First, you need to establish the desired pricing point for your product.

If the on-premise customers you're wanting to work with demand $1.00 per oz. cost for their cocktail base spirits, then they would need a roundabout cost of $25/750ml bottle cost. (750ml bottle = 25.36 oz.)

$1 x 25.36oz = $25.36/750ml

If the retailers you want to represent your product need to capture a 25% mark up on the shelf and you want to be selling to the end consumer at $30 per bottle, then your cost to the retailer needs to be $24.00/bt.

$30 / (1 + 25%) = $24.00

Step 2: Consider the current cost of goods sold (COGS)

Next, calculate the cost of goods (COGs) for your product. On the supplier's side this includes the production costs, packaging, and any additional expenses associated with the product to determine the FOB.

The supplier's cost to the wholesaler, plus freight, plus that state's excise taxes are the cost of goods for the wholesaler. Let's assume for the sake of this example the wholesaler's COGs for one case of your product is $120 including freight and tax. (6pk/750ml)

Step 3: Determine the margin requirements

Now, consider the margin requirements of the wholesaler. They typically have a target margin they aim to achieve on each product they sell.

For our following examples, let's assume the wholesaler aims for a 25% margin on your product. This is for the sake of the equation, not a generalized assumption of wholesale margin expectations.

Step 4: Asses the necessary cost adjustment to the wholesaler

To calculate the net cost to the wholesaler, subtract the Depletion Allowance from the COGs. (COGs = FOB+freight+Tax) The Depletion Allowance is the billback amount that gets the COGs to match what's needed to hit a margin and a price point to the wholesaler's customer.

On premise: The necessary DA billback needed for the wholesaler to be able to capture 25% margin, while selling the product at $25/750ml to the customer, would be $7.50 per case.

Off premise: The necessary DA billback needed for the wholesaler to be able to capture 25% margin, while selling the product at $24/750ml to the retail customer, would be $12.00 per case.

Typically, the DA support that a supplier is able to offer comes from a predetermined marketing expense budget. Look back to my chapter on FOBs to read more about building marketing budgets into FOBs. If trying to hit a particular price point exactly, it may take a little trial an error to see where in an acceptable margin range and target selling price the DA amount will fall.

Calculations: All these words written out as formulas and examples

Net Cost to Wholesaler = COGs - Depletion Allowance

Net Cost to Wholesaler EXAMPLE #1: $120 - $7.50 = $112.50 per case. ($18.75/750ml)

Net Cost to Wholesaler EXAMPLE #2: $120 - $12.00 = $108.00 per case. ($18.00/750ml)

Wholesaler Margin = (Selling Price to customer – Net cost to wholesaler) / selling price to customer

Wholesaler Margin EXAMPLE #1: $7.50/case DA: ($25-$18.75) / $25 = 25% margin

Wholesaler Margin EXAMPLE #2: $12.00/case DA: ($24-$18.00) / $24 = 25% Margin

Retailer Margin = (Retail Price – Wholesale Price) / Retail Price * 100

Retailer Margin EXAMPLE: ($30 - $24) / $30 * 100 = 20%

*Note that this is 25% "mark up" which is also 20% "Margin"

On Premise Pour cost = cost per serving / selling price for cocktail

On Premise Pour Cost EXAMPLE: (Assuming a 2oz Pour and $1 per oz. cost, and the drink being $11 on the menu) $2 / $11 = 18.2% pour cost

By carefully calculating the Depletion Allowance, you can maintain the desired pricing point while ensuring both the wholesaler and the retailer/bar/restaurant maintain their respective margins.

Beneficiaries of Depletion Allowances

Depletion Allowances benefit all parties involved in the pricing process. Suppliers can support desired price points without compromising their own overall profitability. Wholesalers can maintain healthy margins and offer competitive pricing to their customers. Retailers and bars benefit from receiving attractive pricing for products that align with their target price points. Ultimately, the strategic use of Depletion Allowances helps build strong relationships and drive business growth for everyone.

Strategic Implementation and Considerations

To effectively utilize Depletion Allowances, it's important to consider the specific pricing strategies, market dynamics, and customer demands of each market or customer segment. By analyzing your target markets, understanding price sensitivity, and aligning your pricing structure with customer expectations, you can strategically implement DAs to drive sales, increase market share, and enhance profitability.

**Important Note: Many states have unique rules, tax structures and nuance differences. The formulas in this document are general and will need to be modified for several states and municipalities.

Understanding the definition, mechanisms, and calculations behind Depletion Allowances is essential for leveraging their power in your pricing strategies. By defining DAs, understanding their mechanisms, mastering the calculations, and considering strategic implementation, you can confidently utilize DAs to support specific price points, maintain healthy margins, and drive business growth.

Review Questions:

1) What is the primary purpose of Depletion Allowances (DAs) in the alcohol industry?
2) Which system is involved in the mechanisms of DAs that allows wholesalers to generate a chargeback to the supplier?
3) Calculate the net cost to the wholesaler if the COGs is $150 per case and the Depletion Allowance is $10. *Net Cost to Wholesaler = COGs - Depletion Allowance*
4) If a wholesaler sells a product to a customer at $28 per 750ml and the net cost to the wholesaler is $21 per 750ml, what is the wholesaler's margin? *Wholesaler Margin = (Selling Price to customer – Net cost to wholesaler) / selling price to customer*
5) For a retailer, if the retail price of a product is $35 and the wholesale price is $27, what is the retailer's margin? *Retailer Margin = (Retail Price – Wholesale Price) / Retail Price * 100*
6) Why is it essential for suppliers to consider specific pricing strategies, market dynamics, and customer demands when utilizing DAs?
7) What is the difference between "mark up" and "margin" as mentioned in the article regarding retailer pricing?

Article 3: Beneficiaries of Depletion Allowances; Maximizing Profits for Wholesalers, Suppliers, and Sales Teams

Depletion Allowances (DAs) serve as a pivotal tool in the alcohol industry, aiming to maximize profits across various stakeholders. This article delves into the multifaceted benefits of DAs, emphasizing their role in enhancing profitability for wholesalers, suppliers, and sales teams.

Wholesalers: Balancing Profitability and Market Competitiveness Wholesalers, being a central cog in the distribution machinery, leverage DAs to harmonize their profit margins with competitive market pricing. By tactically employing DAs, they can:

- Align with desired pricing structures.
- Attract a broader customer base.
- Boost sales volumes. The essence lies in striking an equilibrium between ensuring business sustainability and staying competitive in the market.

Suppliers: Nurturing Brand Growth Through Strategic Pricing Suppliers harness DAs to:

- Tailor their wholesaler's pricing in line with market nuances and consumer predilections.
- Offer specific incentives, fostering deeper wholesaler relationships.
- Enhance brand proliferation and market ingress. DAs, thus, become an indispensable instrument for suppliers, fostering brand visibility and market share expansion.

Sales Teams: Catalyzing Market Reach and Revenue Growth Sales teams, the vanguard of product promotion, benefit immensely from DAs by:

- Gaining pricing malleability, driving sales momentum.
- Showcasing product value propositions effectively.

- Negotiating and securing pivotal brand placements.

Beyond sheer financial metrics, DAs amplify their negotiation prowess, facilitating brand adoption and market expansion.

Building Trust and Long-Term Partnerships The ramifications of DAs transcend mere monetary advantages. Strategic DA utilization fosters trust, fortifying relationships between wholesalers, suppliers, sales teams, and their clientele. This collaborative approach, underpinned by competitive pricing and sales drive, nurtures long-standing business success.

Depletion Allowances stand as a cornerstone for wholesalers, suppliers, and sales teams, accentuating profit margins and market dominance. Their judicious application ensures sustained margins, robust pricing strategies, and an uptick in sales volumes. A transparent and collaborative approach to DAs paves the way for synergistic partnerships, underlining profitability and enduring growth.

Review Questions:

1. Multiple Choice: Which of the following best describes the primary purpose of Depletion Allowances (DAs)?
   a. a) To increase the production cost for suppliers.
   b. b) To maintain healthy margins for wholesalers while offering competitive pricing.
   c. c) To reduce the sales volume for sales teams.
   d. d) To decrease brand visibility in the market.
2. True/False: Suppliers use DAs primarily to decrease their brand proliferation and market ingress.
3. Fill in the Blank: Sales teams benefit from DAs by gaining _____, which helps in driving sales

momentum and showcasing product value propositions effectively.

4. Multiple Choice: Beyond financial metrics, DAs play a crucial role in:
   a. a) Reducing the negotiation prowess of sales teams.
   b. b) Amplifying the negotiation prowess of sales teams.
   c. c) Decreasing brand adoption.
   d. d) Limiting market expansion.
5. True/False: A transparent and collaborative approach to DAs can hinder the formation of synergistic partnerships and reduce profitability.

Article 4: Strategic Implementation of Depletion Allowances: Making Informed Decisions for Pricing Success

The alcoholic beverage industry is characterized by its dynamic nature and competitive landscape. Within this context, Depletion Allowances (DAs) emerge as a pivotal tool. However, the mere application of DAs isn't enough; their strategic implementation is what drives pricing success. Following are the intricacies of deploying DAs effectively.

Understanding Market Dynamics and Margins

The first step towards strategic DA implementation is comprehending the market's pulse. This involves:

- Conducting market research to discern pricing trends.
- Analyzing competitor pricing strategies.
- Understanding the margin requirements of wholesalers.

Such insights pave the way for informed decisions regarding the level of DAs to be offered.

Assessing Product Performance and Demand

A product's performance in the market and its demand trajectory are critical determinants for DA application. It's prudent to:

- Align DAs with products showcasing potential for sales growth.
- Focus on products that resonate with consumer demand.

Collaborating with Wholesalers

A symbiotic relationship with wholesalers can amplify the effectiveness of DAs. This involves:

- Engaging in transparent discussions about margin requirements and pricing strategies.
- Crafting a DA strategy that is mutually beneficial.

Setting Clear Goals and Metrics

For any strategy to succeed, clear goal-setting is paramount. When it comes to DAs:

- Define specific pricing targets.
- Establish sales volume objectives.
- Set profitability thresholds.

Regular monitoring and data-driven adjustments ensure the strategy remains on course.

Continuously Evaluating and Adapting

The market is not static; it's a living entity that evolves. Hence, continuous evaluation and adaptation of DA strategies are essential. This involves:

- Regular product performance reviews.
- Gathering feedback and incorporating insights.

Strategic implementation of Depletion Allowances is not just a choice but a necessity for pricing success in the alcoholic beverage industry. By adopting a structured approach that encompasses market understanding, product assessment, wholesaler collaboration, goal setting, and continuous evaluation, suppliers can navigate the market's challenges and harness the full potential of DAs.

Review Questions:

1. Multiple Choice: Which of the following is NOT a step towards strategic DA implementation?
    a. Understanding market dynamics
    b. Assessing product performance
    c. Ignoring competitor pricing strategies
2. Collaborating with wholesalers
3. True/False: Regularly monitoring the performance of your products and evaluating the impact of DAs on profitability is unnecessary.
4. Fill in the Blank: A Depletion Allowance is a mechanism that allows _____ or _____ to support specific price points for their products.
5. Written: Explain the importance of collaborating with wholesalers when implementing Depletion Allowances.

6. Multiple Choice: What should suppliers focus on when assessing product performance for DA implementation?
   a. Products with declining sales
   b. Products that have the potential for higher sales growth
   c. Products with the least market potential
   d. Products that are least popular among consumers

Article 5: Margin Control with Depletion Allowances: Maintaining Desired Margins for Long-Term Profitability

Now that we've journeyed through some of the intricacies of pricing, from FOB pricing to the strategic implementation of Depletion Allowances (DAs), our focus now shifts to the essence of margin control with DAs. This article underscores the significance of DAs in ensuring desired margins, which is paramount for long-term profitability.

Recap of Previous Articles:

I. The Power of Depletion Allowances: Enhancing Pricing Strategies:
   a. Introduced DAs and their influence on pricing strategies.
   b. Emphasized the optimization of pricing and profitability through DAs.
II. Demystifying Depletion Allowances: Definition, Mechanisms, and Calculations:
   a. Offered a comprehensive definition and elucidation of DAs.

b. Delved into the mechanisms and calculations integral to DA implementation.

III. Beneficiaries of Depletion Allowances: Maximizing Profits for Wholesalers, Suppliers, and Sales Teams:
   a. Investigated the advantages DAs offer to wholesalers, suppliers, and sales teams.
   b. Stressed the collaborative essence in maximizing DAs.

IV. Strategic Implementation of Depletion Allowances: Making Informed Decisions for Pricing Success:
   a. Presented key considerations for strategic DA implementation.
   b. Accentuated the importance of market dynamics comprehension and goal-setting.

Ensuring Margins Align with Pricing Objectives:
DAs serve as a tool for suppliers, granting them the capability to align and maintain specific desired margins by modulating the net cost of goods sold. This ensures a harmonious blend of pricing flexibility, profitability, and market competitiveness. Typically speaking, wholesalers have a bottom margin line and a blended target of over all sales. Often times the only way to negotiate down a lower wholesaler price to the bar/restaurant/retailer is to support it with a billback.

Balancing Wholesaler Margins and Supplier Profitability:
Through DAs, wholesalers find support in reaching their margin aspirations, thereby solidifying partnerships. Concurrently, suppliers can bolster these margins and the financial add to the partnership without jeopardizing their own overall profitability.

Adapting to Market Dynamics and Competitive Landscape:
The fluid nature of market conditions necessitates agile pricing

strategies. DAs offer the adaptability to modify pricing based on these ever-shifting conditions, ensuring enduring profitability amidst market fluctuations.

Leveraging DAs for Long-Term Profitability:
DAs aren't just short-term tools; they're strategic assets for long-term brand establishment, market penetration, and profitability. They can also be adeptly employed to manage overstocked inventory, paving the way for new product introductions.

Margin control, facilitated by Depletion Allowances, is instrumental in upholding desired margins, ensuring long-term profitability in the alcoholic beverage sector. I hope this pricing odyssey has illuminated the multifaceted role of DAs, their strategic applications, and the myriad benefits they offer. With a keen understanding of market dynamics, collaboration, and the agility to adapt, businesses can harness DAs to bolster profitability and foster sustainable growth.

In the ever-evolving landscape of the alcoholic beverage industry, continuous evaluation, adaptation, and collaboration are the cornerstones of success. With strategic pricing and tools like Depletion Allowances at your disposal, the path to industry success becomes clearer.

Review Questions:

1. Multiple Choice: Which of the following is NOT a benefit of Depletion Allowances?
   a. Ensuring pricing flexibility
   b. Adapting to market dynamics
   c. Ignoring market trends

d. Maintaining desired margins

2. True/False: Depletion Allowances can only be used as a short-term strategy.

3. Fill in the Blank: DAs enable suppliers to control and maintain _____ by adjusting the net cost of goods sold.

4. Written: Explain the role of Depletion Allowances in balancing wholesaler margins and supplier profitability.

5. Multiple Choice: What is the primary purpose of Depletion Allowances in the context of the alcoholic beverage industry?
a. To increase product inventory
b. To ignore market trends
c. To maintain desired margins for long-term profitability
d. To reduce collaboration with wholesalers

Sub-chapter 5.3: SPAs - Special Purchase Agreements: Enhancing Pricing Flexibility

Welcome to the next phase of our exploration into the alcoholic beverage industry's pricing intricacies. This chapter shines a spotlight on SPAs, or Special Purchase Agreements. These agreements are pivotal in offering a nuanced approach to pricing, granting suppliers and wholesalers the dexterity to adeptly maneuver through the fluctuating market dynamics.

Why SPAs Matter:

- SPAs transcend the limitations of fixed pricing models, introducing a more adaptable pricing structure.
- They pave the way for pricing arrangements tailored to specific criteria such as volume, timing, or other bespoke factors.
- By harnessing SPAs, suppliers and wholesalers can adeptly respond to market shifts, optimizing profitability. This approach not only offers suppliers a cost-efficient support method but also endows wholesalers with a blended margin flexibility.

What are SPAs?

- At their core, SPAs are purchasing contracts forged between suppliers and wholesalers.
- They champion customized pricing blueprints tailored to distinct purchase orders.
- An illustrative example: A wholesaler procuring a pallet of product from a supplier might receive 1 layer of the product free of charge.

Who Benefits from SPAs?

- Suppliers find themselves in a position to propose volume-centric discounts, promotional pricing, and incentives, fostering increased purchases and fortifying customer loyalty.
- Wholesalers, equipped with SPAs, can swiftly adapt to market oscillations, positioning their pricing competitively to seize a larger market share.
- Retailers and bars reap the benefits of more appealing product pricing, aligning seamlessly with their pricing objectives.

How to Structure Effective SPAs:

- The foundation of an effective SPA lies in delineating the agreement's scope, duration, and pricing parameters.
- Factors such as volume commitments, minimum purchase stipulations, and performance-driven incentives should be at the forefront.
- The linchpin for successful SPAs is the cultivation of transparency, open communication, and collaboration between the involved suppliers and wholesalers.

When to Use SPAs:

- SPAs come into their own especially when the market is in flux and pricing demands adaptability.
- They find their application in diverse scenarios, be it specific promotions, seasonal market shifts, or targeting distinct customer demographics.

Where SPAs Apply:

- SPAs are exclusive agreements between the supplier and wholesaler. While they reduce the Cost of Goods (COGs) for the wholesaler, the Freight on Board (FOB) price remains unchanged for the supplier. This arrangement empowers the wholesaler to offer competitive market pricing while upholding their margin expectations. For the supplier, supporting price through product, as opposed to specific financial billbacks, often proves more cost-efficient.

In the forthcoming articles, we will delve deeper, unraveling the mechanics, considerations, and strategies pivotal for the effective deployment of SPAs. Here's a sneak peek:

Article 1: Customized Pricing Structures

Delve into the nuances of how SPAs facilitate bespoke pricing arrangements. Understand how suppliers can incentivize purchases and fortify brand loyalty through volume-centric discounts and promotional pricing.

Article 2: Structuring Effective SPAs: Mechanics and Calculations

Grasp the essential components and considerations pivotal for crafting effective SPAs. Learn to define the agreement's scope, duration, pricing parameters, and volume commitments.

Article 3: Cultivating Transparency and Communication in SPA Pricing

Understand the paramount importance of fostering transparent communication in SPAs. Realize how market insights, collaborative pricing dialogues, and periodic business reviews amplify the efficacy of SPAs.

Article 4: Incentives and Promotional Programs in SPAs: Driving Sales and Boosting Market Penetration

Dive into the role incentives and promotional programs play within SPAs. Discover strategies to align incentives with sales goals, customize them for wholesaler requirements, and offer robust promotional support.

Article 5: Collaboration and Evaluation in SPAs: Building Long-Term Success

Comprehend the significance of collaboration in the successful implementation of SPAs. Recognize the value of continuous evaluation, feedback, and adaptability in fortifying partnerships and ensuring long-term success.

Embark on this enlightening journey into the world of Special purchase agreements, where pricing flexibility and win-win agreements are the order of the day. By harnessing the potential of SPAs, you're poised to carve a niche for yourself in the ever-evolving alcoholic beverage industry landscape.

Article 1: Customized Pricing Structures in SPAs

This article focuses on the concept of customized pricing structures, highlighting how SPAs enable suppliers and wholesalers to adapt their pricing strategies based on specific market needs and opportunities.

Customized Pricing Structures:
Through SPAs, suppliers and wholesalers have the capability to design tailored pricing arrangements influenced by factors such as volume, timing, and target customer segments. By aligning pricing structures with distinct customer needs, suppliers can cater to diverse market segments more effectively.

Volume-Based Discounts:
One of the primary features of SPAs is the provision for tiered pricing based on purchase order volumes. This structure incentivizes bulk orders, promoting increased sales volumes and offering potential cost efficiencies for wholesalers. An example would be getting a case price discount for ordering larger quantities. Another possible structure would be a number of cases provided at no charge, when a certain quantity is reached in purchases.

Promotional Pricing:
SPAs facilitate the introduction of temporary promotional pricing, which can be strategically employed during specific

periods like holidays, seasonal promotions, or product launches. Such pricing can also address inventory that has been stagnant for extended periods.

Targeted Pricing for Specific Customer Segments:
By recognizing and targeting specific markets, suppliers can offer pricing structures that resonate with the preferences of those segments. Through SPAs, suppliers can provide differentiated pricing for items more specifically designed for retail chains, on-premise establishments, or regional markets, optimizing their market presence.

Geographically Based Pricing:
Geographic considerations play a pivotal role in pricing decisions. SPAs allow suppliers to adjust pricing based on regional factors such as market demand, cost of living, and local competition. This ensures that pricing strategies are attuned to local market conditions, enhancing competitiveness. This could also include freight options where suppliers cover the cost of shipping as a savings due to specific shipping lanes.

Loyalty Programs and Special Incentives:
Incorporating loyalty programs or special incentives within SPAs can further strengthen the bond between suppliers and wholesalers. Such programs, which might offer additional discounts or access to exclusive products, foster sustained partnerships and encourage product promotion.

Customized pricing structures, facilitated by SPAs, present suppliers and wholesalers with opportunities for enhanced growth, profitability, and market penetration. The adaptability inherent in SPAs allows for informed pricing decisions tailored to the unique challenges and opportunities of the alcoholic beverage industry.

Review Questions:

1. Multiple Choice: Which of the following is NOT a benefit of using SPAs in the alcoholic beverage industry?

    a. Tailored pricing based on volume
    b. Temporary promotional pricing during holidays
    c. Fixed pricing for all customer segments
    d. Geographically based pricing adjustments

2. Fill in the Blank: SPAs allow suppliers to offer tiered pricing based on the _____ of purchase orders.
3. True/False: SPAs are primarily used to increase the price of products in response to high demand.
4. Written: Explain the significance of loyalty programs and special incentives within the context of SPAs.
5. Multiple Choice: What is the primary purpose of geographically based pricing in SPAs?

    a. To account for differences in shipping costs
    b. To adjust pricing based on regional market demand and local competition
    c. To offer the same price across all regions
    d. To prioritize sales in regions with the highest population

Article 2: Structuring Effective SPAs: Mechanics and Calculations
    Special Purchase Agreements (SPAs) play a pivotal role in the alcoholic beverage industry, offering tailored pricing arrangements that cater to specific needs and opportunities. This article elucidates the mechanics and considerations pivotal to

structuring SPAs effectively, encompassing lift analysis and relevant mathematical formulations.

Defining the Scope and Duration
An effective SPA begins by delineating its scope and duration. It's imperative to identify the products or categories encompassed and the agreement's temporal span. This gives clarity on priority items or brands.

Establishing Pricing Parameters
Determining pricing parameters is central to SPAs. Consider the following structures based on the agreement's objectives:

- **Percentage Discounts:**
   Wholesalers receive a percentage discount off the standard price contingent on specified quantities or sales targets. Occasionally, a mutually managed "bank" might be integrated for added complexity.
   Formula: Discounted Price = Regular Price - (Regular Price * Discount Percentage)
- **Fixed Pricing Tiers:**
   Pricing is pre-established based on volume tiers, incentivizing larger orders.
   Formula: Total Price = Price per Unit * Quantity

Volume Commitments and Minimum Purchase Requirements
For a win-win agreement, articulate volume commitments and minimum purchase prerequisites. This facilitates effective inventory and production management for suppliers and sets clear purchasing expectations for wholesalers.

Performance-Based Incentives
For established brands, integrate performance-based incentives in SPAs. These rewards, based on sales or market share growth

targets, can be offered as credit or free products in subsequent orders, considering inventory management.

Formula: Incentive = Total Sales * Incentive Percentage

Lift Analysis

Lift analysis gauges the influence of discounts or promotions on sales, determining the additional sales volume required to counterbalance the discount and sustain or enhance profitability. It's a balancing act between offering wholesalers enticing deals and ensuring a robust profit margin. When structuring SPAs, juxtapose lift analysis with other determinants for a holistic pricing arrangement.

Monitoring and Evaluation

Consistent monitoring and evaluation, using Key Performance Indicators (KPIs) like sales, margins, and market share, are paramount. This data-driven approach facilitates SPA effectiveness assessment, allowing for requisite adjustments.

Review Questions:

1. Multiple Choice: What is the primary purpose of defining the scope and duration in an SPA?

    a. To determine the products' color and design.
    b. To set the agreement's temporal span and identify the products or categories encompassed.
    c. To decide the marketing strategy for the products.
    d. To choose the suppliers for the products.

2. Fill in the blank: In the Percentage Discounts structure, the Discounted Price is calculated as _____.

3.   True or False: Lift analysis is used to measure the impact of advertisements on brand awareness. True or False?

4.   Explain the significance of monitoring and evaluation in the context of SPAs and how they can influence future pricing decisions.

5.   Multiple Choice: Which of the following is NOT a common pricing structure used in SPAs?

      a.   Percentage Discounts
      b.   Fixed Pricing Tiers
      c.   Seasonal Packaging
      d.   Volume Commitments and Minimum Purchase Requirements.

Article 2.5: Mechanisms and Calculations Expanded - Lift Analysis:

Lift analysis is a valuable technique used in pricing strategies to measure the impact of discounts or promotions on sales. It helps determine the additional sales volume needed to offset the discount and maintain the same profit level or achieve a desired profit increase.

Step 1: Define the baseline scenario:

Identify the baseline sales volume, profit per unit, and total profit from the baseline sale.

Step 2: Calculate the profit per unit with the discount:

Determine the profit per unit when the discount is applied. This is the profit per unit under the special pricing agreement.

Step 3: Calculate the break-even volume on profit:

Divide the total profit from the baseline sale by the profit per unit with the discount to find the break-even volume on profit.

Step 4: Evaluate the additional units needed:

Compare the break-even volume on profit with the baseline sales volume to determine the additional units needed to maintain the same profit level or achieve the desired profit increase.

Example 1: Break-even Volume on Profit (Discount Percentage)

Let's consider a scenario where a supplier normally sells 10 units at a time, making a profit of $5 per unit. They decide to offer a 20% discount. How many more units do they need to sell to maintain the same profit level?

Step 1: Define the baseline scenario:

Baseline sales volume = 10 units

Profit per unit (baseline) = $5

Total profit from the baseline sale = Profit per unit (baseline) * Baseline sales volume = $5 * 10 = $50

Step 2: Calculate the profit per unit with the discount:

Profit per unit (with discount) = Profit per unit (baseline) * (1 - Discount percentage) = $5 * (1 - 0.20) = $4

Step 3: Calculate the break-even volume on profit:

Break-even volume = Total profit from the baseline sale / Profit per unit (with discount) = $50 / $4 = 12.5 units

Step 4: Evaluate the additional units needed:

Additional units needed = Break-even volume - Baseline sales volume = 12.5 units - 10 units = 2.5 units

In this example, the supplier would need to sell an additional 2.5 units (or maintain the same sales volume) to offset the discount and maintain the same profit margin. The supplier should carefully evaluate whether offering this discount is beneficial in terms of overall profitability and market positioning.

Example 2: Quantity-based Free Goods Deal

Suppose the supplier offers a quantity-based free goods deal of 2 free cases for every purchase of 20 cases. The supplier normally sells 50 cases at a profit of $15 per case. We will calculate the additional cases needed for the supplier to maintain or increase their profit level.

Step 1: Calculate the baseline profit:

Baseline sales volume = 50 cases

Profit per case (baseline) = $15

Total profit from the baseline sale = Baseline sales volume * Profit per case (baseline) = 50 * $15 = $750

Step 2: Calculate the profit per case with the free goods offer:

Profit per case (with free goods promotion) = (Profit per case baseline * number of paid goods) / total number of goods sold with the deal

Profit per case (with free goods) = ($15 * 20) / 22 = $13.63 per case

Step 3: Calculate the break-even volume on profit:

Break-even volume = Total profit from the baseline sale / Profit per case (with free goods) = $750 / $13.63 = 55 cases (approximately)

Step 4: Evaluate the additional cases needed:

Additional cases needed = Break-even volume - Baseline sales volume = 55 - 50 = 5 cases

In this example, the supplier would need the wholesaler to purchase an additional 5 cases (beyond the baseline sales volume of 50 cases) to maintain the same profit level when offering the equivalent of 2 free cases for every purchase of 20 cases. The supplier should consider whether the increase in volume justifies the decrease in profit per case and evaluate the overall profitability and market impact.

Now, let's explore a scenario where the wholesaler purchases 60 cases, qualifying for 6 free cases. The math is all the same, but the quantity comes out differently with the 60 cases minimum purchase requirement to receive the 2 on 20 deal.

In this scenario, if the wholesaler purchases 60 cases, qualifying for 6 free cases, the supplier's total profit becomes $899.58 ($13.63 * 66 cases). This represents an increase in total profit compared to the baseline sale of 50 cases at a profit of

$750. The supplier would need the wholesaler to buy an additional 10 cases to achieve this increase in profit.

The supplier should carefully analyze the trade-off between profit per case and overall profit, taking into account the additional cases required and the market impact of the quantity-based free goods deal.

The win-win here would be giving the wholesaler a cost of goods equal to them purchasing a 2 on 20 case deal, but with the supplier's profit per order increasing by implementing a 60 case minimum to keep things even keel.

Lift analysis is a powerful tool for both suppliers and wholesalers to assess the impact of promotional offers and incentives in SPAs. By calculating the lift, businesses can make informed decisions about pricing structures and determine the necessary volume increases to maintain profitability. It helps strike a balance between providing attractive offers to wholesalers and ensuring a healthy profit margin.

When structuring SPAs, it's important to consider the lift analysis alongside other factors, such as volume commitments, minimum purchase requirements, and performance-based incentives. This comprehensive approach allows for effective pricing arrangements that benefit both suppliers and wholesalers.

Review Questions:

1.   What is the primary purpose of lift analysis in pricing strategies?

2.   In the context of a discount percentage, if the regular profit per unit is $5 and a 20% discount is applied, what would be the profit per unit with the discount?

3. For a quantity-based free goods deal, if a supplier offers 2 free cases for every purchase of 20 cases and normally sells 50 cases at a profit of $15 per case, what is the profit per case with the free goods promotion?

4. True or False: In lift analysis, the break-even volume on profit is calculated by dividing the total profit from the baseline sale by the profit per unit with the discount.

5. In a scenario where a wholesaler purchases 60 cases, qualifying for 6 free cases, and the supplier's profit per case with the free goods promotion is $13.63, what would be the supplier's total profit for 66 cases?

Article 3: Fostering Transparency and Communication in SPA Pricing

Transparency and communication play pivotal roles in the realm of Special Purchase Agreements (SPAs). This chapter underscores the significance of cultivating these elements in SPA pricing. The essence of thriving pricing strategies lies in the establishment of robust and reciprocally advantageous relationships between suppliers and wholesalers. Through the lens of transparency and open communication, both entities can proficiently steer through the intricacies of SPAs, realizing their pricing aspirations.

Clear and Open Communication: It's imperative to delineate clear communication channels between the suppliers and wholesalers engaged in the SPA. Consistent discussions about pricing, prevailing market scenarios, and potential alterations that might influence the agreement are crucial. A conducive environment for open dialogue can preemptively address concerns, eliminating potential misunderstandings or disputes. The overarching goal is mutual growth, achieved in tandem.

Shared Market Insights: Disseminating market insights and pertinent industry data with collaborators can be instrumental. This encompasses consumer trend analytics, competitive examinations, and market prognostications. Equipped with these insights, both suppliers and wholesalers can formulate informed pricing determinations, synchronizing their strategies to augment sales and profit margins. It's often more beneficial to seek insights than to merely share them.

Collaborative Pricing Discussions: Engaging in joint pricing deliberations ensures a comprehensive understanding of each party's viewpoints, limitations, and objectives. Delve into various pricing scenarios, contemplate diverse models, and collaboratively identify solutions that resonate with both profitability and market competitiveness.

Regular Performance Reviews: Periodic evaluations of the SPA's efficacy, gauging its influence on sales, margins, and market share, are paramount. These reviews serve as platforms to discuss performance metrics, address potential impediments, and pinpoint avenues for enhancement in the pricing blueprint. While annual and midyear business assessments are standard, monthly reviews can pave the way for advanced planning and organization.

Adaptability and Flexibility: The dynamic nature of the market necessitates that SPA pricing remains malleable. Periodic assessments, coupled with requisite modifications to pricing, terms, or incentives, ensure the SPA's sustained relevance and efficiency.

Trust and Collaboration: The bedrock of prosperous SPA pricing relationships is trust. Coupled with collaboration, it ensures a harmonious partnership, working in unison towards mutual objectives. Upholding transparency, honoring commitments, and nurturing cooperation fortify this partnership, setting the stage for enduring success.

By championing transparency and communication in SPA pricing, suppliers and wholesalers can forge resilient, collaborative bonds that propel growth, profitability, and customer contentment. It's pivotal to remember that triumphant pricing strategies are an amalgamation of continuous collaboration, adaptability, and a joint pledge to mutual success.

Review Questions:

1. Why is clear and open communication essential in SPA pricing?
2. True or False: Sharing market insights with collaborators is not beneficial in SPA pricing.
3. What is the primary purpose of regular performance reviews in SPA pricing?
4. Why is adaptability and flexibility important in SPA pricing?
5. Fill in the blank: _____ is the foundation of successful SPA pricing relationships.

Article 4: Incentives and Promotional Programs in SPAs: Driving Sales and Boosting Market Penetration

Incentives and promotional programs can also play a pivotal role in Special Purchase Agreements (SPAs). These tools, when effectively employed, can drive sales and enhance market penetration. In this article, we probe into the intricacies of incentives and promotional programs, illustrating their significance in SPAs.

Understanding Incentives and Promotional Programs:
Incentives: These are rewards or benefits extended to

wholesalers and retailers to motivate them to meet specific sales targets or objectives. Incentives can be either financial (discounts, rebates, performance bonuses) or non-financial (exclusive access to new products, marketing support). *Example:* Wholesalers achieving a 20% increase in sales of core items from the previous year are rewarded with 10% more of a limited or highly sought-after seasonal item.

Promotional Programs: These are marketing strategies aimed at amplifying product visibility, stimulating consumer demand, and propelling sales. Such programs can encompass trade promotions, point-of-sale materials, advertising campaigns, and product demonstrations. *Example:* For every 150 units of a product purchased by the wholesaler, the supplier commits to 25 trade demos at retail locations.

Aligning Incentives with Sales Objectives:

- Clearly define sales objectives in line with overarching business goals and desired market penetration.
- Design incentives and promotional programs that resonate with these sales objectives, offering wholesalers the impetus to champion and vend your products.

Tailoring Incentives to Wholesaler Needs:

- Understand the distinct needs and motivations of various wholesalers.
- Propose incentives that cater to each wholesaler's unique requirements, such as bespoke marketing materials or exclusive partnership opportunities.

Performance-Based Incentive Structures:

- Adopt performance-based incentive structures anchored to tangible sales targets or key performance indicators (KPIs).
- Set transparent guidelines and tracking systems to ensure equitable and precise performance measurement and incentive eligibility.

Promotional Support and Co-Marketing:

- Furnish wholesalers with robust promotional backing, including marketing collateral and promotional events.
- Explore collaborative marketing ventures where both suppliers and wholesalers jointly undertake promotional campaigns, pooling their strengths and resources for maximum effect.

Monitoring and Evaluation:

- Consistently assess the efficacy of incentive and promotional programs.
- Gather feedback from wholesalers to gauge program satisfaction, pinpoint areas for enhancement, and recalibrate strategies to optimize outcomes.

Incentives and promotional programs are instrumental in propelling sales and amplifying market penetration within SPAs. By aligning these incentives with sales goals, customizing them to cater to wholesaler needs, and offering comprehensive promotional backing, suppliers can craft a mutually beneficial scenario that spurs wholesalers to actively champion and vend their products.

Review Questions:

1. What are the two main types of incentives mentioned in the article?

2. True/False: Promotional programs are solely about advertising campaigns.

3. Fill in the blank: Performance-based incentive structures are tied to measurable _____ or key performance indicators (KPIs).

4. Which of the following is NOT a benefit of co-marketing as mentioned in the article?

    1. Enhanced product visibility
    2. Access to new products
    3. Joint promotional campaigns
    4. Leveraging each other's strengths

5. Why is it essential to continuously monitor the effectiveness of incentive and promotional programs?

Article 5: Collaboration and Evaluation in SPAs: Building Long-Term Success

Collaboration between suppliers and wholesalers is crucial for the effective implementation and execution of SPAs. By working together, both parties can align their strategies, leverage their respective strengths, and achieve shared goals. Collaboration means asking a lot of questions, active listening, and approaching different departments with those questions. Talk to sales leaders, sales consultants, and the portfolio manager.

If you implement an ongoing purchasing agreement, it can be hard to dial that back, because ultimately what you're doing if you remove that agreement is giving the market a price increase. Be sure that what you're supporting is impactful, and if it's not, pull it back and rework your strategy.

Here are some key aspects of collaboration in SPAs:

Transparent Communication:

Establish open and transparent lines of communication with your wholesalers. Regularly discuss sales performance, market insights, and any challenges or opportunities that arise. Reviewing performance means looking at the % of business that uses the targeted and supported price points or price tiers.

Respectfully, don't ask questions that you can find the answers to yourself. If you have an observation in the market, share that and build a dialog around it. There are opportunities to investigate sales portals that your distributor may offer or recommend, including third party options like VIP, Salesforce, etc.

Seek feedback and input to better understand needs and market dynamics. This will enable you to make informed decisions and tailor your strategies accordingly.

Joint Business Planning:

Collaborate with wholesalers on joint business planning to align objectives, establish targets, and develop action plans. Timing conflicts can be everywhere. If there is a gap in other priorities or objectives on the wholesale side, jump at the opportunity to align a short-term SPA and offer pulse pricing to the market. As important as catering to the end consumer, is providing tools to the sales force when they need them.

Training and Education:

You stand to make a greater impact on product education by making 20-30 second videos on social media and developing a following with the sales teams you work with, than by doing an hour-long training at a sales meeting. The presentation may feel better, but the regular constant reminders are of greater value long term. Again, this is good to work on regularly but if you're offering a short-term incentive you need to turn up the presence on social media and marketing to lean into the opportunities.

If you're offering financial support through SPAs you had better be focusing of fostering a collaborative learning environment where both suppliers and wholesalers can exchange insights and best practices. Provide training and education programs to wholesalers to enhance their product knowledge, selling skills, and customer service capabilities. The more passive and flexible the better.

Ongoing Evaluation in SPAs:

Regular evaluation is essential to assess the effectiveness of your SPAs, identify areas for improvement, and ensure long-term success.

Here are some key aspects of ongoing evaluation in SPAs:

Performance Metrics:

Define relevant performance metrics and key performance indicators (KPIs) to measure the success of your SPAs. These metrics may include sales volume, (dollars or units sold) market share, (accounts or points of distribution within your key accounts) customer satisfaction, (pull through in active accounts) and promotional effectiveness, (ROI on spend vs. increase in sales).

Regularly track and analyze these metrics to evaluate the impact of your SPA strategies and identify trends or areas requiring attention.

Feedback and Reviews:

Seek feedback from wholesalers on their experience with the SPA. Conduct regular reviews or surveys to gather their insights, suggestions, and any challenges they may be facing. Regular can be 1-2 times per year, or it can be quarterly. If you're meeting monthly to manage these things, you may not be allowing enough time for new processes to gain traction. Patience and discipline turn into success.

Use this feedback to refine your strategies, address concerns, and strengthen your partnership with wholesalers.

Adaptability and Flexibility:

Be flexible and adaptable in your approach. The market landscape and dynamics may change, requiring adjustments to your SPA strategies. Even is cases where you may disagree, give people the opportunity to be wrong. You may find yourself pleasantly surprised with their success!

This may sound like a broken record but regularly evaluate market conditions, consumer trends, and competitive factors to stay ahead of the curve and ensure your SPAs remain relevant and effective.

Recap: Key Highlights of Collaboration and Evaluation in SPAs

· Collaboration is crucial for effective SPA implementation: Establish transparent communication channels and actively seek feedback to align strategies, understand market dynamics, and make informed decisions.

·   Joint business planning ensures objective alignment: Collaborate with wholesalers to set targets, develop action plans, and seize short-term opportunities that align with their priorities.

·   Training and education programs empower wholesalers: Utilize social media and short videos to enhance product education and create a collaborative learning environment.

·   Ongoing evaluation is essential for success: Define performance metrics and regularly track sales volume, market share, customer satisfaction, and promotional effectiveness to identify areas for improvement.

·   Solicit feedback and conduct regular reviews: Gather insights from wholesalers to refine SPA strategies, address concerns, and strengthen partnerships.

·   Be adaptable and flexible: Continuously evaluate market conditions, consumer trends, and competitive factors to adjust SPA strategies and stay ahead of the curve.

·   Collaboration and evaluation drive long-term success: Building strong relationships and driving sustained growth in the marketplace requires ongoing collaboration and evaluation efforts.

By prioritizing collaboration and evaluation in SPAs, suppliers and wholesalers can establish mutually beneficial partnerships and achieve long-term success in the adult beverage industry.

Review Questions:

1. True/False: Collaboration in SPAs primarily involves transparent communication and joint business planning.
2. Which of the following is NOT a performance metric for evaluating SPAs?

    1. Sales volume
    2. Market share
    3. Number of training sessions
    4. Promotional effectiveness

3. Fill in the blank: Regular _____ sessions can significantly enhance product knowledge and selling skills of wholesalers.
4. Why is adaptability crucial in the execution of SPAs?
5. Which of the following best describes the role of feedback in SPAs?

    1. To refine strategies
    2. To increase sales volume
    3. To set new targets
    4. To reduce costs

Formula Recap: The Math Summary and formula Cheat Sheet

Chapter 5 talks about the intricacies of pricing strategies tailored for the adult beverage industry. Building on the foundational concepts introduced in the previous chapters, this section provides a detailed exploration of pricing mechanisms, their mathematical underpinnings, and their practical applications in real-world scenarios.

Key Themes and Topics:

Lift Analysis in Pricing:

- **Main Theme:** Lift analysis is a technique used to measure the impact of discounts or promotions on sales. It helps businesses determine the additional sales volume needed to offset discounts and maintain or achieve desired profit levels.
- **Formula Summary:** The chapter introduced formulas to calculate the break-even volume on profit, profit per unit with discounts, and the additional units needed to maintain profit levels.

Transparency and Communication in SPA Pricing:

- **Main Theme:** The importance of fostering transparency and open communication between suppliers and wholesalers for successful pricing strategies. Clear communication ensures mutual understanding, alignment of goals, and effective navigation of SPA complexities.
- **Key Concepts:** Shared market insights, collaborative pricing discussions, regular performance reviews, and the significance of adaptability and flexibility in SPA pricing.

Incentives and Promotional Programs in SPAs:

- **Main Theme:** The role of incentives and promotional programs in driving sales and boosting market penetration. These tools can be leveraged to motivate wholesalers and retailers to promote products more aggressively.

- **Examples:** The chapter provided real-world examples, such as offering a percentage discount or a quantity-based free goods deal, to illustrate the application of these concepts.

Collaboration and Evaluation in SPAs:

- **Main Theme:** The significance of collaboration between suppliers and wholesalers for effective SPA implementation and the importance of ongoing evaluation to ensure the long-term success of these agreements.
- **Key Concepts:** Transparent communication, joint business planning, training and education, performance metrics, feedback and reviews, and the need for adaptability and flexibility.

Recap of Important Concepts:

- **Pricing Mechanisms:** Throughout the chapter, various pricing mechanisms like FOBs, DAs, and SPAs were explored in depth, highlighting their unique characteristics, benefits, and challenges.
- **Mathematical Underpinnings:** The chapter emphasized the importance of understanding the mathematical formulas behind pricing strategies. From lift analysis to break-even calculations, the mathematical aspect ensures that businesses can make informed and profitable decisions.
- **Real-world Applications:** Practical examples and scenarios were provided to help readers grasp the real-world implications of these pricing strategies. These examples serve as a bridge between theoretical knowledge and practical application.

- **Collaboration and Communication:** Emphasized throughout the chapter was the importance of collaboration and communication. Whether it's between suppliers and wholesalers or within an organization, effective communication ensures that all stakeholders are aligned and working towards common goals.
- **Evaluation and Adaptability:** The dynamic nature of the market necessitates regular evaluations and adaptability. Businesses need to be agile, adjusting their strategies based on market feedback, performance metrics, and changing circumstances.

Additional Review tool: Pricing Formula Summary List

For your convenience, here's a summary of the key formulas covered in the chapters. Reference the respective articles in each chapter for detailed calculations.

Chapter 1: FOBs - Freight on Board: Designing Effective Pricing Models

Formula 1: FOB Price Calculation:

FOB Price = FOB Price + State Tax / (1 + Wholesaler Markup Percentage)

Formula 2: Suggested Retail Price (SRP) Calculation:

SRP = Price to Retail * (1 + Retailer Markup Percentage)

Chapter 2: DAs - Depletion Allowances: Optimizing Pricing and Margin Control

Formula 1: Net Cost to Wholesaler Calculation:

Net Cost to Wholesaler = COGs - Depletion Allowance

Formula 2: Wholesaler Margin Calculation:

Wholesaler Margin = (Selling Price to Customer - Net Cost to Wholesaler) / Selling Price to Customer *100

Formula 3: Retailer Margin Calculation:

Retailer Margin = (Retail Price - Wholesale Price) / Retail Price * 100

Formula 4: On-Premise Pour Cost Calculation:

On-Premise Pour Cost = Cost per Serving / Selling Price for Cocktail

Chapter 3: SPAs - Special Purchase Agreements: Enhancing Pricing Flexibility

Formula 1: Percentage Discount Calculation:

Discounted Price = Regular Price - (Regular Price * Discount Percentage)

Formula 2: Fixed Pricing Tiers Calculation:

Total Price = Price per Unit * Quantity

Formula 3: Volume Commitments and Minimum Purchase Requirements Calculation:

No specific formula mentioned, but ensure clear volume commitments and minimum purchase requirements are established.

Formula 4: Performance-Based Incentives Calculation:

Incentive = Total Sales * Incentive Percentage

Additional: Lift Analysis

Formula 1: Break-even Volume on Profit Calculation:

Break-even Volume = Total Profit from Baseline Sale / Profit per Unit with Discount

Example 1: Break-even Volume on Profit (Discount Percentage)

Example 2: Quantity-Based Free Goods Deal Calculation:

There is no one, single, formula. Evaluate additional cases needed to maintain or increase profit level based on break-even volume calculation.

Key take away:

By utilizing the formulas outlined in this comprehensive recap, businesses can effectively design pricing models, calculate depletion allowances, establish pricing parameters for special purchase agreements, and analyze the impact of discounts and promotions through lift analysis. These formulas provide valuable insights and guidance for making informed pricing decisions and optimizing profitability in the alcoholic beverage industry.

Remember to reference the respective articles in each chapter for detailed calculations and consider the specific context of your business and market dynamics when applying these formulas.

Here's a little cheat sheet of a few pocket formulas. Please feel free to print and cut this out or keep a photo in your phone for math on the move.

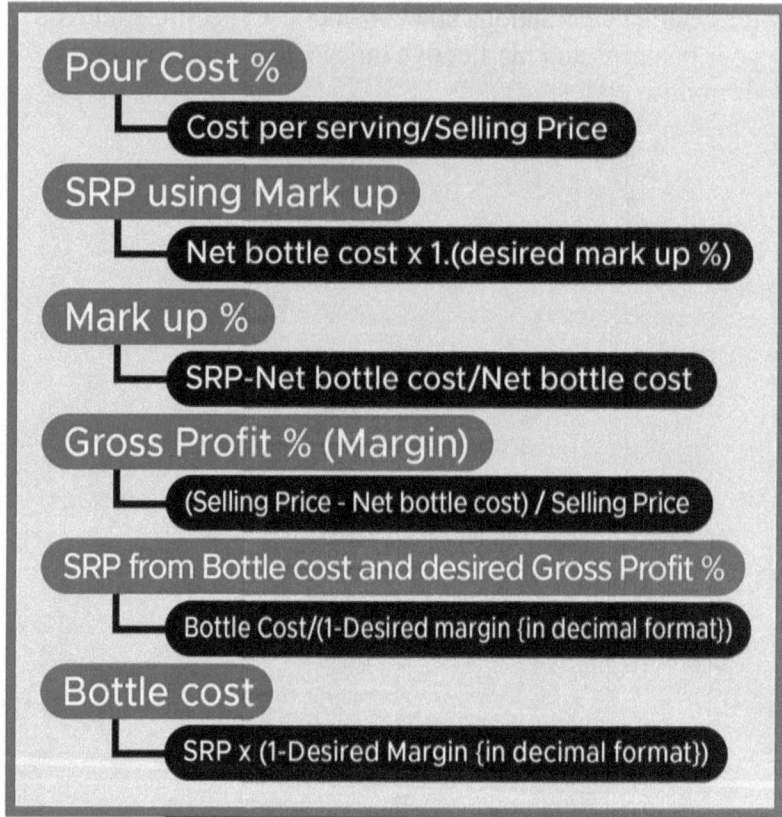

Pour Cost %
Cost per serving/Selling Price

SRP using Mark up
Net bottle cost x 1.(desired mark up %)

Mark up %
SRP-Net bottle cost/Net bottle cost

Gross Profit % (Margin)
(Selling Price - Net bottle cost) / Selling Price

SRP from Bottle cost and desired Gross Profit %
Bottle Cost/(1-Desired margin {in decimal format})

Bottle cost
SRP x (1-Desired Margin {in decimal format})

Chapter 6: Financial Management and Profitability

Ok so we just finished a chapter filled with formulas and calculations, so it's probably superfluous to follow it with a chapter about how important it all is. But now that I've acknowledged that, let me just say, financial management serves as the cornerstone of the alcohol industry's economic structure, underpinning the operational and strategic decisions that drive profitability and growth. This chapter will dissect the essential financial practices and principles that govern the industry's unique business environment.

The alcohol industry operates within a framework of stringent regulations and complex market dynamics, which necessitates a wide understanding of financial management. Each segment of the industry—from production to distribution to retail—must navigate its own set of financial considerations to not only survive but to thrive economically.

In the following sections, we will examine those critical components.

Budgeting and Financial Planning: We will outline the process of constructing a comprehensive budget that accounts for the industry's revenue streams and cost structures, ensuring that businesses can plan for both stability and growth.

Cost Control and Margin Optimization: We will explore strategies for managing costs without compromising product quality, and for optimizing profit margins in a highly competitive marketplace.

Cash Flow Management: We will delve into the techniques for managing the inflows and outflows of cash, a vital aspect of maintaining business solvency and supporting expansion in the alcohol industry.

Evaluating ROI: We will discuss methodologies for assessing the return on investment for various business activities, from marketing campaigns to new product development, ensuring that resources are allocated efficiently.

This chapter aims to equip readers with the financial tools and knowledge necessary to navigate the alcohol industry's economic landscape effectively. Whether you are a financial manager in a large beverage corporation, a small distillery owner, or a student of the industry, the insights provided here will be instrumental in fostering a deep understanding of the financial mechanisms at play in the alcohol industry.

Article 1: Budgeting and Financial Planning for Alcohol Businesses

Understanding Revenue Streams

Long term, producers primarily generate revenue in the USA through sales to wholesalers. Additionally, many producers enhance their revenue and marketing efforts through on-site distilleries or tasting rooms, which can also foster brand loyalty. Wholesalers typically adopt a 'cost-plus' model to maintain margins, accounting for storage, transportation, and marketing costs in their pricing strategies. A subset of wholesalers operates with a focus on logistics, earning revenue through delivery and split case fees. Retailers face varying financial challenges based on their business models, from club stores with thin margins and membership fee-based profits to regional chains that capitalize on market presence for higher margins.

The Art of Effective Budgeting

Budgeting in the alcohol industry serves as a strategic tool for navigating market trends, consumer behavior, and unforeseen challenges.

Key budgeting activities include:

Forecasting Sales: Employing historical data, market research, and industry trends to anticipate future sales, crucial for production cycle planning. Investment in advanced forecasting software, increasingly enhanced by AI, is considered valuable. But if you have access to raw data and know how to work a pivot table, you're on the right path.

Allocating Resources: Ensuring optimal allocation of resources for marketing, staffing, or material procurement. Return on investment (ROI) considerations should include both measurable outcomes and intangible factors such as company culture and integrity.

Risk Management: Addressing regulatory, market, and external challenges through robust budgeting to absorb potential shocks and maintain business continuity, including preparation for potential sales declines.

Capital Expenditure Planning: Providing a framework for timely and strategic investments in expansion, diversification, or facility upgrades, aligned with long-term business objectives.

The Power of Financial Planning

Financial planning offers a comprehensive perspective on a business's financial health, encompassing the setting of financial objectives and the development of strategies to achieve them. This process may involve expansion into new markets, product line introductions, or optimization of the current operational footprint. It also includes risk assessment and the formulation of mitigation strategies to address potential regulatory changes or market downturns, ensuring sustained profitability and growth.

While the alcohol industry is often celebrated for its products and heritage, the foundation of any successful alcohol business is robust financial planning and budgeting. Further exploration of this chapter will reveal additional tools, strategies, and insights to support business success in this sector.

Review Questions:

1. True/False: The primary revenue stream for producers in the alcohol industry is the sale of products to end consumers.
2. Multiple Choice: What is a common revenue model for wholesalers in the alcohol industry?

    a. Subscription-based model
    b. Cost-plus model
    c. Flat-rate model
    d. Commission-based model

3. Fill in the Blank: When planning for capital expenditures, alcohol businesses must ensure that investments are _____, feasible, and aligned with long-term business goals.
4. Short Answer: Why is it important for alcohol businesses to include both measurable outcomes and intangible factors in ROI considerations?

5. Match the following components of financial planning with their correct descriptions.
>   a.Forecasting Sales
>   b.Allocating Resources
>   c.Risk Management
>   d.Capital Expenditure Planning

   i.   Involves anticipating future sales using historical data and market analysis.

   ii.   Ensures resources are distributed effectively for various business needs.

   iii.   Acts as a financial cushion against market fluctuations and regulatory changes.

   iv.   Provides a strategic framework for investments in business growth and infrastructure.

Article 2: Cost Control and Margin Optimization: The Balancing Act in the Alcohol Industry

Managing costs and optimizing margins are critical for the success of businesses in the alcohol industry. This sector's unique challenges stem from its complex supply chains, diverse product offerings, and constantly changing consumer preferences. Effective financial management in this context means ensuring quality while maintaining a strong financial foundation.

Deciphering the Cost Matrix

Costs in the alcohol industry are diverse, encompassing raw materials, packaging, marketing, and distribution.

They can be categorized as follows:

Variable Costs: Costs that fluctuate with production volume.

Formula: Variable Cost = Number of Units Produced x Cost per Unit

Example: For 1,000 bottles at $5 each, the variable cost totals $5,000.

Fixed Costs: Costs that remain unchanged regardless of production volume.

Formula: Total Cost = Variable Cost + Fixed Cost

Example: With fixed costs of $10,000 and variable costs of $5,000, the total cost equals $15,000.

Strategies for Effective Cost Control

Effective cost control can be achieved through:

Leveraging Relationships: Building strong supplier relationships can lead to better pricing and terms. This sounds obvious but always network and consider using your network to find the best options.

Bulk Purchasing and Contracts: Utilizing economies of scale to negotiate better prices.

Formula: Savings = (Original Price per Unit - Discounted Price per Unit) x Number of Units

Example: A $0.50 saving per bottle for 1,000 bottles results in $500 savings.

Operational Efficiency: Investing in technology and training to streamline operations can reduce costs over time.

Mastering Margin Optimization

Margins represent the difference between the selling price and the cost of production.

Strategies for optimizing margins include:

Diverse Product Offerings: Catering to various market segments with products at different price points can enhance profitability.

Formula: Gross Margin = (Selling Price - Cost of Goods Sold) / Selling Price x 100%

Example: A bottle sold for $20, costing $10 to produce, yields a 50% gross margin.

Pricing Quantities: Implementing bulk discounts or promotional offers can attract different customer segments.

Formula: Discounted Margin = (Discounted Price - Cost of Goods Sold) / Discounted Price x 100%

Example: A discounted bottle sold for $18, with production costs of $10, has a margin of 44.44%.

Regular Price Reviews: Adjusting prices in response to market changes can maintain or improve margins.

Formula: New Margin = (New Selling Price - Cost of Goods Sold) / New Selling Price x 100%

Example: If the selling price increases to $22 while production cost stays at $10, the new margin is 54.55%.

The Road Ahead

The alcohol industry demands agility in financial management. Businesses must continuously review their cost structures and margin strategies to adapt to market changes. The forthcoming articles will further explore cash flow management, working capital considerations, and ROI evaluation, providing the knowledge to navigate the financial aspects of the alcohol industry confidently.

Review Questions:

1. True/False: Variable costs in the alcohol industry remain constant regardless of how much is produced.
2. Fill in the Blank: The formula for calculating total cost is Total Cost = Variable Cost + _____.
3. Multiple Choice: What is the benefit of leveraging relationships with suppliers?
   A) To receive moral support
   B) To gain better pricing and favorable payment terms
   C) To increase the cost of goods
   D) To create more paperwork
4. Short Answer: Explain how bulk purchasing can affect cost control in the alcohol industry.
5. Calculation: If a company decides to offer a 10% discount on a product that originally costs $15 to produce and is sold for $30, what is the new discounted margin percentage?

Article 3: Cash Flow Management and Working Capital Considerations in the Alcohol Industry

Cash flow management and working capital are critical components of financial stability in the alcohol industry, which is characterized by unique production cycles, regulatory challenges, and market dynamics. Effective management of these financial elements is essential for the sustainability and growth of businesses within this sector.

Cash Flow Challenges in the Alcohol Industry

Production Cycles: The production of certain alcoholic beverages, particularly those requiring aging, involves a significant delay between production and sales, leading to capital being tied up in inventory for long durations.

Regulatory Delays: Obtaining necessary licenses and approvals can introduce delays in sales and revenue recognition. For example, label approval by regulatory bodies like the TTB can vary from a few weeks to several months, depending on the specifics of the submission.

Seasonal Demand: The industry often sees seasonal demand spikes, such as during holidays, resulting in irregular cash inflows. While sales history can improve forecasting, establishing a reliable pattern for these fluctuations requires time.

Strategies for Managing Cash Flow

Forecasting: Effective cash flow forecasting enables businesses to anticipate and plan for potential cash shortages or surpluses, facilitating strategic financial decisions.

Diversifying Revenue Streams: Producers can achieve more consistent cash inflows by diversifying revenue streams, including on-premise sales through tasting rooms or events, which can be particularly lucrative in the early years of operation.

Negotiating Terms: Securing favorable payment terms with suppliers and customers can help synchronize cash inflows with outflows. This may include quantity purchase agreements, payment terms for shipments, and structured marketing funds.

Working Capital Management

Working capital, the liquidity measure of current assets minus current liabilities, is indicative of a company's short-term financial health. In the alcohol industry, where inventory often constitutes a large part of current assets, managing working capital efficiently is crucial.

Inventory Management: Effective inventory strategies prevent excessive capital from being locked in stock, which may involve just-in-time inventory practices or optimized reorder levels.

Receivables Management: Maintaining strict credit policies and diligently collecting overdue accounts can reduce days sales outstanding, thereby enhancing cash flow.

Flexible Financing: Access to lines of credit or other financing options provides a financial buffer in times of cash flow constraints. However, it is important to avoid over-leveraging to safeguard against unforeseen expenses.

Navigating the financial landscape of the alcohol industry requires a keen understanding of cash flow management and working capital. By implementing robust financial strategies and maintaining flexibility, businesses can ensure their financial performance remains strong amidst the industry's challenges.

Flexible Financing Expanded

1) **Line of Credit**
   a) Where: Traditional banks or credit unions.
   b) How to Ask: "I'm interested in establishing a business line of credit to manage fluctuations in our cash flow. What are your terms and qualifications?"
   c) More Info: U.S. Small Business Administration
   d) https://www.sba.gov/
2) **Business Credit Card**
   a) Where: Most major banks offer business credit cards.
   b) How to Ask: "What benefits and features come with your business credit cards? I'd like to apply for one."
   c) More Info: NerdWallet's Best Business Credit Cards
   d) https://www.nerdwallet.com/best/credit-cards/small-business
3) **Equipment Financing**
   a) Where: Banks, dedicated equipment financiers, or online lenders.
   b) How to Ask: "I'm looking to finance some equipment purchases for our distillery. What are your terms for equipment loans?"
   c) More Info: Equipment Leasing and Finance Association
   d) https://www.elfaonline.org/
4) **Inventory Financing**
   a) Where: Asset-based lenders or specialized inventory financing firms.
   b) How to Ask: "Our winery needs flexible financing tied to our inventory. Can you provide inventory-based loans?"
   c) More Info: Fit Small Business Inventory Financing Guide
   d) https://fitsmallbusiness.com/
5) **Merchant Cash Advances**
   a) Where: Online lenders or dedicated MCA providers.

b) How to Ask: "We're considering a merchant cash advance based on our card sales. What are your rates and terms?"

c) More Info: Investopedia on Merchant Cash Advances

d) https://www.investopedia.com/

6) **Trade Credit**

a) Where: Directly from suppliers.

b) How to Ask: "We value our relationship and are looking to negotiate extended payment terms. Would you consider net-30 or net-60 terms?"

c) More Info: Investopedia on Trade Credit

d) https://www.investopedia.com/terms/t/trade-credit.asp

7) **SBA (Small Business Administration) Loans**

a) Where: Approved SBA lenders, usually banks.

b) How to Ask: "We're exploring SBA loan options for our business expansion. Can you guide us on how to apply?"

c) More Info: U.S. Small Business Administration Loans

d) https://www.sba.gov/funding-programs/loans

8) **Factoring or Invoice Financing**

a) Where: Factoring companies or online platforms like BlueVine.

b) How to Ask: "We're interested in advancing our unpaid invoices. What are your rates for invoice factoring?"

c) More Info: BlueVine

d) https://www.bluevine.com/

9) **Revenue-based Financing**

a) Where: Online lenders specializing in revenue-based loans.

b) How to Ask: "Our distillery is interested in revenue-based financing. What are your criteria and terms?"

c) More Info: Lighter Capital

d) https://www.lightercapital.com/

10) **Crowdfunding or Community Shares**

a) Where: Platforms like Kickstarter, Indiegogo, or local community share platforms.

b) How to Ask: This is more about pitching your idea or project to the public, so it's more about crafting a compelling story.
c) More Info: Kickstarter and Indiegogo
d) https://www.kickstarter.com/
e) https://www.indiegogo.com/

Remember, when considering any form of financing, it's essential to do thorough research and understand all terms, rates, and potential obligations. Consulting with a financial advisor or business consultant can also be invaluable.

The Path Forward

Cash flow and working capital management are not just about numbers; they're about ensuring that businesses have the financial flexibility to seize opportunities and weather challenges. As the alcohol industry continues to evolve, businesses that prioritize these financial aspects will be better positioned to thrive.

Review Questions:

1. True/False: Seasonal demand spikes in the alcohol industry can lead to consistent cash inflows throughout the year.
2. In the alcohol industry, the time lag between production and sales for beverages requiring aging is a significant challenge to _____ management.
3. Which of the following is NOT a strategy for managing cash flow in the alcohol industry?

   a) Forecasting future sales and cash requirements
   b) Diversifying revenue streams through on-premise sales and events

    c) Ignoring payment terms with suppliers and customers
    d) Negotiating favorable payment terms with suppliers and customers

4. Match the following financing options with their correct sources:

    a) Line of Credit
    b) Business Credit Card
    c) Factoring or Invoice Financing

Sources:

    I.   Traditional banks or credit unions
    II.   Most major banks
    III.   Factoring companies or online platforms like BlueVine

5. What does working capital represent in a business, and why is it particularly important in the alcohol industry?

Article 4: Evaluating Return on Investment (ROI) and Financial Performance in the Alcohol Industry

Entering the alcohol industry often stems from a passion for the craft or the business itself. However, for sustained success, it's essential to measure and understand the return on investments (ROI). This is particularly important in the alcohol sector due to its long production cycles, regulatory challenges, and market dynamics. This article examines ROI and the evaluation of financial performance in the alcohol industry.

The Importance of ROI in the Alcohol Industry

Guiding Investments: Understanding potential ROI is crucial for decision-making and resource allocation, such as in new distillery setups, marketing campaigns, or market expansions.

Performance Measurement: ROI serves as a quantifiable metric to assess the effectiveness of strategies and initiatives, enabling continuous refinement and optimization.

Stakeholder Communication: ROI provides stakeholders, from investors to employees, with a transparent view of the company's financial health and prospects.

Calculating ROI in the Alcohol Sector

$$ROI = \frac{\text{Net Profit from Investment - Cost of Investment}}{\text{Cost of Investment}} \times 100\%$$

The calculation of ROI in the alcohol industry must consider several industry-specific factors:

Long-Term Investments: Products requiring aging necessitate a long-term perspective on ROI, as returns may not be realized for years.

Regulatory and Compliance Costs: Significant costs in the industry, including federal and variable state fees, must be included in investment costs.

Brand Building and Marketing: The intangible and long-term nature of returns from brand-building efforts complicates ROI calculations. Early investments in marketing may not yield immediate returns but are crucial for long-term brand viability.

Strategies for Optimizing ROI

Diversified Portfolio: A range of products can mitigate market volatility and provide steadier returns. Starting with entry-level items can establish brand presence, with higher-tier products introduced later to improve profitability.

Efficient Production: Cost reductions through streamlined production and technology adoption can enhance ROI. It's important to plan purchases and operations to avoid unnecessary expenditures.

Data-Driven Marketing: Employing data analytics in marketing can lead to more effective strategies and better investment returns.

Evaluating Financial Performance

In addition to ROI, other financial metrics offer a comprehensive view of a company's performance:

Profit Margin Analysis: Analyzing profitability across different products or segments helps in targeting growth in profit dollars.

Liquidity Ratios: These ratios indicate the company's capacity to meet short-term obligations, considering factors like seasonal sales and inventory requirements. For financial summaries of the beer industry, refer to "Boston Beer Financial Ratios for Analysis 2009-2023 | SAM | MacroTrends" (https://www.macrotrends.net/stocks/charts/SAM/boston-beer/financial-ratios-for-analysis).

Debt Ratios: Metrics like the debt-to-equity ratio provide insight into a company's leverage and long-term payment capabilities. For more on the debt-to-equity ratio in the food & beverage industry, see "Average D/E Ratio for the Food and Beverage Sector" (https://www.investopedia.com/articles/personal-finance/061915/average-debt-equity-ratio-food-beverage-sector.asp).

Evaluating ROI and financial performance involves more than numerical analysis; it requires an understanding of what the figures indicate about a company's strategic decisions and future direction. As the alcohol industry evolves, prioritizing financial evaluation will position businesses to make well-informed decisions and foster growth. Future articles will delve into the financial management nuances within the alcohol industry, providing a thorough understanding of the topic.

Review Questions:

1. True/False: In the alcohol industry, the return on long-term investments such as aged products can be realized shortly after production.
2. What is a significant factor to consider when calculating ROI in the alcohol industry?
   a. The color of the packaging
   b. Immediate sales after product launch
   c. Regulatory and compliance costs
   d. The CEO's personal taste preferences
3. When optimizing ROI, having a _____ can help mitigate market volatility and provide steadier returns.
4. Explain why it is important to use data analytics in marketing strategies within the alcohol industry.
5. Discuss the importance of evaluating both ROI and other financial metrics, such as profit margin analysis

and debt ratios, in understanding the financial performance of a company in the alcohol industry.

Article 5: The Future of Financial Management in the Alcohol Industry: Trends and Innovations

The alcohol industry is constantly undergoing significant transformation due to the emergence of non-alcoholic products, craft breweries, the rise of artisanal spirits, and evolving consumer preferences. These changes are driving an evolution in financial management within the sector. As we look ahead, several trends and innovations are anticipated to reshape financial strategies for businesses in the alcohol industry.

Digital Transformation and Financial Management: The digital revolution is impacting the alcohol industry, particularly in financial management. Technologies such as automated inventory systems and AI-driven sales forecasting are transforming traditional financial practices:

Blockchain in Supply Chain: Blockchain technology ensures transparency and traceability in transactions, from procurement to final sales. It establishes a secure digital ledger that records transactions, which, once verified, cannot be altered. This technology is integrated into supply chain management software, using smart contracts and decentralized applications to automate and validate processes.

AI and Machine Learning: These technologies facilitate predictive analytics that can forecast sales, refine pricing strategies, and predict market trends, enabling businesses to make informed financial decisions.

Sustainable Financing: Sustainability has become a critical factor in business operations and investment decisions in the alcohol industry:

Sustainability-Linked Loans (SLLs)

Where: Available from commercial lenders or peer-to-peer lending platforms.

How to Ask: Inquire by stating, "We're interested in loans that offer terms linked to our sustainability performance. Can you provide details on your SLLs?"

More Info: Harvard Business School Online provides additional information on SLLs at https://online.hbs.edu/courses/sustainable-business-strategy/.

Sustainability Bonds

Where: Obtainable from bond issuers that focus on green and social projects.

How to Ask: Request information by asking, "We're looking to finance a mix of green and social projects. Can you provide details on your sustainability bonds?"

More Info: Further insights on Sustainability Bonds can be found at Harvard Business School Online at https://online.hbs.edu/courses/sustainable-business-strategy/.

Green Loans

Where: Accessible through commercial lenders or peer-to-peer lending platforms.

How to Ask: Seek information by stating, "We're initiating environmentally friendly projects and are seeking financing. Can you provide details on your green loans?"

More Info: Harvard Business School Online discusses Green Loans at https://online.hbs.edu/courses/sustainable-business-strategy/.

Direct-to-Consumer (DTC) Sales and Financial Implications: The expansion of e-commerce and regulatory changes have made DTC sales a significant source of revenue for alcohol brands:

Cash Flow Management: DTC sales can result in quicker payment cycles, affecting cash flow management.

Tax Implications: Direct sales to consumers across various jurisdictions can lead to complex tax implications, necessitating sophisticated financial management.

Risk Management in a Globalized World: The global nature of the alcohol industry introduces several financial risks:

Currency Fluctuations: Businesses that import materials or export products are subject to the financial impact of currency market volatility.

Geopolitical Risks: International trade can be influenced by political conflicts, tariffs, and trade disputes, affecting the cost of doing business.

Continuous Learning and Financial Education: The rapid evolution of the industry highlights the need for continuous learning:

Professional Development: Organizations are investing in financial management training for their teams. Notable courses include:

Financial Management Capstone by Coursera at https://www.coursera.org/learn/financial-management-capstone

Finance and Accounting Online Training by LinkedIn Learning at https://www.linkedin.com/learning/topics/finance-and-accounting

Professional Development in Finance by New York Institute of Finance at https://www.nyif.com/

Collaborative Learning: Industry forums and seminars offer venues for shared learning and knowledge exchange. Noteworthy platforms include:

eLearning Learning: Facilitates finance-related discussions and collaborative learning.

Education Forum by AFAANZ: A conference that promotes the advancement of accounting education and collaborative excellence among its members.

The future of financial management in the alcohol industry is characterized by dynamic changes driven by technological innovations, consumer behavior, and global economic trends. By staying informed and adaptable, businesses can effectively navigate these changes, ensuring profitability and growth in the years ahead.

Review Questions:

1. Fill in the blank: In the context of financial management in the alcohol industry, _____ technology ensures transparency and traceability in supply chain transactions.

2. Multiple choice: What type of loans are linked to a company's sustainability performance?

    a. Commercial Loans
    b. Sustainability-Linked Loans (SLLs)
    c. Green Loans
    d. Peer-to-Peer Loans

3. True/False: Direct-to-Consumer (DTC) sales do not affect cash flow management strategies in the alcohol industry.
4. Fill in the blank: The course
"_____" by Coursera is recommended for professional development in financial management within the alcohol industry.
5. Multiple choice: Which of the following is a risk associated with the global nature of the alcohol industry?

    a. Currency Fluctuations
    b. Fixed pricing strategies
    c. Localized marketing campaigns
    d. Domestic supply chain management

Chapter 6 Recap: Financial Mastery in the Alcohol Industry: A Comprehensive Guide

The Blueprint of Success: Budgeting and Financial Planning

Key Takeaway: Effective budgeting and financial planning are crucial for any alcohol business, underpinning resource allocation and risk management.

Discussion: Producers depend on sales to wholesalers and also use on-site distilleries or tasting rooms for marketing. Wholesalers employ a 'cost-plus' model to maintain margins, while retailers must carefully plan their revenue streams.

The Balancing Act: Cost Control and Margin Optimization

Key Takeaway: Proficiency in cost control and margin optimization is key to profitability and long-term viability in the alcohol industry.

Discussion: Costs range from raw materials to distribution. Strategies for cost control include supplier negotiations, bulk purchases, and operational efficiencies. Margin optimization involves managing product ranges, pricing strategies, and regular price assessments.

Navigating Financial Waters: Cash Flow and Working Capital

Key Takeaway: The adept management of cash flow and working capital is vital for the financial robustness and expansion of alcohol industry entities.

Discussion: The industry faces unique cash flow challenges due to production, regulation, and demand. Key considerations include inventory management, receivable strategies, and flexible financing.

Measuring Success: ROI and Financial Performance

Key Takeaway: Evaluating ROI and other financial metrics is essential for a comprehensive understanding of a business's strategic direction and potential.

Discussion: ROI is used for guiding investments, evaluating performance, and stakeholder communication. Additional metrics such as profit margin analysis, liquidity ratios, and debt ratios offer further insight into business performance.

The Future Landscape: Trends and Innovations

Key Takeaway: Emerging technological advancements, sustainable financing, and global market trends will shape the future of financial management in the alcohol industry.

Discussion: The financial landscape will be transformed by digitalization, eco-conscious financing, DTC sales, international risk management, and the imperative of ongoing education.

The financial terrain of the alcohol industry is multifaceted, influenced by production, regulatory environments, and international developments. As the sector progresses, the emphasis on astute financial management becomes paramount. Businesses that master these financial principles will be poised to thrive, ensuring profitability, sustainability, and growth in a dynamic marketplace.

Chapter 7: Supply Chain and Logistics within the Three-Tier System

Chapter 7 is where we discuss the physical check points in the Three-Tier Alcohol System of the U.S. alcoholic beverage market. This chapter is designed to provide a clear and comprehensive understanding of the system's supply chain, logistics, and the challenges and opportunities it presents.

Understanding the Three-Tier Alcohol System

The U.S. alcoholic beverage market operates under a unique regulatory framework known as the Three-Tier Alcohol System. This system shapes the way alcohol is distributed and sold, creating a complex network of logistics and regulations. Our focus in this chapter is to unravel these complexities, offering a detailed analysis of how the system functions and its impact on the industry.

Key Objectives of This Chapter:

Clarifying the Complexities: We aim to simplify the intricate aspects of alcohol distribution laws and the challenges faced in alcohol distribution jobs, providing a clear understanding of the industry's framework.

Empowering with Knowledge: Whether you are an entrepreneur assessing the market value of the alcoholic beverage industry or a student exploring career opportunities, this chapter is designed to arm you with practical insights and knowledge.

Learning from Success Stories: By examining case studies and real-world examples, we will explore how industry leaders have successfully managed challenges such as unpredictable lead times and supplier relationship optimization.

This chapter is an essential guide for anyone looking to navigate the U.S. alcoholic beverage market. The goal is to equip you with the necessary knowledge and tools to understand and excel within the Three-Tier System.

Article 1: Navigating the Waves of Unpredictable Lead Times in the Three-Tier Alcohol System

Mastering the art of managing lead times is paramount, especially within the unique regulatory framework of the Three-Tier System. This system distinctly separates alcohol producers, distributors, and retailers, adding complexity to the supply chain.

The Ripple Effect of Delays Every bottle of wine, beer, or spirit has a journey through a vast supply chain. Delays can occur due to various reasons like global shipping congestion, customs clearance backlogs, or unforeseen weather events. These delays can lead to stock shortages, empty shelves, and disappointed consumers, significantly impacting product launches or promotional events.

Strategies to Weather the Storm

Robust Forecasting: Implementing advanced forecasting tools for analyzing historical sales data, seasonal trends, and market shifts. Regularly updating forecasts to reflect real-time market conditions.

Diversified Supply Sources: Establishing relationships with multiple suppliers across different regions. Conducting regular supplier assessments to ensure reliability and quality standards.

Transparent Communication: Utilizing collaborative platforms for real-time information sharing. Holding regular meetings with stakeholders to discuss supply chain performance and risks.

The Balancing Act of Stock Management Balancing demand and supply is crucial. Overstocking ties up capital and storage space, while stockouts can lead to lost sales. Achieving this balance requires understanding market dynamics, leveraging technology for real-time inventory tracking, and fostering strong relationships across the supply chain.

Unpredictable lead times pose a unique challenge. With the right strategies, tools, and collaborative spirit, industry players can navigate these challenges and thrive.

Review Questions:

1. True/False: The Three-Tier Alcohol System in the U.S. simplifies the supply chain for alcohol distribution.
2. What can cause delays in the alcohol supply chain?
   a. Global shipping congestion
   b. Customs clearance backlogs
   c. Unforeseen weather events
   d. All of the above
3. Robust forecasting in the alcohol industry should include analyzing _____ data, seasonal trends, and market shifts.
4. What is a key strategy for managing supply sources in the alcohol industry?

   a. Relying on a single supplier
   b. Diversifying suppliers across different regions
   c. Ordering only as needed
   d. Ignoring supplier quality standards
5. True/False: Overstocking in the alcohol industry can lead to tied-up capital and potential spoilage of products.

Article 2: Navigating Regulatory and Compliance Factors in Alcohol Distribution

Understanding the Three-Tier Alcohol System The U.S. alcoholic beverage industry operates under the Three-Tier Alcohol System, a regulatory framework established post-Prohibition. This system mandates a clear separation between alcohol producers, distributors, and retailers to prevent monopolies, promote accountability, and ensure product quality. However, the complexity increases with each state having its own set of rules, creating a diverse regulatory landscape.

Federal Oversight: The Role of the TTB The Alcohol and Tobacco Tax and Trade Bureau (TTB) oversees production, labeling, advertising, and import/export of alcoholic beverages at the federal level. Compliance with TTB regulations is crucial for maintaining legal adherence, industry integrity, and consumer trust.

State-Specific Mandates Each state in the U.S. has its own alcohol regulatory body and set of rules, ranging from licensing requirements to distribution limits and regulations for "dry" counties. Understanding and adhering to these state-specific mandates is essential for businesses operating in multiple states.

Temperature Control in Transportation Regulations around temperature-controlled shipments are particularly important for certain alcoholic beverages like wines and craft beers. These mandates ensure that the quality of these products is maintained from producer to consumer.

Embracing Compliance as a Competitive Advantage

Navigating the regulatory landscape of the Three-Tier System is challenging but offers unique opportunities. Businesses that excel in compliance can position themselves as trustworthy industry leaders. This adherence to regulations can be a competitive advantage, especially in an era where consumers value transparency and authenticity.

Review Questions:

1. True/False: The Three-Tier Alcohol System was established to promote monopolies in the alcohol industry.
2. What is the primary role of the Alcohol and Tobacco Tax and Trade Bureau (TTB) in the U.S. alcoholic beverage industry?
   a. Overseeing production, labeling, advertising, and import/export of alcoholic beverages.
   b. Directly selling alcoholic beverages to consumers.
   c. Producing alcoholic beverages.
3. Each state in the U.S. has its own _____ regulatory body and set of rules for alcohol distribution.
4. True/False: Temperature control during transportation is only a recommendation and not a regulatory requirement for certain alcoholic beverages.
5. How can businesses turn regulatory compliance into a competitive advantage in the alcohol industry?
   a. By ignoring state-specific mandates.

      b. By embracing compliance and positioning themselves as trustworthy industry leaders.

      c. By focusing solely on federal regulations.

Article 3: Mastering Inventory Management in the Three-Tier Alcohol System

Inventory Management: The Heartbeat of the Alcohol Supply Chain At its core, inventory management in the alcoholic beverage industry is about ensuring the right product is in the right place at the right time. This objective becomes intricate when considering the variables of production, distribution, and retail within the Three-Tier System. The wholesale model is a cost-plus goods business where the end game is to capture a calculated margin expectation and mitigate the risks associated with that process.

Direct Import (DI) vs. Domestic Ordering: The Strategic Choice

Direct Import (DI) Overview

Control and Forecasting: DI requires a significant level of trust in forecasting from producers. It involves ordering directly from the production location, often overseas.

Lead Times: Lead times for DI can range from 60 to 120 days. This requires wholesalers to forecast demand accurately for at least three months ahead, as they place orders while receiving current stock.

Risk and Reward: DI offers better pricing and cost benefits due to bulk purchasing and eliminating an additional layer of domestic freight costs. However, it also presents higher risks due to longer lead times and potential for overstock or understock situations.

Stateside Ordering Overview

Convenience and Speed: Stateside inventory, stored in domestic warehouses, offers quicker access to products, reducing lead times significantly.

Warehousing Costs: While it provides logistical ease, stateside ordering involves additional warehousing costs borne by the producer or importer.

Pricing Implications: Products ordered stateside typically have higher FOB (Freight on Board) costs due to domestic freight charges or due to producers/importers incurring import freight costs, impacting the final pricing.

Harnessing Technology for Precision and Efficiency
Modern inventory management isn't just about manual counts and spreadsheets. Advanced systems, like Blueridge software, provide real-time visibility into stock levels, seasonal demand trends, and supply chain dynamics. These tools, when used effectively, can predict demand surges, prevent stockouts, and optimize inventory turnover. The more sales history, the better the predictive models. Algorithm functionality has grown at exponential rates, and AI's integration into these models is a future prospect to watch.

Demand Forecasting: Forecasting demand for alcoholic beverages is both an art and a science. Seasonality, market trends, and shifting consumer preferences play a role. Historical sales data, predictive analytics, and soon, even AI can be harnessed to create accurate demand projections. This proactive approach ensures alignment between production, distribution, and retail demand.

Collaborative Inventory Management: The Three-Tier System thrives on collaboration. Open communication channels between suppliers and wholesalers can lead to shared insights, synchronized production schedules, and timely deliveries. This synergy ensures a seamless flow of products, from producers to consumers, enhancing the overall efficiency of the supply chain.

Case Spotlight: A Craft Brewery's Triumph Over Inventory Challenges While I'll leave it unnamed, please consider a craft brewery that faced inventory imbalances due to unpredictable demand surges. By integrating advanced inventory management systems and fostering open communication with its distributor, the brewery could predict demand spikes, optimize stock levels, and ensure timely deliveries. This collaborative approach transformed potential losses into increased sales and enhanced brand reputation. While not famous, the small investment in better inventory management software made the difference in a year of profits that could have been losses.

Review Questions:

1. True/False: In the Three-Tier Alcohol System, inventory management primarily focuses on ensuring products are available at the right place and time.
2. What is a significant risk associated with Direct Import (DI) in inventory management?
   a. Reduced product variety
   b. Shorter lead times
   c. Longer lead times and potential for overstock
   d. Lower warehousing costs

3. Advanced inventory management systems, like
   _____, provide real-time visibility into stock
   levels and demand trends.
4. What is a key benefit of stateside ordering in inventory
   management?
   a. Lower FOB costs
   b. Longer lead times
   c. Quicker access to products
   d. Higher pricing benefits
5. True/False: Collaborative inventory management in
   the Three-Tier System does not significantly impact
   the efficiency of the supply chain.

Article 4: Building and Nurturing Supplier Relationships in the
Three-Tier Alcohol System

Why Supplier Relationships Matter In an industry where
product quality, timely delivery, and regulatory compliance are
paramount, the bond between suppliers and wholesalers
becomes the backbone of success.

A harmonious relationship ensures:

Consistent Product Quality: Ensuring that the beverages
reaching consumers are of the highest standard. For example,
avoiding the shipment of wine in unrefrigerated trucks to
southern markets during a heat wave is a basic yet crucial
consideration.

Supply Chain Efficiency: Minimizing disruptions and
ensuring smooth operations. Wholesalers who prioritize brand
integrity and intentionality often gain priority in supply chain
crunches. It's about being more than just a sales outlet.

Regulatory Adherence: Collaborative efforts to meet state and federal regulations are essential. Keeping everyone away from regulatory risk is as important as maintaining integrity.

Strategies for Strengthening Supplier Bonds

Transparent Communication: Regular check-ins and open discussions about challenges and shared goals foster trust. This means being available when needed and avoiding turning regular issues into crises.

Collaborative Forecasting: Sharing sales data, market insights, and future plans can help align production and distribution strategies. Advance notice is key, as wholesalers often need to pivot through multiple departments to change purchasing strategies.

Contract Clarity: Clear, fair contracts that outline terms, responsibilities, and dispute resolution mechanisms lay a solid foundation. While contract breaches are common, ensuring that the terms are worth the potential risks is vital.

Feedback Mechanisms: Constructive feedback, both positive and negative, helps in continuous improvement. Understanding what perfection looks like from the partner's perspective can reveal key priorities and deal breakers.

Leveraging Technology for Enhanced Collaboration

Modern technology offers tools that can streamline communication, order management, and even dispute resolution between suppliers and wholesalers. Platforms that offer real-time data sharing, inventory tracking, and demand forecasting can revolutionize supplier-wholesaler interactions.

Case Study: A Californian winery faced challenges with its glass bottle supplier, including delays and quality inconsistencies. Instead of severing ties, the winery and supplier embarked on a collaborative journey. They integrated their IT systems for real-time data sharing, co-invested in quality control mechanisms, and established monthly review meetings. The result was improved bottle quality, timely deliveries, and a relationship that became a benchmark in the industry. The winery's flexibility in changing the glass for their red wine and reshaping their rosé bottles exemplified a partnership that embraced challenges and worked towards mutual growth.

Review Questions:

1. True/False: In the Three-Tier Alcohol System, the relationship between suppliers and wholesalers is primarily transactional, not based on partnership.
2. What is a key benefit of maintaining a harmonious supplier-wholesaler relationship?
   a. Increased regulatory risks
   b. Consistent product quality
   c. Reduced communication needs
   d. Simplified contract terms
3. Transparent communication in supplier relationships helps to foster _____.
4. What role does technology play in supplier-wholesaler relationships?
   a. Reducing the need for personal communication
   b. Streamlining communication and enhancing collaboration
   c. Making contracts obsolete
   d. Increasing dependency on manual processes
5. True/False: A Californian winery improved its relationship with a glass bottle supplier by severing ties and finding a new supplier.

Article 5: Case Studies and Best Practices in the Three-Tier Alcohol System

The U.S. alcoholic beverage industry, governed by the unique Three-Tier System, offers a rich landscape of challenges, innovations, and success stories. Article 5 presents insightful case studies and best practices, providing a comprehensive view of the industry's dynamics.

Case Study 1: Localized Distribution - A Craft Brewery's Success

Background: An Oregon craft brewery struggled to expand beyond state lines, hindered by the complexities of interstate alcohol distribution.

Solution: The brewery shifted focus to intensifying its local presence. They partnered with regional distributors, optimized their supply chain for shorter distances, and actively participated in local events.

Outcome: The brewery's sales skyrocketed, making it a beloved brand in Oregon. This success underlined the importance of establishing a strong local base before expanding nationally, as local market performance often influences retailer decisions in other regions.

Case Study 2: Overcoming Regulatory Challenges through Technology

Background: A New York wine importer was frequently entangled in the web of evolving state regulations, causing delays and compliance issues.

Solution: Investment in a regulatory technology platform enabled real-time updates on state laws, automated compliance processes, and efficient documentation management.

Outcome: A dramatic 90% reduction in regulatory challenges, resulting in quicker shipments and a solid reputation for compliance. Utilizing specialized software or outsourcing compliance tasks can free up resources to focus on growth and revenue generation.

Best Practice 1: Digital Transformation in the Supply Chain

Embracing digital solutions is crucial. Implementing supply chain software that provides real-time tracking, demand forecasting, and regulatory compliance is essential for navigating today's Three-Tier System efficiently.

Best Practice 2: Cultivating Collaborative Relationships

Building trust-based, transparent relationships with suppliers, distributors, and regulators is key. Regular communication, joint problem-solving, and shared objectives can elevate mere transactions to strategic alliances.

Case Study 3: Expanding through Direct-to-Consumer Channels

Background: A Californian winery, facing stiff competition, sought to diversify its distribution strategy.

Solution: The winery maintained its traditional Three-Tier System presence while developing a robust Direct-to-Consumer (DTC) channel, focusing on e-commerce and personalized marketing.

Outcome: Sales increased by 70%, with DTC contributing significantly to revenue. This approach not only broadened the customer base but also enhanced brand loyalty, positively impacting wholesale sales nationally. Taking it one step further, their shipment data was shared with their wholesale partners; making stronger inroads in heavy shipment areas, helping to identify opportunity areas geographically.

Best Practice 3: Commitment to Continuous Education and Training

Navigating the Three-Tier System requires ongoing learning. Regular staff training, industry seminars, and staying abreast of the latest publications are vital to maintaining a competitive edge.

Review Questions:

1. True/False: The craft brewery in Oregon expanded its reach nationally to overcome distribution challenges.
2. What solution did the New York-based wine importer implement to navigate regulatory challenges?
   a. Expanded their physical distribution network
   b. Invested in a regulatory tech platform
   c. Reduced the number of products imported
3. Investing in _____ is essential in today's Three-Tier Alcohol System for real-time tracking, demand forecasting, and regulatory compliance.
4. What was the outcome of the Californian winery's implementation of a Direct-to-Consumer (DTC) channel?
   a. Decrease in overall sales
   b. 70% increase in sales
   c. No significant change in sales

5. True/False: Continuous education and training are unnecessary in the Three-Tier System as long as the business is established.

Chapter 7 Summary: Mastering the Three-Tier Alcohol System's Supply Chain and Logistics

In this chapter, we explored the complexities and nuances of the U.S. alcoholic beverage industry within the Three-Tier System. Each section provided in-depth insights into different aspects of supply chain and logistics, equipping readers with a comprehensive understanding of the industry.

Navigating Unpredictable Lead Times and Consolidation Challenges

Key Insights: Understanding the unpredictability of lead times and mastering the art of consolidation are essential in managing the alcohol supply chain effectively.

Strategic Focus: Emphasize robust forecasting, diversified supply sources, and transparent communication to navigate these challenges.

Regulatory and Compliance Factors in Alcohol Distribution

Key Insights: Navigating the complex regulatory landscape is crucial for maintaining compliance and ensuring the integrity of the alcohol industry.

Strategic Focus: Stay informed about federal and state-specific regulations, and leverage technology for compliance and efficiency.

Inventory Management Strategies for Alcohol Producers and Wholesalers

Key Insights: Effective inventory management is central to aligning supplier expectations with wholesaler goals, with technology playing a key role.

Strategic Focus: Utilize advanced tools for data-driven decision-making, demand forecasting, and understanding the nuances of Direct Import versus domestic ordering.

Optimizing Supplier Relationships within the Three-Tier System

Key Insights: Building and nurturing strong supplier relationships are fundamental to the success and efficiency of the supply chain.

Strategic Focus: Develop transparent, collaborative relationships, and use technology to enhance communication and partnership.

Case Studies and Best Practices in the Three-Tier Alcohol System

Key Insights: Real-world case studies highlight the importance of adaptability, partnership, and strategic thinking in overcoming industry challenges.

Strategic Focus: Adopt best practices such as effective communication, dynamic forecasting, and embracing innovative distribution channels like direct-to-consumer.

Chapter 8: Distribution and Channel Management

As someone with extensive experience on the wholesale distributor side, it's hard for me to encourage the idea of *managing* a distributor. That's why I wouldn't do it. What I will say is that knowing why and how a distributor and specific channels work is paramount. Success in this industry is only possible through collaboration and true partnership. The wholesaler and the supplier have to work symbiotically or they end up fighting each other, and in that battle, no one wins.

Understanding the Importance of Distribution and Channel Management In the ever evolving landscape of the alcohol industry, effective distribution and channel management have become essential elements for market success. This chapter will guide suppliers through the nuances of market dynamics, emphasizing the need for adaptable strategies to meet changing consumer preferences. We will explore how suppliers can establish a strong market presence through strategic partnerships, innovative distribution channels, and enduring relationships with distributors and retailers.

A Comprehensive Exploration of Distribution Strategies This chapter offers a detailed exploration of distribution and channel management, examining the importance of distributor relationships, the effectiveness of various channels, and the impact of data-driven strategies in today's digital era. Readers will gain a deeper understanding of how to navigate these aspects effectively.

Demystifying the Three-Tier System A foundational aspect of this chapter is an in-depth look at the Three-Tier System, the cornerstone of alcohol distribution in the United States. This system dictates the flow of alcohol from producers to consumers and is crucial for understanding the industry's distribution landscape.

Suppliers: At the top tier, suppliers are the creators and branders of alcoholic beverages. This section will delve into their role in crafting and marketing products that resonate with consumers.

Distributors: As the middle tier, distributors are the vital link between suppliers and retailers. We will explore their role in logistics, brand introduction, and market penetration.

Retailers: At the consumer level, retailers represent a diverse array of establishments where alcohol is sold. This section will discuss their role in presenting products to consumers and influencing purchasing decisions.

Exploring Regional Differences in Wholesale Alcohol Sales The chapter will also address the varying state laws and market dynamics across the United States, highlighting the unique challenges and opportunities in different regions. From government-controlled distribution to open markets, these differences significantly impact distribution strategies.

Embarking on a Journey of Discovery As we progress through the chapter, we will investigate regional market trends, the optimization of distribution channels, the growing importance of direct-to-consumer sales, and the development of strong distributor relationships. This exploration will be enriched with data-driven insights and case studies.

Charting a Course in Alcohol Distribution This chapter aims to equip readers with the knowledge and tools necessary to navigate and succeed in this complex field. Let's embark on this journey together, advancing one step closer to mastering the art of alcohol distribution.

Article 1: Navigating Regional Market Trends and Optimizing Distribution Channels

The alcohol distribution landscape is characterized by its dynamic nature, significantly influenced by regional market trends. This article delves into these trends and their impact on distribution strategies, offering a comprehensive guide to optimizing distribution channels for sustained success.

Understanding Regional Market Trends The key to successful distribution lies in understanding the unique characteristics of each regional market. Suppliers must be adept at identifying local consumer preferences and tailoring their strategies accordingly. For instance, California's preference for agave spirits, the Midwest's inclination towards whiskey, and Florida's penchant for rum are examples of regional tastes that suppliers must consider. This understanding enables suppliers to uncover opportunities and align their products and marketing efforts with local preferences.

Adapting to Market Shifts in Supplier-Distributor Collaborations Market shifts can significantly impact supplier-distributor relationships. Suppliers must remain agile, adapting their strategies in response to changes in consumer preferences and market conditions. This adaptability is crucial for maintaining strong partnerships with distributors, ensuring alignment with market demand, and securing a competitive advantage.

Diversity of Distribution Channels The alcohol industry presents a variety of distribution channels, each with distinct advantages and challenges. Suppliers must navigate between traditional retail channels, which offer personal customer experiences, and e-commerce platforms, which provide access to a broader digital market. Understanding these channels is crucial for suppliers to strategically position their brands for maximum visibility and accessibility. Researching major players in each channel, such as Total Wine, Darden, Lettuce Entertain You, Wine.com, and others, is essential for understanding how to achieve a widespread market presence.

Timeless Strategies for Channel Selection Choosing the right distribution channels involves strategic planning and foresight. Suppliers should adhere to timeless principles such as conducting comprehensive market research, understanding consumer demographics, and ensuring that channel choices align with their brand identity. These strategies form the foundation for successful channel optimization.

Fostering Strong Distributor Partnerships Building and maintaining strong, transparent relationships with distributors is vital for successful distribution. These partnerships should be rooted in trust, collaboration, and mutual understanding. Suppliers should engage with distributors to align goals, understand their needs, and create incentives that drive sales and support long-term success.

Sustaining Long-Term Growth and Market Presence To ensure long-term growth and maintain market presence, suppliers must continuously evaluate and adapt their distribution strategies in response to evolving regional trends. Embracing innovation, responsiveness, and change is essential for suppliers to stay competitive in the alcohol market.

Constantly analyze not just who is buying the product, but how they are consuming it. Are people drinking canned cocktails out of the can, or are they pouring them into a glass? Why would that be important to marketing and strategy?

Embracing the Journey of Distribution Optimization
Navigating regional market trends and optimizing distribution channels is a continuous journey in the world of alcohol distribution. By understanding regional nuances, leveraging strategic channel selection, and nurturing strong distributor relationships, suppliers can confidently navigate this ever-changing landscape. This journey, driven by insights and innovation, is crucial for achieving long-term growth and success in the dynamic world of alcohol distribution.

Review Questions:

1. True/False: California's preference for agave spirits significantly influences the distribution strategies of alcohol suppliers in the region.
2. When market conditions change, suppliers must adapt their strategies. This adaptation is crucial for maintaining:
   a. Product quality.
   b. Fruitful partnerships with distributors.
   c. The same distribution channels.
   d. Fixed pricing strategies.
3. In the alcohol industry, _____ offers a vast digital marketplace, while traditional retail provides a personal touch and in-store experiences.
4. Timeless strategies for selecting the most suitable distribution channels include:
   a. Ignoring market research.
   b. Focusing solely on brand identity.

    c. Conducting thorough market research and analyzing consumer demographics.

    d. Relying only on past successes.

5. True/False: Building robust and transparent relationships with distributors is not essential for securing shelf space and market support.

Article 2: Building and Sustaining Strong Distributor Relationships

I'll repeat it here, the collaboration between distributors and suppliers forms the cornerstone of brand success. These partnerships transcend mere transactions, weaving a tapestry of shared success. This article tunnels into the critical role of these collaborations, offering insights on establishing and nurturing robust, mutually beneficial relationships with distributors.

Distributor-Supplier Collaborations and Motivations: Recognizing this interdependence is key to fostering meaningful collaborations based on trust and transparency. Distributors aim for revenue growth year over year. Suppliers should balance allocation-based models and low-profit, high-volume items to create equilibrium.

Foundations for Mutually Beneficial Partnerships

Establishing a strong distributor-supplier partnership requires balancing cooperation and independence. Suppliers should clearly understand their brand identity, target consumers, and sales goals. Articulating these elements helps in finding distributors who share similar visions and values, laying the groundwork for mutual growth. Remember the importance of "independence." Mutual success is achieved by demonstrating and providing value from both sides. Be cooperative with pricing and inventory, be independent with sales and merchandising. Once those are managed successfully, all will blend into harmony.

Evolving Expectations and Needs: As market dynamics and consumer preferences shift, distributors' expectations and needs also evolve. Modern distributors look for brands that add value to their portfolio and contribute to their growth. Suppliers should actively engage with distributors to understand their objectives, challenges, and market demands, tailoring strategies to meet these evolving needs. Align your brand with the most value in your desired market segment, rather than focusing on internal competition.

Utilizing Market Insights for Enhanced Brand Presence Market insights guide suppliers in managing distributor relationships. Suppliers with robust data can better understand market trends, consumer behaviors, and competitor activities. These insights enable suppliers to refine marketing strategies, pricing, and product positioning, enhancing brand presence and driving sales. Invest in data tracking systems like Nielsen, IRI, or Sip Source for long-term benefits.

The Importance of Data-Driven Approaches Data-driven strategies are vital in effective distributor management. Leveraging data helps suppliers set realistic goals, evaluate distribution efforts, and make informed adjustments. Monitoring sales figures and the impact of promotional activities enables precise navigation of market complexities. Often times the anecdotes of the market are explained with clear direction through the data. Seek transparency and visibility in sales data through distributor portals or third-party sites. Share plans with partners at all levels. VIP, Salesforce, etc.

Setting Realistic Goals and Expectations Setting realistic goals and expectations is crucial in alcohol distribution.

Suppliers and distributors should collaborate to define clear, measurable objectives. A mutual understanding of sales targets, marketing initiatives, and distribution goals lays the foundation for success. Realistic expectations enhance the sense of achievement and strengthen the distributor-supplier partnership.

The essence of successful alcohol distribution lies in building and sustaining strong relationships with distributors. Recognizing the importance of these collaborations, suppliers should commit to mutual growth and shared success.

Review Questions:

1. What is the primary focus of distributor-supplier relationships in the alcohol industry?
   a. Transactional exchanges
   b. Building brand awareness
   c. Establishing shared success and growth
   d. Competitive positioning
2. True/False: Distributors in the alcohol industry are primarily interested in products, not the brands behind them.
3. When establishing partnerships with distributors, it is important for suppliers to have a clear understanding of their _____, _____, and _____.
4. What role do market insights play in distributor-supplier relationships?
   a. They are irrelevant in modern distribution strategies.
   b. They help in understanding market trends and consumer behaviors.
   c. They are only used for financial forecasting.
   d. They are exclusively for tracking competitor activities.

5. True/False: Setting realistic goals and expectations with distributors is not necessary for the success of alcohol distribution.

Article 3: Embracing the Power of Direct-to-Consumer (DTC) Sales in the Alcohol Industry

A digital revolution has significantly transformed the alcohol industry, presenting unique opportunities for suppliers to engage directly with consumers. This isn't new but is still in its earliest stages as we see AI develop. This article explores the burgeoning realm of Direct-to-Consumer (DTC) sales and e-commerce, highlighting its strategic importance and functionality in the market. This article explores new insights into integrating DTC channels with traditional distribution models.

The Rise of DTC Sales and E-Commerce

The advent of e-commerce has revolutionized consumer-brand interactions, with the alcohol industry being no exception. DTC sales enable suppliers to bypass traditional distribution channels, directly reaching consumers and opening new avenues for growth, brand engagement, and market expansion. Collaborations with established online retailers like wine.com, flaviar, or goPuff offer suppliers access to a broader audience, leveraging these platforms' digital presence and catering to consumers who value convenience. These mechanisms are changing and developing daily. By the time you read this, the ones I have named are likely going to be working with or consumed by other similar partnerships.

Successfully integrating DTC channels with existing distribution models requires a strategic and balanced approach. Suppliers must view DTC sales as a complementary extension of their overall distribution strategy, enriching the brand experience and expanding market reach. For instance, coordinating with wholesale distributors for a unified approach ensures that DTC efforts align seamlessly with traditional retail channels, allowing suppliers to capitalize on both digital and physical marketplaces.

Navigating the Benefits and Challenges of DTC Sales

Direct sales offer numerous benefits, including access to valuable consumer data and preferences. This information enables suppliers to engage in personalized marketing and targeted promotions, tailoring their offerings to meet consumer demands and enhancing customer satisfaction and loyalty. DTC channels are also ideal for A/B testing of product mixes, artwork, and marketing strategies, offering high returns on investment.

Despite its advantages, DTC sales present several challenges, particularly in navigating the complexities of state laws, shipping regulations, and age verification. Compliance is crucial, and effective SEO marketing plays a vital role in ensuring adherence to regulations while enhancing online visibility. Suppliers can collaborate with SEO experts to develop strategies that improve product visibility on online retail platforms, using targeted keywords and optimized product listings to attract a wider consumer base.

Empowering Reach to a Wider Audience and Direct Consumer Engagement

Direct-to-Consumer (DTC) sales enable suppliers to establish a more intimate connection with their audience. By leveraging insights into consumer preferences and behaviors, suppliers can craft personalized experiences, offers, and promotions that resonate deeply with their target audience. This level of personalization fosters a sense of brand loyalty, transforming consumers into enthusiastic brand advocates who actively promote the products within their networks.

Collaboration with DTC platforms is key to effective consumer engagement. Suppliers can implement exclusive discounts and promotions for DTC channel consumers, creating a perception of exclusivity and added value. An effective strategy, for instance, is to offset or completely cover shipping costs, addressing a common barrier to online purchasing. Such tactics not only enhance the appeal of DTC purchasing but also encourage repeat business and customer loyalty.

DTC Sales and Brand Experience: Crafting a Memorable Journey

In today's digital landscape, the brand experience significantly influences consumer decision-making. DTC sales offer suppliers a unique opportunity to create an immersive and memorable brand journey. This can be achieved through interactive websites, engaging content, and storytelling that authentically represents the brand's ethos and values. Such experiences are not only memorable but also shareable, encouraging consumers to spread the word about their positive experiences.

Investing in compelling branding and storytelling on DTC platforms is crucial. This approach helps suppliers stand out in a crowded market, creating a distinctive brand identity that captivates consumers. By weaving a compelling narrative around their products and brand, suppliers can create a lasting impression that extends beyond the initial purchase, fostering a community of loyal customers.

A Timeless Strategy for Long-Term Growth

Embracing DTC sales is a strategic decision with long-term benefits. Suppliers should recognize the importance of direct engagement with consumers and invest in developing robust DTC channels. These channels should complement and synergize with traditional distribution methods, allowing suppliers to maximize their market reach and enhance brand visibility.

Establishing strong partnerships with wholesale distributors and key online platforms is essential for sustainable growth. A long-term approach to DTC sales involves continuously evolving strategies to adapt to market changes, ensuring ongoing relevance and success. By balancing the strengths of both traditional and DTC channels, suppliers can create a resilient and dynamic presence in the alcohol market.

Charting a New Course in the Alcohol Industry through DTC Sales

As we have explored in this comprehensive examination of Direct-to-Consumer (DTC) sales in the alcohol industry, it is evident that the digital revolution has not just altered, but fundamentally enriched the landscape of alcohol distribution and consumer engagement. DTC sales have emerged not merely as a trend, but as a pivotal strategy that enables suppliers to directly connect with their consumers, offering a unique blend of personalization, convenience, and brand experience.

The integration of DTC sales into the traditional distribution models represents a harmonious blend of innovation and tradition. It allows suppliers to extend their reach beyond conventional boundaries, tapping into a market that values the direct interaction and personalized touch that DTC channels provide. This approach does not replace traditional methods but rather enhances them, creating a comprehensive distribution ecosystem that caters to diverse consumer preferences and behaviors.

The journey through DTC sales is one of continuous learning and adaptation. Suppliers are called to navigate the challenges of compliance, digital marketing, and evolving consumer expectations, all while maintaining the essence of their brand identity. The successful implementation of DTC strategies hinges on the ability to balance these elements, ensuring that each step taken is in sync with the overarching goal of sustainable growth and market relevance.

Looking ahead, the future of the alcohol industry appears increasingly dynamic, with DTC sales playing a crucial role in shaping its trajectory. Suppliers who embrace this model will find themselves at the forefront of a consumer-centric market, equipped with the tools and insights to create meaningful connections, drive brand loyalty, and ultimately, carve a distinct niche in a competitive landscape.

The power of DTC sales in the alcohol industry is unmistakable. It offers a pathway for suppliers to not only survive but thrive in a rapidly evolving digital world. By embracing this model, suppliers can look forward to building stronger, more resilient brands that resonate deeply with their consumers, setting the stage for a future where direct engagement and personalized experiences are not just valued, but expected. As the industry continues to evolve, those who adapt and innovate will undoubtedly lead the way, marking a new era of growth and success in the vibrant world of alcohol distribution.

A few links to websites mentioned here:

https://www.wine.com/

https://www.flaviar.com/

https://www.gopuff.com/

https://www.ttb.gov/

Search for "[State Name] Department of Revenue" for specific state regulations.

Review Questions:

1. True/False: DTC sales in the alcohol industry allow suppliers to bypass traditional distribution channels and directly reach consumers.

2. Which of the following online retailers is mentioned in the article as a partner for suppliers to access a broader audience?
   A) Amazon
   B) eBay
   C) wine.com
   D) Etsy

3. In order to successfully integrate DTC channels with existing distribution models, suppliers must view DTC sales as a _____ extension of their overall distribution strategy.

4. True/False: One of the challenges of DTC sales is complying with various state laws, shipping regulations, and age verification measures.

5. What is a key benefit of Direct-to-Consumer sales for suppliers?

    a. Reduced marketing costs
    b. Access to consumer data and preferences
    c. Longer shipping times
    d. Higher production costs

6. To enhance the appeal of DTC purchasing, suppliers can offer exclusive _____ or cover shipping costs.

7. True/False: Investing in compelling branding and storytelling on DTC platforms is not essential for creating a memorable brand experience.

8. What is the role of SEO marketing in the context of DTC sales?

    a. To reduce product prices
    b. To ensure compliance and optimize online visibility
    c. To increase production speed
    d. To design product packaging

Mastering Distribution and Channel Management in the Alcohol Industry

The Three-Tier System: Ensuring Compliance and Promoting Fair Play

At the heart of the U.S. alcohol industry lies the three-tier system, a regulatory framework that separates suppliers, distributors, and retailers. This system not only ensures compliance with legal standards but also fosters fair competition and protects consumer interests. Suppliers must deeply understand this system, as it significantly influences distribution dynamics and strategies.

Adapting to Regional Market Trends: A Tailored Approach

The alcohol market is not monolithic; it varies significantly across different regions. Suppliers must be adept at recognizing and adapting to these regional market trends. This adaptability enables them to tailor their strategies effectively, ensuring they meet the unique demands of each market and capitalize on specific growth opportunities.

Diversifying Distribution Channels: Maximizing Market Reach

The alcohol industry presents a spectrum of distribution channels, each offering unique opportunities and challenges. Suppliers need to judiciously select channels that align with their brand identity and target audience. This strategic channel selection is crucial for maximizing market reach and enhancing brand visibility.

Building and Sustaining Strong Distributor Relationships

The essence of a successful distributor-supplier partnership lies in a balanced blend of cooperation and independence. Suppliers should engage in these partnerships with a clear vision of their brand and objectives, seeking distributors who share their values and goals. Such synergistic relationships pave the way for mutual growth and success.

Embracing the Digital Frontier: The Power of DTC Sales and E-Commerce

The digital revolution has opened up new avenues for suppliers through Direct-to-Consumer sales and e-commerce. These channels allow suppliers to connect directly with consumers, offering personalized experiences and gaining valuable insights from consumer data. Integrating DTC sales with traditional distribution models enables suppliers to leverage the strengths of both approaches, enhancing brand visibility and driving profitability.

Charting a Path to Success in Alcohol Distribution

This chapter has equipped suppliers with the knowledge and strategies needed to navigate the intricate world of alcohol distribution. From understanding the foundational three-tier system to embracing the digital revolution of DTC sales, suppliers are now prepared to optimize their distribution efforts, build robust partnerships, and adapt to the ever-changing market dynamics.

As we continue to explore and innovate in this sector, it is crucial to remain adaptable, embrace new opportunities, and foster strong relationships. The future of alcohol distribution is bright, filled with potential for growth and success. By staying informed, embracing change, and prioritizing strategic partnerships, suppliers can thrive in this competitive landscape.

Disclaimer

The information in this chapter is based on a combination of publicly available sources and industry insights. For the most current regulations and compliance requirements, readers should consult the Alcohol and Tobacco Tax and Trade Bureau (TTB) and state Departments of Revenue (DOR).

Resources for further education:

1. **Alcohol and Tobacco Tax and Trade Bureau (TTB)**: *For comprehensive federal regulations and compliance guidelines related to the alcohol industry, visit the TTB website.*
   a. *Website: https://www.ttb.gov/*
2. **State Departments of Revenue (DOR)**: *For state-specific regulations and compliance requirements in the alcohol industry, consult the website of your state's Department of Revenue. A simple search for "[Your State Name] Department of Revenue" will lead you to the relevant site.*
3. **National Alcohol Beverage Control Association (NABCA)**: *Access information on control state systems, regulations, and industry insights through the NABCA website.*
   a. *Website: https://www.nabca.org/*
4. **Distilled Spirits Council of the United States (DISCUS)**: *Explore industry trends, policy issues, and comprehensive market data on the DISCUS website.*
   a. *Website: https://www.distilledspirits.org/*
5. **Wine Institute**: *For detailed information specific to the wine industry, including Direct-to-Consumer shipping laws and guidelines, the Wine Institute is a valuable resource.*
   a. *Website: https://www.wineinstitute.org/*

6. ***Brewers Association***: *Gain insights into the beer industry, including distribution and market trends, by visiting the Brewers Association website.*
   a. *Website: https://www.brewersassociation.org/*

These resources provide authoritative and up-to-date information, essential for navigating the complex landscape of alcohol distribution and channel management.

Chapter 9: Incentive Programs in the Adult Beverage Industry

Welcome to an in-depth exploration of incentive programs within the adult beverage industry. This chapter, specifically tailored for wholesale distributors, producers, and importers, examines the critical role of incentives towards driving sales and fostering business relationships. Understanding the nuances of designing, implementing, and executing effective incentive programs is essential in a market characterized by intense competition and evolving consumer preferences.

Throughout this chapter, we will examine various facets of incentive programs, drawing upon industry expertise and real-world examples. We will investigate how incentives influence different stages of the product life cycle, adapt to specific market segments, and respond to regional market dynamics. This comprehensive approach aims to equip you with the knowledge and tools necessary to maximize the effectiveness of your incentive initiatives.

Article 1: The Importance of Incentives

This article will dissect how incentives impact product life cycles and market growth, and the strategic use of different incentive types—volume, points of distribution (POD), and account-based. Understanding these distinctions is key to crafting targeted and effective incentive programs that not only drive sales but also cement lasting industry relationships.

Article 2: Designing Effective Incentive Programs

Next, we guide you through the intricacies of creating successful incentive programs. This article will cover essential considerations like budget determination, balancing marketing exposure with time-sensitive objectives, and aligning incentives with fiscal timelines. These insights are crucial for developing incentive programs that not only motivate your sales team but also yield measurable results.

Article 3: Implementing and Executing Incentive Programs

Focusing on the practical aspects, this article will offer strategies for effectively utilizing sampling and point-of-sale (POS) materials to boost product visibility and stimulate sales. We will also delve into market working techniques and the importance of hiring sales professionals with relevant experience, prioritizing sales acumen over extensive product knowledge. These strategies are crucial for the successful rollout and execution of incentive programs.

Insert/Expansion: Hiring the Right Personnel for the Market

The success of your incentive programs heavily relies on the personnel driving them. This section will explore the essential qualities and experiences to consider when recruiting sales professionals. Emphasis will be placed on industry knowledge, relationship-building skills, and a comprehensive understanding of the adult beverage market. Additionally, we will offer insights into conducting effective interviews and evaluating candidates, ensuring they align with your organizational goals and culture.

Article 1: The Significance of Incentives in the Adult Beverage Industry

Incentives emerge as a pivotal force in catalyzing sales growth and forging robust relationships across the distribution chain. This article delves into the critical role of incentives, examining their impact on various stages of the product life cycle and overall market growth. By harnessing the power of well-crafted incentives, businesses can create a compelling force that propels their brand to new heights.

Motivating Sales Teams: The Power of Incentives

Incentives act as dynamic motivators for sales teams, spurring efforts to boost sales volumes, expand points of distribution (POD), and acquire new accounts. Attractive rewards, ranging from monetary bonuses to gift cards and recognition, can ignite a sales team's ambition, driving them to excel in promoting products. This motivational aspect is especially crucial during a brand's nascent stages, where establishing a firm market presence is key.

Differentiating Incentive Types: Volume, POD, and Account-Based

Crafting effective incentive programs necessitates a clear distinction between various incentive types, each aligned with specific business goals. Volume incentives, aimed at hitting sales targets, are ideal for boosting overall sales and capturing market share. POD incentives, on the other hand, focus on increasing the number of outlets where products are available, thereby enhancing brand visibility and market penetration. Account-based incentives are tailored to deepen relationships with key accounts, fostering long-term partnerships and consistent sales within these accounts. Distinguishing between volume, POD, and account-based incentives enables strategic program design tailored to distinct business objectives.

Choosing the Right Incentive Approach

Selecting the most suitable incentive approach depends on multiple factors, including the brand's growth stage, market dynamics, and strategic goals. Emerging brands might find POD incentives more beneficial for establishing market presence and expanding distribution networks. Established brands, conversely, may leverage volume incentives to sustain sales growth and maintain market dominance.

A thorough assessment of market position, competitive landscape, and consumer demand is crucial in determining the most fitting incentive strategy. Understanding your target market's preferences allows for the creation of incentive programs that resonate not just with sales teams but also with end consumers. The choice of incentive approach should be informed by factors like brand maturity, market conditions, and strategic aims.

Incentives stand as a formidable tool in the adult beverage industry, essential for driving sales and building strong stakeholder relationships. By effectively motivating sales teams, differentiating between incentive types, and aligning strategies with business objectives, the impact of incentive programs can be maximized. It's important to tailor these programs to the unique needs and dynamics of your market, continuously evaluating and refining them to maintain their efficacy. With strategic, well-designed incentives, businesses can achieve substantial sales growth and carve out a competitive advantage in the industry.

Review Questions:

1. True or False: Incentives are only effective for established brands in the adult beverage industry.
2. What is the primary goal of POD incentives?

   a. Increase overall sales volume
   b. Expand the number of outlets offering the product
   c. Focus on individual account performance

3. Account-based incentives are designed to foster _____ with key accounts.
4. True or False: Volume incentives are most effective for brands in the early stages of their life cycle.
5. What is a key factor in choosing the right incentive approach?

   a. The color of the product packaging
   b. The brand's stage of growth and market dynamics
   c. The CEO's personal preference

Article 2: Designing Effective Incentive Programs for Success

The creation of effective incentive programs is a cornerstone of a thriving sales strategy. The process of designing these programs demands meticulous planning, astute budgeting, and a deep understanding of various influencing factors. This article aims to unpack the essential components of crafting incentive programs that not only drive sales but also yield substantial, positive outcomes. Through the implementation of well-structured programs, businesses can energize their sales teams, accomplish business objectives, and cultivate enduring relationships with wholesalers, retailers, and customers.

Allocating an Appropriate Budget

A strategic approach to incentivizing sales consultants involves allocating a specific dollar amount per case sold within a set period. This method allows suppliers to fully utilize their budget while ensuring that sales consultants receive substantial incentives. For instance, with a $20 per case budget for a 12-bottle case, an incentive of $5 per POD (consisting of 3 bottles) can be established. This strategy not only ensures equitable distribution of incentives but also motivates sales consultants to strive for higher PODs. Budgeting incentives based on a per-case basis optimizes expenditure and offers significant rewards to sales consultants.

Depending on the stage of the brand though you must appropriately factor for sharing this incentive budget with a marketing budget. What I mean by that is to initially gain distribution, you'll have to make some upside down spends. Once a footprint is established it becomes much more financially responsible to expand in smaller percentage size doses.

Balancing Marketing Exposure and Targeting: Strategic Alignment

Achieving a balance between marketing exposure and precise targeting is key. For long-term incentives, such as annual volume goals, targeting senior leadership with strategically aligned incentives can be effective. Mid-level management can be the focus for quarterly or semi-annual financial incentives. Offering trips to a mix of management and sales levels can cultivate brand ambassadors and reward performance. For short-term incentives, targeting sales consultants directly is ideal, ensuring that the incentives align with the specific goals and timeframes relevant to each segment of the sales team. Customizing incentives to suit the roles and timeframes of different sales team segments enhances their impact.

Leveraging Tactical and Specific Tools and Supports

While maintaining simplicity in the incentive structure for ease of tracking and understanding, it's equally important to provide tactical and specific supports during the incentive period. Collaborating closely with sales consultants at the local level to focus on strategic placements, such as menu print placements and high-volume accounts, can lead to significant wins. Targeting specialist positions like spirits specialists or key account managers (KAMs) can drive specific placements and achieve desired outcomes. Providing these targeted supports can significantly enhance the effectiveness of the incentive programs. Utilizing tactical and specific tools and supports during the incentive period can lead to significant sales achievements and drive desired outcomes. Targeting the *right* accounts for your brand can be more important than targeting wide sweeping sales. I highly suggest catering your approach to targets that make sense for your product specifically.

Considering When and Where to Run Incentives: Strategic Timing

When planning incentive programs, thoughtful consideration of the timing and location is crucial. Aligning the timing of the incentive with the fiscal timelines of your business and wholesaler partners is essential. Additionally, understanding market dynamics, consumer preferences, and regional variations enables the customization of incentives for maximum impact. Strategic timing and targeting of incentives can optimize results and establish a competitive edge in the adult beverage industry. Carefully considering the timing and targeting of incentives ensures better alignment with fiscal timelines and market dynamics, enhancing their effectiveness.

Deepening the Understanding of Incentive Program Options

Incentive programs, when designed thoughtfully, can be a game-changer in the adult beverage industry. Let's delve deeper into various incentive program options, exploring their nuances and strategic applications.

Volume-Based Incentives: Amplifying Sales and Market Share

Volume-based incentives focus on setting and achieving sales volume targets. These incentives are particularly effective in driving higher sales volumes and increasing market share. For instance, setting case volume or gross sales targets incentivizes sales consultants to push for larger orders, thereby boosting overall sales. This approach is especially beneficial when a brand is looking to establish a stronger position in fewer accounts. (Creating *partner* accounts).

New Account Incentives: Expanding Market Reach

Incentives for acquiring new accounts are crucial, especially for brands in the introductory phase. The challenge of getting a brand into new accounts is significant, and incentives can effectively motivate sales consultants to overcome this hurdle. This type of incentive is vital for brands looking to establish a foothold in the market, as it encourages the expansion of the brand's reach and opens up new business opportunities.

POD Incentives: Enhancing Brand Visibility

POD incentives are designed to increase the number of placements or points of distribution within a territory. This approach is rooted in the "Billboard Effect," where increased visibility of a brand leads to higher sales for each product. By incentivizing sales consultants to secure more placements, brands can significantly improve their visibility and accessibility, which is a key factor in consumer purchasing decisions.

Targeted Placement Incentives: Strategic Brand Positioning

Targeted placement incentives focus on securing strategic placements such as menu print placements, premium shelf positions, or high-traffic on-premise accounts. These placements are crucial for enhancing brand positioning and visibility. However, tracking and managing these incentives can be challenging. It's essential to have dedicated personnel in the market to manage these incentives effectively and support sales representatives in achieving these strategic placements.

Understanding the Potential Results

Incentive programs can yield a variety of impactful results. Let's explore these potential outcomes in more detail:

Increased Sales Volumes: Boosting Revenue

Well-designed incentive programs are a direct driver of sales growth. By motivating sales consultants to achieve higher sales volumes, these programs can lead to increased revenue for both suppliers and sales consultants. The direct correlation between incentives and sales performance is a fundamental principle in sales strategy.

Market Expansion: Penetrating New Markets

Incentives that focus on acquiring new accounts or expanding points of distribution are instrumental in market expansion. This approach, emphasizing growth outward before upward, is critical for brands looking to increase their market presence. Expanding the number of accounts before focusing on volume within existing accounts allows for a broader market penetration and a solid foundation for future growth.

Brand Visibility: Establishing Market Presence

Strategic placements and targeted incentives play a significant role in enhancing brand visibility. For new brands, the initial years are all about making the market aware of their existence. By focusing on strategic placements and visibility, brands can establish a strong presence in the market, which is essential for long-term success.

Stronger Relationships: Building Brand Ambassadors

Incentive programs are not just about immediate sales results; they also play a crucial role in fostering strong, long-term relationships between suppliers and sales consultants. Programs like trip incentives and long-term goals help in creating brand ambassadors who have a personal connection to the brand. These relationships are invaluable, as they lead to increased loyalty and long-term partnership.

Crafting a Competitive Edge

Designing effective incentive programs is a multifaceted process that requires careful consideration of various elements. By understanding the different types of incentives and their strategic applications, suppliers can create programs that not only motivate sales teams but also drive significant sales growth. The key lies in aligning these programs with market dynamics, consumer preferences, and the specific goals of the brand. Through thoughtful design and implementation, incentive programs can be a powerful tool in establishing a competitive edge in the adult beverage industry.

Review Questions:

1. True/False: Volume-based incentives are primarily focused on acquiring new accounts rather than increasing sales volumes.
2. What is the primary goal of New Account Incentives in the adult beverage industry?
   a. To reduce product prices
   b. To acquire new accounts and expand market reach
   c. To increase the number of products per account
   d. To enhance the quality of the products
3. POD Incentives are designed to increase the number of _____ or points of distribution within a territory, thereby improving brand visibility and accessibility.
4. True/False: Targeted Placement Incentives, such as securing premium shelf positions, are easy to track and manage without dedicated personnel in the market.
5. Which of the following is a key consideration when designing effective incentive programs?
   a. Focusing solely on short-term sales

b. Ignoring market dynamics and consumer preferences
c. Aligning incentives with fiscal timelines and market dynamics
d. Avoiding budget allocation for incentives

Article 3: Implementing and Executing Incentive Programs for Optimal Results

This article will focus on the importance of tracking, communication, and hiring the right personnel. These elements are crucial for success.

Tracking Information in Real-Time: To ensure the effectiveness of incentive programs, it is essential to track progress and results in real-time. This allows for timely adjustments and recognition of achievements. Utilize digital tools and software to monitor sales data, distribution points, and other key metrics. Real-time tracking helps in identifying trends, understanding market dynamics, and making informed decisions. It also enables quick recognition and reward of sales consultants' efforts, boosting morale and motivation.

Effective Communication During the Incentive Period: Communication is key during the incentive period, but don't communicate something unless it has value. Regular updates, feedback, and encouragement are vital to keep the sales team informed and engaged. Establish clear communication channels, whether through meetings, emails, or digital platforms, to disseminate information about the incentive program's progress, successes, and areas for improvement. Effective communication fosters a sense of team spirit and keeps everyone aligned with the program's goals.

Hiring the Right Personnel for the Market: The success of incentive programs heavily relies on having the right personnel in place. This includes state managers, regional managers, and brand ambassadors who understand the market, have strong relationships with key stakeholders, and possess the skills to drive sales and execute the program effectively.

State Managers: They play a crucial role in overseeing the implementation of incentive programs at the state level. They should have a deep understanding of the local market, regulatory environment, and key accounts. Their leadership and ability to motivate sales teams are essential for the program's success.

Regional Managers: These individuals are responsible for managing multiple states or territories. They should have strong strategic planning skills, the ability to analyze market trends, and the capacity to coordinate efforts across different regions.

Brand Ambassadors: Brand ambassadors act as the face of the brand. They should be knowledgeable about the product, skilled in customer engagement, and capable of creating excitement and loyalty among consumers and sales teams.

Enhanced Tracking and Data Utilization: Real-time tracking is pivotal in managing incentive programs effectively. Leveraging technology solutions like CRM systems, sales tracking software, or mobile apps can provide a comprehensive view of program performance. These tools can track sales figures, distribution metrics, and even individual sales consultant performance. Advanced analytics can offer insights into market trends, product performance, and customer preferences, enabling more strategic decision-making. Additionally, integrating data from wholesalers and third-party sources can enrich your understanding of market dynamics and help tailor future incentives. A few systems that you'll run into or should seek out: VIP, MicroStrategy, DivePort, Salesforce, etc. Ask your wholesaler what type of system they use to share data in live time.

Optimizing Communication Strategies: Effective communication is more than just regular updates; it's about engaging your team in a way that resonates. Utilize a mix of communication channels - emails, texts, social media, and even virtual meetings - to maintain a dynamic and interactive dialogue. Short, engaging videos or infographics can convey progress and motivate teams more effectively than traditional emails. Personalized messages acknowledging individual or team achievements can significantly boost morale. Also, consider periodic virtual town halls or Q&A sessions to address concerns, gather feedback, and keep everyone aligned with the program's objectives.

Strategic Personnel Hiring and Training: Hiring the right personnel is a strategic investment. Look for candidates with a blend of industry experience, sales acumen, and a passion for the adult beverage sector. Once onboard, invest in comprehensive training programs that cover not just your products but also sales techniques, market trends, and customer engagement strategies. Encourage continuous learning and development to keep your team sharp and informed. Sales training from Wilson Learning is one of the best I have encountered.

Regional Managers: These individuals should be adept at translating national strategies into actionable regional plans. They should be skilled in data analysis, market forecasting, and team leadership. Their role is to bridge the gap between corporate objectives and local market realities.

State Managers: Focus on hiring individuals with strong local market knowledge and networks. They should excel in operational management, stakeholder engagement, and tactical execution of incentive programs. Their insights into local market nuances are invaluable, which means great relationships should come along with this hire.

Brand Ambassadors: Look for charismatic, knowledgeable, and engaging individuals. They should be adept at storytelling, customer engagement, and creating memorable brand experiences. Their role is to humanize your brand and create emotional connections with your audience.

Long-Term Personnel Engagement: While incentives are temporary, your relationship with your employees should be long-term. Foster a culture of recognition, growth, and loyalty. Encourage career progression within the company, offer regular training and development opportunities, and create a work environment that values and rewards contributions. This approach not only enhances the effectiveness of your incentive programs but also builds a dedicated and motivated workforce committed to your brand's success.

The successful implementation and execution of incentive programs in the adult beverage industry hinge on a holistic approach encompassing advanced tracking, dynamic communication, strategic personnel management, and fostering long-term employee engagement. By embracing these strategies, you can create a healthy framework that drives sales, strengthens relationships, and positions your brand for sustained success in a competitive market. Continuously adapt and refine your strategies to stay ahead of market trends and ensure the ongoing effectiveness of your incentive programs.

Review Questions:

1. True/False: Sampling initiatives and the use of Point-of-Sale (POS) materials are essential strategies for creating brand awareness and driving product trial in incentive programs.
2. When implementing incentive programs, what is crucial for tracking the progress and performance of the programs?
   a. Regular team meetings
   b. Real-time data tracking using technology solutions
   c. Annual performance reviews
   d. Customer feedback surveys
3. Effective communication during the incentive period should be **positive** and **brief** to keep participants engaged and motivated.
4. True/False: Hiring the right personnel for the market, such as regional managers, state managers, and brand ambassadors, is not as important as the incentive program itself.
5. What is a key role of regional managers in implementing and executing incentive programs?
   a. Handling customer complaints
   b. Translating national strategies into actionable regional plans
   c. Directly selling products to end consumers
   d. Designing the incentive programs

Incentive Programs: Driving Sales and Building Relationships

Chapter 3 delves into the multifaceted world of incentive programs in the adult beverage industry, underscoring their pivotal role in catalyzing sales growth and forging robust relationships. This chapter not only illuminates the strategic use of incentives at various product life cycle stages and market growth phases but also stresses the criticality of aligning these incentives with fiscal timelines and the imperative of valuing sales expertise in personnel recruitment.

Article 1: The Importance of Incentives in Driving Sales and Market Growth This article unpacks the diverse array of incentives, including volume, points of distribution (PODs), and account-based approaches. It showcases how these incentives can be dynamically adapted to suit different stages of the product life cycle, market conditions, and specific business objectives. Tailoring incentive programs to the product life cycle stages enables businesses to optimize strategies for maximal impact. A deep understanding of incentives, coupled with customization to meet specific goals, empowers businesses to not only boost sales but also to nurture enduring industry relationships.

Article 2: Designing Effective Incentive Programs Here, the focus shifts to the intricacies of crafting effective incentive programs. It covers the nuances of budgeting for incentives, calculating spend per case/POD, and the crucial alignment of these incentives with the fiscal timelines of both the wholesaler and the business. The article also emphasizes the need for customizing incentives to resonate with specific market segments and regions. Aligning incentives with fiscal timelines and market segments enhances program effectiveness, driving desired outcomes. Effective program design demands a nuanced understanding of budget allocation, a balance between marketing exposure and time-sensitive goals, and a deep comprehension of target market dynamics.

Article 3: Implementing and Executing Incentive Programs This article offers a roadmap for the successful implementation and execution of incentive programs. It highlights the strategic use of sampling, point-of-sale (POS) materials, and effective market engagement techniques. Additionally, it underscores the importance of recruiting sales professionals with relevant experience, prioritizing sales acumen over product knowledge. Leveraging sampling, POS materials, and effective sales strategies enhances brand visibility, drives sales, and fosters strong customer and team relationships. Successful implementation hinges on real-time tracking, robust communication, and the deployment of skilled personnel, ensuring program efficacy.

In implementing incentive programs, it's vital to tailor them to specific goals and market dynamics. Emphasize aligning incentives with fiscal timelines, strategically use sampling and POS materials, and prioritize hiring sales professionals with industry relevance. Such strategic actions are key to driving sales growth, building strong relationships, and securing a competitive edge in the dynamic adult beverage industry.

Chapter 10: Charting the Future: Trends and Evolving Consumer Preferences

This magnificent industry is a fascinating blend of tradition and innovation. It reflects the ebb and flow of societal changes, preferences, and aspirations. In this extensive chapter, we journey through a historical context, current landscape, and future outlook, providing an expansive view of consumer engagement in the beverage alcohol industry.

Historical Context and Cultural Evolution Our exploration begins with a deep dive into the historical roots of alcoholic beverages. From the ancient wines of Mesopotamia to the medieval ales of Europe, these drinks have served as more than mere refreshments; they are emblems of societal norms, economic status, and cultural evolution. This historical perspective sets the stage for understanding how past practices and preferences have shaped the present industry.

Modern Landscape and Consumer Trends Transitioning to the present, we examine the multifaceted modern landscape of the adult beverage industry. Today's market is a global phenomenon, driven by informed, value-driven consumers who seek more than a drink; they are in pursuit of experiences that resonate with their identities and values. This section delves into the current consumer trends, emphasizing the informed and adventurous nature of modern consumers and their quest for meaningful experiences.

Power of Data in Shaping Trends In the digital age, data has become a critical tool for understanding and predicting market trends. We explore how platforms like Shanken, SipSource, and industry newsletters offer a pulse on consumer behavior, preferences, and purchasing patterns, providing essential insights for industry players.

Global Influence and Sustainability Globalization's impact on the industry is profound, creating a world where consumers enjoy a global palate, from Japanese whiskies to South African wines. Alongside this, we address the increasing importance of sustainability and ethical production, highlighting how modern consumers prioritize eco-friendly methods and ethical sourcing, making this a movement rather than a mere trend.

Emerging Trends, Technological Advances, and Future Predictions As we look to the future, understanding and staying ahead of emerging trends and technological advancements becomes crucial. This chapter will cover various forward-looking topics, including the rise of on-premise experiences, the burgeoning ready-to-drink (RTD) and ready-to-serve (RTS) market, non-alcoholic offerings, and the role of technology in shaping the industry. We'll explore the increasing importance of sustainability, technological innovations like blockchain and AI, and the strategic implications of global market expansions.

Comprehensive Overview of the Industry This chapter comprises nine articles, each meticulously crafted to provide a well-rounded understanding of the forces shaping the alcohol industry's past, present, and future. From technological innovations to global expansions, these articles are designed to equip readers with the knowledge needed to navigate this dynamic industry.

Unraveling the Intricacies As we navigate through the complexities of the industry, each article offers not just a deep dive into its respective topic but also elucidates how these trends are interlinked with the broader industry objectives. The insights provided are tailored to provoke thought, inspire action, and ultimately, drive forward the enduring success of ventures within the alcohol realm.

Envisioning the Future This chapter is more than an informational guide; it's a beacon for innovation and strategic foresight essential for thriving in the ever-evolving narrative of the alcohol industry. With a blend of captivating narratives and actionable insights, this journey through the industry's past, present, and future promises to be both enlightening and invigorating.

Article 1: Decoding Consumer Behavior and Key Market Trends in the Adult Beverage Industry

Ancient Beginnings: The Divine Elixirs The historical journey of alcoholic beverages reveals each civilization's unique imprint. Ancient Egyptians not only consumed beer but revered it, incorporating it into religious ceremonies and daily life. This era's importance is highlighted by artifacts like hieroglyphics depicting brewing processes and tombs with beer jugs.

In ancient Greece, wine was more than a beverage; it symbolized pleasure, festivity, and even had medicinal properties. The Greeks' celebration of Dionysus, the god of wine, underscores the beverage's significance in their society.

The Middle Ages: The Monastic Legacy During the Middle Ages, European monasteries were at the forefront of beer and spirit production. Monks' meticulous brewing techniques and spirit distillation, like the 15th-century Boomsma Cloosterbitter, laid the groundwork for the diverse spirits enjoyed today. Their preservation of brewing secrets played a crucial role in maintaining and advancing these traditions.

Global Influence: A Melting Pot of Flavors The age of exploration brought new flavors and techniques, enriching the global beverage palette. The introduction of drinks like bourbon, spiced rum, and botanical gins illustrates the cultural and commercial exchanges of this era. For instance, the British-influenced gin and tonic in India exemplifies the fusion of different cultures in the beverage industry.

Modern-Day Nuances: Craftsmanship and Eco-Consciousness Today's industry blends traditional methods with modern innovation. The craft movement, initially led by breweries like Dogfish Head and Sierra Nevada, focuses on artisanal production and unique flavors. Additionally, the growing demand for sustainable and organic beverages reflects a shift towards environmental responsibility and consumer consciousness.

The Role of Data Analytics: Predicting the Future Data analytics, illustrated by platforms like Shanken and SipSource, has become crucial in understanding and predicting market trends. The rise of low-alcohol or alcohol-free beverages among millennials and Gen Z, driven by health considerations, exemplifies this trend. The potential integration of AI and machine learning in predicting consumer behavior marks a significant advancement in the industry.

The adult beverage industry mirrors society's evolving values and preferences. Understanding its historical roots, global influences, and current trends allows for a deeper appreciation of the beverages and the industry's trajectory.

Additional resources:

I. **Ancient Egyptian Beer Reference:**
   a. **Title:** "A sip of history: ancient Egyptian beer"
   b. **Source:** British Museum
   c. **Description:** This reference provides historical insights into the brewing and consumption of beer in ancient Egypt. It includes information on the cultural significance of beer, depicted in hieroglyphics and archaeological findings.
   d. https://www.britishmuseum.org/blog/sip-history-ancient-egyptian-beer

II. **Monastic Brewing and Distillation Reference:**
   a. **Source:** Chicago Tribune
   b. **Description:** This source discusses the role of monasteries in the development of beer and spirit production during the Middle Ages. It highlights the contribution of monks in enhancing beer quality and pioneering the distillation of spirits, with a special mention of Boomsma Cloosterbitter, a spirit based on a 15th-century recipe.
   c. https://www.chicagotribune.com/dining/drink/sc-boomsma-drink-food-0113-20170111-story.html

Review Questions:

1. **True or False:** The ancient Egyptians considered beer a sacred drink, used only in religious ceremonies.

2. Which era is known for the monastic legacy in beer and spirit production?
   a. Ancient Greece
   b. The Middle Ages
   c. Modern-Day
   d. Age of Exploration

3. The British-influenced drink developed to combat malaria in India was _____.

4. **True or False:** Today's adult beverage industry is characterized by a shift towards high-alcohol content and traditional flavors.

5. Which platform is mentioned as a tool for understanding current market trends in the adult beverage industry?
   a. Facebook
   b. SipSource
   c. YouTube
   d. TikTok

Article 2: Mastering Key Market Trends in the U.S. Adult Beverage Industry

The adult beverage industry is constantly evolving, influenced by cultural shifts, health trends, technological advancements, and consumer preferences. This article examines key market trends and how businesses can harness them for growth.

Health and Wellness Movement The growing health-conscious consumer base has sparked a surge in low-alcohol, alcohol-free, and organic beverages. Brands are innovating products like low-calorie wines and gluten-free beers to align with wellness goals. Data from Nielsen and IRI Data supports this trend, showing a significant shift in consumer preferences towards healthier beverage options.

Premiumization and Craft Movement Quality is becoming more important than quantity for consumers. The rise of small-batch distilleries, artisanal wineries, and craft breweries highlights this trend. Resources like the Shanken newsletter provide insights into the premium and craft movement, showcasing successful brands and effective strategies.

Sustainability and Ethical Practices Environmental responsibility is becoming a crucial factor in consumer choices. Businesses are adopting sustainable practices like eco-friendly packaging and water conservation. SipSource offers valuable data on sustainable trends, emphasizing the need for brands to align their values with those of consumers.

Technology and Personalization Technological advancements are transforming consumer interactions with beverages. Augmented reality, AI-driven recommendations, and personalized offerings are gaining traction. Keeping up with updates from industry newsletters can help businesses navigate this tech-driven landscape.

Cultural Influences and Global Flavors Global flavors and cultural influences are increasingly shaping consumer preferences. The popularity of beverages like Japanese sake and traditional spirits like mezcal in the U.S. reflects this trend. Resources like Overproof provide insights into the impact of cultural influences on the alcohol industry.

E-commerce and Direct-to-Consumer Sales The shift towards e-commerce and direct-to-consumer channels has been accelerated by the pandemic. Platforms like IRI Data offer insights for optimizing online presence and expanding reach.

Understanding and leveraging these key market trends is essential for businesses in the adult beverage industry to resonate with consumers and foster growth. Staying informed and adaptable is key to thriving in this dynamic landscape.

Summary of References for further reading

I. Nielsen
   a. Overview: Provides analytics on health and wellness trends in the beverage industry.
   b. Link: https://nielseniq.com/global/en/landing-page/beval-hub/
II. IRI Worldwide (State of the Beverage Alcohol Industry)
   a. Overview: Similar to Nielsen, IRI Worldwide offers detailed insights and analytics, including those related to the beverage alcohol industry.
   b. Link: https://www.iriworldwide.com/en-us/insights/publications/state-of-the-beverage-alcohol-industry
III. Haus Alpenz
   a. Overview: Not specifically mentioned in the original details, but Haus Alpenz is known for its unique portfolio of spirits and liqueurs, likely relating to trends in premium and craft beverages.
   b. Link: https://alpenz.com/
IV. Shanken News Daily

      a. Overview: Offers insights into the premiumization and craft movement within the adult beverage industry.

      b. Link: https://www.shankennewsdaily.com/

V.   Overproof

      a. Overview: Discusses the impact of cultural influences on the alcohol industry, particularly with respect to trends and market shifts.

      b. Link: https://overproof.com/2022/11/10/alcohol-trends-2023/

VI. IRI Worldwide

      a. Overview: Offers insights for e-commerce strategy in the beverage industry, likely encompassing data analytics and market trends relevant to online sales and digital marketing.

      b. Link: https://www.iriworldwide.com/en-us

Review Questions

1. **True or False:** The health and wellness movement has led to a decrease in demand for low-alcohol and organic beverages.

2. What does the Shanken newsletter primarily provide insights into?
   a. Health and Wellness Trends
   b. Premiumization and Craft Movement
   c. Technological Advancements
   d. Global Flavors

3. Environmental consciousness in the adult beverage industry is often demonstrated through _____

and water conservation in production.

4. **True or False:** Cultural influences and global flavors have little impact on the U.S. adult beverage industry.

5. Which of the following has accelerated the shift towards e-commerce in the adult beverage industry?
   a. Health and Wellness Movement
   b. The Pandemic
   c. Premiumization
   d. Technological Advancements

Article 3: Embracing Innovation and New Product Development in the Adult Beverage Industry

Innovation is crucial in the adult beverage industry to keep pace with evolving consumer preferences and emerging trends. This article examines the significance of innovation, the new product development (NPD) process, and strategies for businesses to stay competitive and relevant.

The Imperative of Innovation Innovation is essential for brands to differentiate themselves and maintain relevance. It can take various forms, from new flavors and sustainable practices to leveraging technology for unique consumer experiences. Resources like industry newsletters and public industry news forums like Shanken provide updates on industry innovations.

Understanding Consumer Needs Successful innovation starts with understanding consumer needs. Utilizing market research, surveys, and feedback mechanisms is vital. Platforms like Nielsen and IRI Data offer valuable analytics on consumer preferences.

The New Product Development Process NPD is a systematic approach to bringing innovative ideas to market. It involves several stages:

Idea Generation: Includes brainstorming, market research, and trend analysis.

Concept Testing: Evaluates the idea's feasibility through methods like focus groups.

Product Design and Development: Involves formulation, packaging, and branding.

Market Testing: Gathering feedback from select market launches.

Commercialization: Full-scale product launch with appropriate marketing strategies.

Leveraging Technology in NPD Modern NPD increasingly relies on technology, from AI for trend predictions to virtual reality for product testing. Staying informed with platforms like SipSource is essential for insights into tech-driven NPD innovations.

Collaborative Innovation Innovation can be enhanced through collaborations with external entities like research institutions, tech startups, or consumers, bringing in new perspectives and expertise.

Challenges and Overcoming Them Innovation in the alcohol industry faces challenges like regulatory constraints and the risk of unsuccessful ventures. A culture emphasizing learning, agility, and resilience is key to overcoming these hurdles.

Innovation and NPD are fundamental for growth in the adult beverage industry. By focusing on consumer needs, utilizing technology, and fostering a culture of innovation, brands can lead the industry's future.

Summary of References

Shanken: Provides insights into industry trends and innovations.
Nielsen and IRI Data: Offer detailed analytics on consumer preferences and trends.

Review Questions

1. **True or False:** Innovation in the adult beverage industry is limited to introducing new flavors.

2. Which platform offers detailed analytics on consumer preferences in the adult beverage industry?
   a. Shanken
   b. Nielsen
   c. SipSource

3. In the NPD process, _____ involves evaluating the feasibility of a product idea.

4. **True or False:** Collaborative innovation is restricted to partnerships within the same industry.

5. What is a key challenge in innovation for the adult beverage industry?
   a. Flavor development
   b. Regulatory hurdles
   c. Bottle design

d. Marketing strategies

Article 4: Exploring Industry Disruptions and Technological Advances in the U.S. Alcohol Beverage Industry

The U.S. alcohol beverage industry has historically adapted to societal, economic, and technological changes. Currently, it's undergoing a transformation due to technological disruptions. This exploration will shed light on these changes and their implications for the industry.

Digital Transformation: Harnessing the Power of Data and Analytics Data analytics is becoming increasingly important in the industry. Platforms likethe former Drizly or UberEats models use data to inform local market trends and optimize offerings. However, with the collection of more data comes the responsibility of navigating complex regulatory landscapes across different states. Using the right tools and strategies can turn these challenges into opportunities.

Blockchain Technology: Enhancing Transparency and Traceability Blockchain is emerging as a key technology in the alcohol industry, particularly for ensuring product authenticity. Brands like Everledger use blockchain to trace the journey of wines and spirits, combating counterfeiting and enhancing consumer trust. This technology streamlines operations and can automate transactions via smart contracts.

Artificial Intelligence and Machine Learning: Optimizing Operations and Customer Experiences AI and ML are significantly impacting the industry, from consumer interaction to product development. IntelligentX, for instance, uses AI to adapt beer recipes based on consumer feedback. AI-driven tools also assist in inventory management, demand forecasting, and counterfeit detection. However, ethical considerations and potential biases in algorithms must be addressed.

Technological disruptions present opportunities for those in the alcohol beverage industry willing to adapt and innovate. Utilizing data, blockchain, and AI can enhance operations and strengthen consumer connections.

Summary of References

I. Drizly:
   a. Overview: A platform that leverages data analytics for insights on local market trends in the alcohol industry.
   b. Link: https://drizly.com/
II. Everledger:
   a. Overview: Uses blockchain technology for product traceability in the wine and spirits sector.
   b. Link: https://everledger.io/industry-solutions/wine-spirits/
III. IntelligentX (AI-Brewed Beer Video):
   a. Overview: An example of earlier AI application in beer recipe development based on consumer feedback. The video on Vimeo showcases IntelligentX's approach to AI-driven beer brewing.
   b. Link: https://vimeo.com/172395607

Review Questions

1. **True or False:** Blockchain technology in the alcohol industry is primarily used for enhancing digital payment systems.

2. What does Drizly use to provide insights on local market trends?
   a. Blockchain Technology
   b. Data Analytics
   c. AI and ML
   d. Smart Contracts

3. _____ uses AI to adapt beer recipes based on consumer feedback.

4. **True or False:** AI and ML applications in the alcohol industry are limited to product development and consumer interaction.

5. What is a key challenge when implementing technological advancements in the alcohol industry?
   a. Flavor development
   b. Regulatory compliance
   c. Packaging design
   d. Marketing strategies

Article 5: Sustainability and Environmental Considerations in the U.S. Alcohol Beverage Industry

Sustainability, once a mere buzzword, is now a critical component of business strategy, particularly in the U.S. alcohol beverage industry. This industry, with its complex supply chains and resource-intensive processes, has a notable environmental footprint. Progressive brands are recognizing the ethical and business imperatives of adopting sustainable practices. This comprehensive exploration delves into how the industry is tackling environmental challenges.

Eco-Friendly Packaging: Beyond the Basics Packaging is not just about containment and branding; it has significant environmental implications. Traditional materials, especially plastics and non-recyclables, pose a major environmental threat. Innovative companies are countering this by adopting eco-friendly alternatives:

Seedlip's Transition: Seedlip exemplifies this shift with its 100% recyclable packaging.

Craft Breweries' Innovations: Many are moving towards biodegradable six-pack rings, a significant step in protecting marine life.

Extended Producer Responsibility (EPR): This concept encourages brands to be responsible for the lifecycle of their packaging, promoting recycling and reuse.

Sustainable Sourcing and Production: Beyond Organic

Ethical Sourcing: Consumers demand transparency in sourcing, driving brands towards ethical practices.

Organic and Bio-dynamic Farming: These practices are becoming more prevalent, focusing on biodiversity and ecological balance.

Water Conservation: Water usage in brewing and distilling is a critical area, with brands innovating to reduce their water footprint.

Case Study - Patagonia Provisions: Their venture into beer, collaborating with breweries like Rhinegeist and Allagash, emphasizes regenerative farming practices.

Green Initiatives: Leading by Example

Arbikie Highland Estate's Endeavor: Their goal to become the first green hydrogen-powered distillery is a groundbreaking effort in reducing carbon emissions.
Renewable Energy Adoption: More distilleries and breweries are investing in renewable energy sources, like solar and wind power, to fuel their operations.

The circular economy is gaining momentum in the industry:

Waste as Resource: By-products like spent grains and grape pomace are being repurposed for animal feed, compost, and even textiles.
Refill and Reuse Programs: Bottle-refill initiatives, while still emerging, represent a significant step towards reducing single-use packaging.
Collaborations with Sustainability Startups: Partnerships with companies like Loop are exploring innovative packaging solutions tailored for the beverage industry.

Sustainability is more than an ethical choice; it's a strategic business decision:

Market Differentiation: Brands adopting green practices are differentiating themselves in a crowded market.
Consumer Demand: A growing segment of consumers is prioritizing sustainability, influencing their purchasing decisions.
Regulatory Compliance: Adhering to environmental regulations can prevent legal challenges and enhance brand reputation.

The U.S. alcohol beverage industry's journey towards sustainability is a comprehensive endeavor, involving packaging, sourcing, production, and waste management. While challenges are present, the proactive approach of the industry is commendable. For industry stakeholders, integrating sustainability is not just ethical but also essential for long-term business viability and brand resonance.

Summary of Resources

I. **Arbikie Highland Estate - Sustainability:**
   a. **Overview:** Arbikie Estate's sustainability page details their commitment to becoming the world's first green hydrogen-powered distillery and their sustainable farming practices.
   b. **Link:** https://arbikie.com/pages/sustainability
II. **Rhinegeist Brewery:**
   a. **Overview:** Rhinegeist Brewery's website offers insights into their beer offerings, which may include sustainable brewing practices, given their collaboration with Patagonia Provisions.
   b. **Link:** https://rhinegeist.com/
III. **Allagash Brewing Company:**
   a. **Overview:** Allagash Brewing Company is known for its craft beers and may also incorporate sustainable brewing practices as part of its collaboration with Patagonia Provisions.
   b. **Link:** https://www.allagash.com/
IV. **Patagonia Provisions - Why Beer:**

a. **Overview:** This page explains Patagonia Provisions' venture into the beer industry, focusing on regenerative organic farming and sustainable practices.
b. **Link:** https://www.patagoniaprovisions.com/pages/why-beer

V. **Seedlip Drinks:**
   a. **Overview:** Seedlip Drinks showcases its non-alcoholic spirits and commitment to sustainable packaging and eco-friendly practices.
   b. **Link:** https://www.seedlipdrinks.com/en-us/

Review Questions

1. **True or False:** Arbikie Highland Estate is aiming to become the world's first green hydrogen-powered distillery.
2. Which brand is known for its 100% recyclable packaging?
   a. Rhinegeist
   b. Allagash
   c. Seedlip
   d. Patagonia Provisions
3. Patagonia Provisions has ventured into the beer industry with a focus on _____ farming.
4. **True or False:** The concept of a circular economy in the alcohol beverage industry only focuses on recycling and does not include reuse principles.
5. What is the primary environmental concern addressed by the use of biodegradable six-pack rings by craft breweries?
   a. Air pollution reduction
   b. Water conservation

    c. Reduction of harm to marine life
    d. Soil health improvement

Article 6: Non-Alcoholic and Low-Alcohol Beverage Trends: A New Era of Conscious Consumption

The U.S. alcohol beverage industry has witnessed a significant shift towards non-alcoholic and low-alcohol beverages. This change reflects a societal move towards mindful consumption, driven by health and wellness trends. This in-depth exploration will examine the industry's response to these evolving consumer preferences.

The non-alcoholic spirits sector is redefining the beverage landscape:

Innovative Brands: Seedlip and Ritual Zero Proof are pioneering the space with sophisticated alternatives to traditional spirits.

Emerging Players: New entrants like Aplos, offering hemp-based spirits, and Wilderton, with its bold non-alcoholic options, are expanding the category.

Consumer Drivers: The shift towards non-alcoholic options is fueled by lifestyle choices and health considerations, demanding high-quality, flavorful alternatives.

Low-alcohol beverages cater to those seeking a moderate drinking experience:

Sessionable Options: Brands are introducing products like session IPAs and low-ABV wines, balancing taste and alcohol content.

Notable Examples: Sotolon Selections and aromatized wines from Haus Alpenz represent quality and variety in this category.

Historical Context: Traditional beverages like Madeira and Vermouth, with their complex flavor profiles and rich history, are seeing renewed interest.

Appeal to a Younger Audience: These classic drinks are attracting younger consumers keen on exploring traditional flavors with a contemporary twist.

The demand for craft and artisanal beverages extends to this sector:

Emphasis on Craftsmanship: Local distilleries and breweries are experimenting with unique ingredients and traditional methods.

Diverse Landscape: This trend has led to a varied beverage market where authenticity and quality are paramount.

The growing popularity of non-alcoholic and low-alcohol beverages marks a shift in the industry's approach to consumer needs. As health and wellness continue to shape consumption patterns, brands that respond with innovative, high-quality offerings will find success.

For industry participants, adapting to this change and prioritizing consumer preferences is crucial. The future of the U.S. alcohol beverage industry lies in its ability to evolve and cater to a diverse, health-conscious market.

Summary of Resources

I.   **Seedlip Drinks:**

a. **Overview:** Pioneers in crafting non-alcoholic spirits, offering a sophisticated and health-conscious alternative to traditional alcoholic beverages.
b. **Link:** https://www.seedlipdrinks.com/en-us/our-story/

II. **Ritual Zero Proof:**
a. **Overview:** Produces non-alcoholic spirits, catering to consumers seeking the cocktail experience without alcohol.
b. **Link:** https://www.ritualzeroproof.com/pages/about-us

III. **Aplos:**
a. **Overview:** Offers hemp-based, non-alcoholic spirits, emphasizing wellness and the benefits of a hemp-infused, relaxing beverage.
b. **Link:** https://www.aplos.world/learn/from-alcohol-to-hemp

IV. **Wilderton Free:**
a. **Overview:** Creates bold, non-alcoholic spirits using global botanicals, focusing on flavor and aroma.
b. **Link:** https://wildertonfree.com/pages/the-story

V. **Alpenz - Cap Corse Blanc:**
a. **Overview:** Features Cap Corse Blanc, a low-alcohol aromatized wine, part of Alpenz's diverse and high-quality offerings.
b. **Link:** https://alpenz.com/product-cap_corse_blanc.html

VI. **Alpenz - Sotolon Selections:**
a. **Overview:** Showcases Sotolon Selections, a range of distinctive, low-alcohol beverages offered by Alpenz.

    b. **Link:** https://alpenz.com/category-sotolon_selections.html

VII.   **Alpenz - Aromatized Wines and Spirits:**

    a. **Overview:** Highlights Alpenz's selection of aromatized wines and spirits, which include traditional and complex-flavored options.

    b. **Link:** https://alpenz.com/category-aromatized.html

Review Questions

1. **True or False:** The rise in non-alcoholic spirits like Seedlip is primarily due to consumer demand for more flavorful soda and mocktail alternatives.
2. What is the primary focus of Aplos, a new entrant in the non-alcoholic spirits market?
   a. Hemp-based spirits emphasizing relaxation.
   b. Traditional alcoholic spirits.
   c. High-alcohol content beverages.
   d. Carbonated soft drinks.
3. Wilderton Free, known for its _____, offers non-alcoholic spirits crafted using raw botanicals sourced globally.
4. **True or False:** Low-alcohol beverages like those from Alpenz are gaining popularity because they offer the same taste and quality as high-alcohol content drinks.
5. What unique approach is Alpenz known for in their low-alcohol beverage offerings?
   a. Mass-produced, generic flavors.
   b. Unique, high-quality selections like Cap Corse Blanc and Sotolon Selections.
   c. Only non-alcoholic options.
   d. Beverages with artificial flavoring.

Article 7: Global Expansions and International Market Opportunities

The U.S. alcohol industry is witnessing a significant shift, with domestic brands gaining popularity and exploring international markets. As the American market matures, the potential of global expansion presents new opportunities for growth.

Recent trends in the U.S. market have seen a shift in consumer preferences:

Growth in Spirits Market Share: According to the Distilled Spirits Council, in 2023 spirits have overtaken beer in revenue, a reflection of changing consumer tastes and the resurgence of cocktail culture.

Popular Segments: Tequila and American whiskey have shown substantial growth, indicating a diversification of consumer preferences.

Several American brands are making successful forays into global markets:

Jack Daniel's International Success: Known for its Tennessee whiskey, Jack Daniel's has a robust presence internationally, adapting to global tastes with innovations like their American single malt whiskey.

Jim Beam's Global Reach: An iconic bourbon, Jim Beam, now part of the Suntory portfolio, enjoys significant popularity in markets like Japan, showcasing the potential of American spirits in Asia.

New Amsterdam Vodka's Expansion: Launched in 2011 and known for its affordability, New Amsterdam Vodka, supported by E&J Gallo's network, is well-positioned for international growth.

The U.S. craft beer industry faces unique challenges in international expansion:

Defining "Craft": The definition of "craft" is contentious, especially with acquisitions by larger conglomerates, as seen with Brooklyn Brewery's partnership with Kirin.

International Appeal: Despite these debates, the "craft" label has considerable appeal in international markets, offering an opportunity for American breweries.

Exploring international markets offers immense potential but also presents challenges:

Emerging Markets: Countries like China and India, with growing economies, present lucrative opportunities. Obviously geopolitical issues have sway over this growth and as the global positioning of brands expands this trend changes regularly.

Cultural and Regulatory Considerations: Understanding local tastes, cultural nuances, and regulatory environments is crucial for successful market entry.

Logistical Challenges: Establishing efficient supply chains and navigating tariffs require careful planning and strategy.

The international market represents a new frontier for growth for the U.S. liquor industry. Brands that can adapt to different cultures, navigate logistical challenges, and leverage their American heritage can significantly benefit from global expansion.

Review Questions

1. **True or False:** According to the Distilled Spirits Council of the United States, spirits have surpassed beer in revenue market share as of 2022.
2. Which American whiskey brand has a significant international presence and recently launched an American single malt whiskey?
   a. Jim Beam
   b. Jack Daniel's
   c. New Amsterdam Vodka
   d. Brooklyn Brewery
3. The acquisition of a stake in Brooklyn Brewery by _____ in 2016 raised discussions about the definition of "craft" beer.
4. **True or False:** New Amsterdam Vodka, known for its affordability, is primarily focused on the domestic U.S. market and has not ventured into international markets.
5. When considering international expansion, U.S. liquor brands need to be particularly mindful of:
   a. Only marketing strategies.
   b. Just supply chain logistics.
   c. Understanding local cultures, tastes, and regulatory environments.
   d. Focusing solely on product quality.

Article 8: Predictions for the Future of the Adult Beverage Industry: Embracing the Digital Revolution

The adult beverage industry is at a pivotal point, integrating cutting-edge technologies such as VR and AR. This integration is not only reshaping marketing strategies but also revolutionizing consumer interactions and experiences.

The potential of VR and AR in beverage marketing is vast:

Immersive Experiences: VR can transport consumers to virtual vineyards or breweries, offering interactive and educational experiences. These virtual tours and tastings create a unique bond between the consumer and the brand.

AR Enhancements: AR brings a new dimension to shopping experiences. Interactive labels, like those pioneered by 19 Crimes Wines, offer detailed product information and storytelling through smartphone integration.

Benefits: VR and AR provide enhanced engagement, educational opportunities, and the ability to offer personalized experiences to consumers.

The current consumer landscape demands more than generic offerings:

Demand for Personalization: Modern consumers seek products that cater to their individual tastes. Brands are responding with tailored experiences, such as custom beer blends or personalized wine recommendations through digital platforms.

Emerging Trends: Beyond personalization, consumers are influencing trends like sustainability, craft beverages, and novel flavor profiles.

The adult beverage industry's future is being shaped by technological advancements and changing consumer preferences. Brands that embrace these changes, integrating technologies like VR and AR and responding to the call for personalization, will lead the industry's evolution.

Review Questions:

1. **True or False:** Virtual Reality (VR) in the adult beverage industry is primarily used for gaming purposes.
2. What does Augmented Reality (AR) offer in the context of the adult beverage industry?
   a. Only gaming experiences
   b. Enhanced shopping experiences with interactive labels
   c. Traditional marketing methods
   d. Product delivery services
3. 19 Crimes Wines is known for its innovative use of _____ in their wine labels to provide a unique consumer experience.
4. **True or False:** The demand for personalized beverage experiences is diminishing in today's consumer landscape.
5. Which technology is being used by wineries and breweries to offer virtual tours and tastings?
   a. Social Media
   b. Virtual Reality (VR)
   c. E-commerce platforms
   d. Traditional advertising

Article 9: The Evolving Landscape of the Adult Beverage Industry: Navigating the Waves of Change

Continuing from our discussion on technology's role in the adult beverage industry, we now turn to other key factors reshaping this sector: evolving consumer preferences, the lasting impact of the pandemic, and future predictions.

The modern consumer's influence extends beyond personalization:

Sustainability and Ethical Production: There's an increasing demand for eco-friendly and ethically produced beverages. Organic distilleries are gaining popularity among environmentally conscious consumers. At the same time "organic" certifications are changing and adapting.

Craft Beverage Trends: While the craft beer market has seen a slowdown, possibly due to market saturation or pandemic challenges, the demand for unique, high-quality beverages remains robust.

The pandemic has catalyzed significant shifts:

Online Sales Surge: The lockdowns led to a boom in online sales and home deliveries, a trend that continues to persist.

Changing Preferences: The equilibrium between wine and distilled spirits sales indicates a diversification in consumer alcohol preferences.

Looking ahead, several trends are likely to shape the industry:

E-Commerce Expansion: Continued growth in online purchasing, with brands enhancing their digital platforms and offering interactive experiences.

Focus on Sustainability: A shift towards sustainable practices in production, packaging, and distribution will become crucial for brand survival.

Product Diversification: Brands may diversify their offerings to cater to a wider range of tastes.

Experiential Marketing: Emphasis on experiences, such as virtual tours and VR-based storytelling, will become a key marketing strategy.

Looking further into the future:

Smart Bottles: Bottles and labels that interact with consumers, offering personalized experiences and dynamic label designs.

AI-Powered Recommendations: Using AI for real-time drink recommendations based on various factors like mood or weather.

Virtual Bars: The rise of the metaverse could lead to the creation of virtual bars for socializing and digital beverage tasting.

The adult beverage industry is navigating through a period of significant change. Brands that can effectively merge tradition with innovation and offer a blend of products and experiences will be at the forefront of this evolution. The future promises exciting possibilities, novel experiences, and a deeper connection between consumers and brands.

Review Questions

1. **True or False:** The demand for sustainable and ethically produced beverages is decreasing in the modern consumer market.
2. What trend has the pandemic catalyzed in the adult beverage industry?
   a. Decrease in online sales
   b. Surge in online sales and home deliveries
   c. Decline in the quality of beverages
   d. Shift towards non-alcoholic beverages only
3. The craft beer market has experienced a slowdown, which could be attributed to market _____ and pandemic challenges.

4. **True or False:** In the next 1-5 years, the adult beverage industry is expected to see a decline in e-commerce and digital marketing.
5. What innovative concept is predicted for the adult beverage industry in the next 10-15 years?
    a. Traditional brick-and-mortar stores only
    b. Elimination of all digital marketing
    c. Virtual bars in the metaverse
    d. Return to pre-pandemic sales methods

Conclusion: Navigating the Future of the Adult Beverage Industry

Embracing the Digital Revolution and Consumer-Driven Change The adult beverage industry stands at a transformative juncture, marked by rapid technological advancements and shifting consumer preferences. The integration of digital technologies like VR, AR, and AI is reshaping marketing strategies, enhancing consumer engagement, and creating personalized experiences. These innovations, coupled with a growing emphasis on sustainability, ethical production, and authenticity, are driving brands to rethink their approach and align with these new consumer values.

Understanding and Adapting to Market Shifts

Consumer Behavior and Preferences: Brands must continuously adapt to the evolving tastes and preferences of consumers, utilizing resources like Nielsen and IRI Data for market insights.

Craft Beverages and Market Trends: While the craft beer market has seen fluctuations, the demand for unique and quality beverages remains strong. This trend presents opportunities for innovation and diversification in product offerings.

Long-Term Impact of Pandemic-Induced Trends The pandemic has accelerated certain trends, particularly in e-commerce, which is likely to continue growing. Online sales and home deliveries have become more prominent, indicating a permanent shift in consumer buying behavior. Brands that successfully leverage digital platforms and offer unique online experiences are well-positioned for growth.

Financial and Strategic Considerations for the Future

E-Commerce and Diversification: The rise in online purchasing and the need for product diversification will be critical areas of focus. Investing in digital capabilities and exploring new product lines are essential strategies for future success.

Sustainability and Ethical Production: As consumer awareness around environmental issues grows, sustainable practices will become increasingly important. Brands that prioritize eco-friendly production methods will likely gain a competitive edge.

The Three-Tier System: Challenges and Opportunities The unique three-tier system in the U.S. continues to play a significant role in the industry. Understanding and effectively navigating this system will be crucial for brands, particularly in adapting to changing market conditions and consumer preferences.

Looking Ahead: Preparing for a Dynamic Future

Innovation and Consumer Engagement: Embracing technological innovations and focusing on consumer-driven trends will be key to thriving in the evolving landscape.

Market Research and Competitive Analysis: Staying informed about market dynamics and competitive movements will enable brands to adapt swiftly and strategically.

Collaboration and Experimentation: Collaborative efforts, both within and outside the industry, can lead to novel products and experiences that resonate with consumers.

Shaping a Bright Future

The future of the adult beverage industry is vibrant and full of potential. For producers, embracing innovation and quality, while exploring new collaborations will be pivotal. Distributors and retailers must strengthen relationships, utilize data effectively, and remain attuned to consumer trends. Consumers, as the driving force behind industry evolution, should continue to explore and engage with the industry's offerings. My hope is that they continue to search for connection and brands that are built on integrity, quality, provenance and most importantly intentionality.

The adult beverage industry is poised for a period of exciting change through innovation. By adopting a customer-centric approach, embracing technological advancements, and remaining adaptable to market changes, stakeholders can look forward to a future marked by success, innovation, and unparalleled consumer experiences.

Review Questions with Answers

Chapter 1

Chapter 1 – Article 1:

1. Why is understanding a distributor's size and reach crucial when choosing one for your brand?

- Answer: Understanding a distributor's size and reach is crucial because it determines how far your products can go in the marketplace. The magnitude and expanse of a distributor are contingent on where your brand currently stands and where you envision it heading. For budding brands, a distributor with a wide reach can simplify entry into diverse territories. For established brands, a distributor that offers focused attention can be more beneficial.

2. How can a brand's engagement with a distributor's sales team influence its market presence?

- Answer: A brand's engagement with a distributor's sales team can significantly influence its market presence because the deeper the engagement, the higher the chances of the brand being promoted to bars, eateries, and retail outlets. Effective collaboration with the sales team ensures that the brand is well-represented and prioritized in the market.

3. Why is it essential for brands to have their own marketing strategies in addition to relying on a distributor's promotional efforts?

- Answer: It's essential for brands to have their own marketing strategies because while a distributor can amplify a brand's market presence, brands shouldn't be solely reliant on them. A brand's marketing blueprint should complement the distributor's promotional endeavors, creating a synergy that boosts brand recognition and adoption. Additionally, brands can harness the power of digital avenues to further bolster their market presence.

4. How can a brand's online presence in today's digital age impact its market visibility and acceptance?

- Answer: In today's digital-driven epoch, a brand's online presence can significantly impact its market visibility and acceptance. A robust online footprint, especially on social media and other digital platforms, can bolster brand recognition, reach a wider audience, and foster direct engagement with consumers. In the current digital age, having a strong online presence is non-negotiable for brands aiming for widespread market acceptance.

Chapter 1 – Article 2:
1. True or False: A distributor's bond with retailers can be the determining factor in a brand's success.
- Answer: True
2. Which role does a portfolio manager typically play within a distributor's organization?
- a) Handling the financial books of the distributor.
- b) Overseeing the bonus services, offering insights into sales figures, and guiding on market trends.
- c) Building relationships with retailers.
- d) Managing the distributor's online advertising.
- Answer: b) Overseeing the bonus services, offering insights into sales figures, and guiding on market trends.
3. True or False: The sole responsibility of nurturing and maintaining ties with retailers lies with the distributor.
- Answer: False
4. What can third-party firms offer brands in terms of value-added services?
- a) Manufacturing the products.
- b) Designing the product packaging.
- c) Tracking sales and maintaining records of account visits.
- d) Handling customer complaints.
- Answer: c) Tracking sales and maintaining records of account visits.

Chapter 1 – Article 3:
1. True or False: The financial health of a distributor is often the primary factor considered by brands.
- Answer: False
2. Which of the following is NOT a common performance metric for evaluating a distributor?
- a) Shipment case volumes
- b) Number of social media followers
- c) Points of distribution (PODs)
- d) Accounts sold
- Answer: b) Number of social media followers
3. True or False: In the early stages of a brand's development, the primary focus should be on the number of high-volume accounts secured.
- Answer: False

4. Why is it beneficial to strike a balance between high-volume accounts and individual placements?
*   a) It ensures maximum profit.
*   b) It facilitates brand visibility and lays a foundation for brand growth.
*   c) It reduces the workload for the distributor.
*   d) It guarantees product exclusivity in the market.
*   Answer: b) It facilitates brand visibility and lays a foundation for brand growth.

Chapter 1 – Article 4:
1. True or False: Cultural fit with a distributor is solely about having aligned business objectives.
*   Answer: False
2. What does a distributor's commitment to DEI indicate?
*   a) Their marketing strategies
*   b) Their approach to sales and understanding of diverse markets
*   c) Their product range
*   d) Their pricing strategies
*   Answer: b) Their approach to sales and understanding of diverse markets
3. True or False: A distributor's team diversity is solely about the varied backgrounds of its members.
*   Answer: False
4. Which of the following is NOT a way to gauge a distributor's commitment to DEI?
*   a) Speaking to their other brand partners
*   b) Checking their social media follower count
*   c) Discussing their DEI strategies directly
*   d) Conducting background research on their initiatives
*   Answer: b) Checking their social media follower count

Chapter 1 – Article 5:

1. Why is understanding a distributor's reputation crucial when choosing a partner for your brand?
*   Answer: A distributor's reputation is a reflection of their past performances, ethics, reliability, and credibility. It provides insights into their professional conduct, service caliber, and standing in the market, which can significantly influence the effectiveness of the collaboration and the trajectory of the brand.
2. True or False: The longevity of a distributor's sales team is the sole indicator of its stability.

- Answer: False. While the longevity of the sales team can indicate stability, it's also essential to consider the quality of service and the blend of experienced and younger sales personnel.
3. What are some effective ways to gauge a distributor's reputation in the market?
- Answer: Engaging with the target audience, visiting bars, restaurants, and liquor stores, conversing with bartenders and managers about their preferred distributors, and asking in-depth questions about the distributor's professional conduct and service quality.
4. How can a brand owner actively contribute to building and maintaining relationships with retailers?
- Answer: By fostering connections, being approachable, exuding warmth, and being supportive. It's essential for brand owners to actively engage, understand the needs of the retailer, and be their pillar of support.
5. Why is it essential for a brand owner to be accessible and supportive to the distributor's sales team?
- Answer: The rapport with and accessibility to the sales team often outweigh organizational tenure. A strong relationship with the sales team ensures better representation of the brand in the market and fosters trust.
6. In the context of the article, what does the metaphor "dance partner for a marathon performance" signify?
- Answer: It signifies the importance of finding a distributor that aligns well with the brand's vision, ethos, and goals, ensuring a long-lasting and harmonious partnership that can navigate the challenges and complexities of the market.

Chapter 2
Chapter 2 – Article 1:

1. What system is described as the backbone of alcohol distribution?
- a. Two-tier system
- b. Four-tier system
- c. Three-tier system
- d. Single-tier system
- Answer: c. Three-tier system
2. Which federal agency is responsible for crafting and enforcing regulations that govern the alcohol industry?
- a. FDA (Food and Drug Administration)
- b. ATF (Bureau of Alcohol, Tobacco, Firearms, and Explosives)
- c. TTB (Alcohol and Tobacco Tax and Trade Bureau)

- d. DOR (Department of Revenue)
- Answer: c. TTB (Alcohol and Tobacco Tax and Trade Bureau)
3. State regulations in the alcohol industry are described as:
- a. Being uniform across all states.
- b. Adding a unique flair or variation to the federal regulations.
- c. Being less important than federal regulations.
- d. Being optional for businesses to follow.
- Answer: b. Adding a unique flair or variation to the federal regulations.

Chapter 2 – Article 2:

1. Which federal agency oversees the licensing and permits for the alcohol industry?
1. FDA
2. ATF
3. TTB
4. DOR
Answer: c. TTB
2. Why is it essential to be familiar with state-specific licensing requirements in the alcohol industry?
1. Each state has the same regulations.
2. State regulations are optional.
3. Each state has its unique set of rules and regulations.
4. Federal regulations cover all state requirements.
Answer: c. Each state has its unique set of rules and regulations.
3. What is the primary purpose of the alcohol producer permit?
1. For importing unique flavors from abroad.
2. For producing brews, wines, or spirits.
3. For selling alcohol directly to consumers.
4. For warehousing and storage of alcohol.
Answer: b. For producing brews, wines, or spirits.

Chapter 2 – Article 3:
1. Why are labels considered essential storytellers in the alcoholic beverages sector?
- Answer: Labels are essential storytellers because they bridge the gap between producers and consumers. They provide clear and accurate information about the product, ensuring transparency in choices. Beyond the basic details like alcohol content, serving size, and health warnings, labels also embody a brand's identity, offering a first impression of the drink within and telling a story of craftsmanship, quality, and the unique spirit of the beverage.

2. How do packaging and labeling together contribute to a consumer's experience?
- Answer: Packaging and labeling together play a pivotal role in the consumer's experience. While labels provide essential information and convey the brand's identity, packaging contributes to the tactile and visual experience. The choice of materials, colors, and the bottle's shape all add to the allure of the product. Together, they ensure accuracy, prevent misbranding, and offer a sensory journey that resonates with consumers.
3. What role do state-specific regulations play in the context of labeling and packaging compliance?
- Answer: State-specific regulations add another layer to the federal framework governing labeling and packaging. Each state might have its nuances and requirements, akin to regional variations. These can include additional labeling elements, specific font sizes for health warnings, or other unique criteria. Adhering to these state-specific regulations ensures that brands are compliant across different regions and resonate with local audiences.

Chapter 2 – Article 4:
1. Why is understanding different tax rates for spirits, beer, and wine crucial for producers?
- Answer: Understanding different tax rates for spirits, beer, and wine is crucial for producers because each beverage category has distinct tax rates tailored to its category. This ensures that producers pay the correct amount in excise taxes, allowing them to maintain compliance with federal regulations and avoid potential legal and financial repercussions.
2. How do state-specific regulations add complexity to alcohol taxation?
- Answer: State-specific regulations add complexity to alcohol taxation because each state has its unique take on excise taxes. This means that producers must be aware of and adhere to varying tax rates and requirements across different states, making the compliance process more intricate. It's akin to each state having its distinct dance in the grand ballet of compliance.
3. Why is meticulous record-keeping essential in ensuring compliance with alcohol taxation?
- Answer: Meticulous record-keeping is essential in ensuring compliance with alcohol taxation because it ensures transparency, accuracy, and fosters trust between producers and regulatory bodies. Proper documentation of transactions and the ability to retrieve and review them when necessary is pivotal in verifying that the correct taxes have been paid and that producers are operating within the bounds of the law.

Chapter 2 – Article 5:

1. Which entity is described as the "tax collector extraordinaire" in the alcohol industry?
- a) Uncle Bob
- b) Uncle Sam
- c) Uncle John
- d) Uncle Steve

Answer: b) Uncle Sam

2. True or False: All states have uniform advertising and trade practice rules.

Answer: False

3. In the context of the article, what is the primary role of labels in alcoholic beverages?
- a) To provide colorful designs
- b) To tell tales of craftsmanship and quality
- c) To display the price of the product
- d) To show the manufacturer's address

Answer: b) To tell tales of craftsmanship and quality

4. Which platform is NOT mentioned as a realm for advertising regulations in the alcohol industry?
- a) Facebook
- b) Snapchat
- c) YouTube
- d) Instagram

Answer: b) Snapchat

5. Fill in the blank: "_____ and packaging compliance is an art of transparency."

Answer: Labeling

Chapter 3
Chapter 3 – Article 1:

1. Multiple Choice: Which of the following is NOT a primary purpose of branding in the adult beverage industry? a. Differentiation b. Building Trust c. Emotional Connection d. Increasing Production Answer: d. Increasing Production

2. True or False: Branding is solely about the visual elements, such as logos and packaging. Answer: False

3. Short Answer: In your own words, describe the role of branding in influencing consumer behavior. Answer: Branding plays a significant role in shaping consumer perceptions, preferences, and purchasing

decisions. It helps differentiate products in a crowded market, builds trust and credibility, and establishes an emotional connection with consumers, influencing their loyalty and advocacy.

4. Fill in the Blanks: Branding in the adult beverage industry serves as a bridge between _____ and _____. Answer: Branding in the adult beverage industry serves as a bridge between producers and consumers.

5. Matching: Match the following branding elements with their descriptions: a. Brand Identity b. Consistency and Coherence c. Authenticity and Transparency d. Engaging Experiences
   - Ensures a brand's promise is kept across all touchpoints.
   - The soul-searching phase of introspection before projection.
   - Being real, open, and accountable to consumers.
   - Making a brand tangible and relatable through events and campaigns.

   Answers: a. The soul-searching phase of introspection before projection. b. Ensures a brand's promise is kept across all touchpoints. c. Being real, open, and accountable to consumers. d. Making a brand tangible and relatable through events and campaigns.

6. Essay: Discuss the importance of emotional appeal in branding within the adult beverage industry. How does it influence consumer loyalty and decision-making? Answer: Emotional appeal in branding is pivotal in the adult beverage industry as it goes beyond transactional relationships to forge deeper connections with consumers. Brands that evoke positive emotions and resonate with consumers' values and lifestyles are more likely to be chosen repeatedly. This emotional connection fosters brand loyalty, ensuring that consumers not only prefer a particular brand but also advocate for it, influencing others in their circle. Emotional branding taps into feelings, memories, and experiences, making the brand more relatable and memorable, which in turn influences purchasing decisions.

7. Multiple Choice: Which of the following is a key aspect to consider when understanding the role of branding in influencing consumer behavior? a. Perception and Recognition b. Price Reduction c. Production Techniques d. Packaging Materials Answer: a. Perception and Recognition

8. True or False: All brands in the adult beverage industry should have the same values and target audience for maximum success. Answer: False

9. Scenario-Based Question: Imagine you are launching a new craft beer. How would you utilize the principles of branding discussed in the article to ensure its success in the market? Answer: To ensure the success of the new craft beer, I would start by defining a clear brand identity, focusing on the beer's unique selling propositions, values, and target audience. Consistency and coherence would be maintained across all

branding touchpoints, from packaging to marketing campaigns. Authenticity and transparency would be prioritized, sharing information about the beer's ingredients, production process, and the story behind its creation. Engaging experiences would be created through events, tastings, and brand activations to foster a deeper connection with consumers and create memorable brand experiences.

10. Multiple Answer: Which of the following are essential components for building a strong brand in the adult beverage industry? (Choose all that apply) a. Brand Identity b. Consistency and Coherence c. Authenticity and Transparency d. Production Speed Answer: a. Brand Identity, b. Consistency and Coherence, c. Authenticity and Transparency

Chapter 3 – Article 2:

1. Which of the following best describes the role of branding in the adult beverage industry? a. Solely focused on logo design. b. Primarily about product packaging. c. Encompasses the overall perception and personality of a brand. d. Only about differentiating from competitors.
Answer: c. Encompasses the overall perception and personality of a brand.

2. True or False: A brand's mission statement should reflect its values and communicate its value proposition to consumers.
Answer: True

3. When determining a brand's personality, which question might be helpful to consider? a. How much does the product cost? b. Would you want to hang out with your brand after work? c. How many competitors are in the market? d. What is the primary ingredient in the product?
Answer: b. Would you want to hang out with your brand after work?

4. On a scale of 1 to 5, where 1 is "Not Important" and 5 is "Extremely Important", how crucial is consistency in visual elements (like logo, typography, and color palette) for enhancing brand recognition?
Answer: 5 (Extremely Important)

5. Which of the following is NOT a key aspect to consider when understanding the influence of branding on consumer behavior? a. Perception and Recognition b. Product Differentiation c. The number of sales in the last quarter d. Emotional Appeal
Answer: c. The number of sales in the last quarter.

Chapter 3 – Article 3:

1. Multiple Choice: Which of the following is NOT a component of SMART goals?
- a) Specific
- b) Sensational
- c) Measurable

- d) Time-bound
- Answer: b) Sensational
2. True/False: Traditional marketing channels, such as print advertising, are outdated and no longer effective.
- Answer: False
3. Scalable Answer: On a scale of 1-5, how important is it to understand your target audience when crafting a marketing strategy? (1 being not important, 5 being extremely important)
- Answer: 5 (extremely important)
4. Multiple Choice: Which tool can help streamline and automate certain marketing tasks?
- a) A magic wand
- b) Marketing Automation tools
- c) A crystal ball
- d) A time machine
- Answer: b) Marketing Automation tools
5. Fill in the Blank: A/B testing is a data-driven approach that helps optimize your _____ efforts.
- Answer: marketing

Chapter 3 – Article 4:
1. Multiple Choice: Which social media platform is described as the "town square" where everyone gathers?
- a) Instagram
- b) LinkedIn
- c) Twitter
- d) Facebook Answer: d) Facebook
2. True/False: On Instagram, it's only about posting visually appealing pictures without considering the ever-evolving algorithm. Answer: False
3. Multiple Choice: Which digital marketing tool is described as the "digital spotlight" highlighting the brand to those actively searching for related keywords?
- a) Display Advertising
- b) Influencer Marketing
- c) Pay-per-Click (PPC) Advertising
- d) User-Generated Content Answer: c) Pay-per-Click (PPC) Advertising
4. True/False: A/B testing is used to experiment with different marketing elements to optimize campaign performance. Answer: True

Chapter 3 – Article 5:

1. Multiple Choice: Which generation is known for their adventurous and experiential consumption habits? a. Baby Boomers b. Gen X c. Millennials d. Generation Z Answer: c. Millennials
2. True/False: Gen X values nostalgia, quality, and convenience in their beverage choices. Answer: True
3. Scaled Response: On a scale of 1 (Not Important) to 5 (Very Important), how crucial is it to tailor branding messages and marketing channels based on the specific preferences of each market segment? Answer: 5 (Very Important)
4. Fill in the Blank: Partnering with _____ can help brands reach and connect with a wider audience and build trust among consumers in the adult beverage industry. Answer: influencers
5. Multiple Choice: Which of the following is NOT a recommended strategy for engaging with the Generation Z market segment in the adult beverage industry? a. Leveraging social media b. Highlighting customization options c. Focusing solely on traditional marketing channels d. Collaborating with influencers Answer: c. Focusing solely on traditional marketing channels

Chapter 4
Chapter 4 – Article 1:

1. Which of the following is NOT a benefit of strategic alliances in the alcohol industry? a) Shared Resources and Expertise b) Increased Market Access c) Limited Product Offerings d) Risk Mitigation
Answer: c) Limited Product Offerings
2. True or False: Collaborations in the alcohol sector only involve producers.
Answer: False
3. Which factor is essential for the success of a strategic alliance? a) Limited Communication b) Ambiguous Goals c) Legal and Contractual Clarity d) Rigidity
Answer: c) Legal and Contractual Clarity
4. What was the primary objective of the collaboration between Lady Gaga and Dom Pérignon? a) Increase sales b) Philanthropic efforts c) Introduce a new flavor d) Expand to new markets
Answer: b) Philanthropic efforts
5. Which of the following collaborations emphasized the importance of exclusive offerings in forging strong partnerships in the industry? a) Lady Gaga x Dom Pérignon b) Liu Wei x Hennessy c) W Aspen's Spring & Dean Single Barrel Club d) Huckberry and High West Whiskey

Answer: c) W Aspen's Spring & Dean Single Barrel Club

Chapter 4 – Article 2:
Review Questions:
1. Which of the following is NOT a segment Coca-Cola focused on in their alcohol venture?
a) Hard seltzers
b) Hard alternatives
c) Hard ciders
d) Pre-mixed cocktails
Answer: c) Hard ciders
2. True or False: Attending industry events is not a recommended method for finding potential partners in the alcohol industry.
Answer: False
3. Which of the following is crucial when approaching potential partners?
a) Making a direct sales pitch
b) Keeping your value proposition a secret
c) Building genuine relationships
d) Avoiding mutual business acquaintances
Answer: c) Building genuine relationships
4. What is one of the primary responsibilities for businesses entering the alcohol category?
a) Ignoring consumer preferences
b) Avoiding collaborations
c) Ensuring responsible consumption
d) Focusing solely on profit
Answer: c) Ensuring responsible consumption
5. True or False: The alcohol industry remains static and does not evolve over time.
Answer: False

Chapter 4 – Article 3:
Review Questions:
1. Which of the following is NOT a reason for collaborating with influencers in the alcohol industry?
a) Boosting sales
b) Enhancing brand image
c) Reducing production costs
d) Tapping into new audiences
Answer: c) Reducing production costs
2. True or False: Influencers with a large following are always the best choice for collaboration.

Answer: False
3. Which of the following is NOT a factor to consider when selecting influencers for collaboration?
a) Relevance
b) Engagement rates
) Number of posts per day
d) Outreach
Answer: c) Number of posts per day
4. Why is transparency important in influencer collaborations?
a) To increase sales
b) To maintain trust with the audience
c) To reduce production costs
d) To increase the number of followers
Answer: b) To maintain trust with the audience
5. True or False: Industry experts in the alcohol sector can provide valuable insights into market trends and consumer preferences.
Answer: True

Chapter 4 – Article 4:
1. Which of the following is NOT a benefit of sponsorships in the alcohol industry?
a) Enhanced brand visibility
b) Reduced production costs
c) Building brand loyalty
d) Brand alignment with events
Answer: b) Reduced production costs
2. True or False: Event partnerships are solely about financial support in exchange for brand visibility.
Answer: False
3. What is a primary advantage of co-branded events?
a) Reducing competition
b) Sharing audiences and pooling resources
c) Increasing production
d) Reducing marketing costs
Answer: b) Sharing audiences and pooling resources
4. Why is it important to measure the ROI of sponsorships and partnerships?
a) To ensure brand loyalty
b) To validate the effectiveness of the collaboration
c) To increase brand visibility
d) To reduce production costs
Answer: b) To validate the effectiveness of the collaboration

5. True or False: Modern consumers value experiences over mere products.
Answer: True

Chapter 4 – Article 5:
1. Multiple Choice: What is a primary benefit of joint marketing initiatives in the alcohol industry?
- a) Limited product range
- b) Amplified reach and visibility
- c) Reduced brand loyalty
- d) Isolation from industry trends
- Answer: b) Amplified reach and visibility
2. True/False: Co-branding in the alcohol industry always involves two alcohol brands collaborating.
- Answer: False
3. Multiple Choice: Which of the following is NOT a challenge associated with joint marketing and co-branding?
- a) Ensuring brand alignment
- b) Equitable distribution of profits
- c) Transparent communication
- d) Limited consumer engagement
- Answer: d) Limited consumer engagement
4. True/False: Jameson's Caskmates series involves the whiskey brand collaborating with craft breweries.
- Answer: True
5. Multiple Choice: What was the primary benefit of the Red Bull and GoPro partnership?
- a) GoPro's entry into the beverage industry
- b) Red Bull's introduction of a new camera line
- c) Access to video marketing opportunities for Red Bull
- d) GoPro's exclusive sponsorship of Red Bull events
- Answer: c) Access to video marketing opportunities for Red Bull
6. Opinion Question: Reflect on the importance of brand alignment in joint marketing initiatives. How do you think it impacts consumer perception and brand loyalty?

Chapter 4 – Article 6:
Review Questions:
1. Which of the following is NOT a benefit of industry associations in the alcohol sector?
- a) Tailored education
- b) Generic seminars
- c) Advocacy and representation

- d) Purposeful networking
- Answer: b) Generic seminars
2. True or False: Trade shows are only beneficial for showcasing products.
- Answer: False
3. What is the primary advantage of a data-driven approach at trade show booths?
- a) Increased costs
- b) Tailored attendee experience
- c) Generic presentations
- d) Reduced brand visibility
- Answer: b) Tailored attendee experience
4. In the context of the article, what does the term "Purposeful Networking" imply?
- a) Exchanging business cards randomly
- b) Curated networking opportunities with meaningful connections
- c) Attending all events without a strategy
- d) Networking without any specific goal
- Answer: b) Curated networking opportunities with meaningful connections
5. Post-event strategies after trade shows are essential for:
- a) Immediate brand discontinuation
- b) Ignoring potential leads
- c) Strengthening connections and following up with potential leads
- d) Reducing brand visibility
- Answer: c) Strengthening connections and following up with potential leads

Reflective Question:
- How do you think the role of trade shows and industry associations will evolve in the next decade, especially considering the rise of digital platforms and virtual events?

Chapter 5.1
Chapter 5.1 – Article 1:
1. What does FOB stand for in the context of pricing in the alcohol industry?
- Freight on Board.
2. Why is understanding the distinction between on-premises and off-premises sales important for FOB pricing?
- Because these two types of sales have different pricing dynamics and margin expectations, which can impact the overall pricing structure.
3. How does FOB pricing play a role in maintaining business operations for a producer or importer?

- The FOB price is the primary revenue source for the business and should cover all costs associated with producing, packaging, and holding the product, ensuring the financial health and growth of the business.
4. How can regional variations in the cost of living influence FOB pricing?
- Retailers in areas with a higher cost of living might have higher margin expectations, requiring adjustments in FOB pricing to ensure products are priced appropriately for different markets.
5. What is the primary purpose of FOB pricing in the alcohol industry?
- FOB pricing is crucial for effectively positioning products at the wholesaler, ensuring competitiveness in the market, and achieving desired retail and cocktail pricing goals.

Chapter 5.1 – Article 2:
Q&A on FOB Pricing and Freight Options
1. What does FOB stand for in the context of pricing?
- a) Freight on Business
- b) Free on Board
- c) Freight on Board
- d) Free on Business
- Answer: c) Freight on Board
2. Which freight method involves transportation by trucks or trailers, typically for domestic shipments?
- a) Rail Freight
- b) Direct Import Freight
- c) Over the Road (OTR) Freight
- d) Air Freight
- Answer: c) Over the Road (OTR) Freight
3. True or False: Direct Import (DI) Freight is commonly used for domestic shipments within the USA.
- Answer: False
4. Why is it recommended to defer to the wholesaler for domestic shipping?
- a) Wholesalers have a wider range of products.
- b) Wholesalers often have contract rates with logistics companies.
- c) Wholesalers prefer handling their own shipments.
- d) Wholesalers have larger storage facilities.
- Answer: b) Wholesalers often have contract rates with logistics companies.
5. True or False: Packaging does not play a significant role in the transportation of products.
- Answer: False

Chapter 5.1 – Article 3:
1. What does FOB stand for in the context of pricing?
- a) Free on Business
- b) Freight on Business
- c) Freight on Board
- d) Free on Board
- Answer: c) Freight on Board
2. Which of the following is NOT a factor to consider when calculating FOB pricing?
- a) Market Factors
- b) Retailer's shoe size
- c) Retailer's Business Model
- d) Negotiation and Flexibility
- Answer: b) Retailer's shoe size
3. True or False: The SRP formula helps determine the retail shelf price based on the price to retail and the retailer's margin percentage.
- Answer: True
4. Which resource is NOT mentioned as a tool for assessing market conditions?
- a) IRI
- b) Sip Source
- c) Netflix ratings
- d) Nielsen ratings
- Answer: c) Netflix ratings
5. True or False: Wholesalers typically operate on a cost-plus business model.
- Answer: True

Chapter 5.1 – Article 4:
1. True or False: On-premise establishments, like bars, primarily focus on selling products for consumption outside their premises.
- Answer: False
2. In which type of markets is it challenging to have different pricing for on-premise and off-premise channels?
- a) Free markets
- b) Control states
- c) Competitive markets
- d) Open markets
- Answer: b) Control states
3. What does the term "National Shelf Pricing" refer to?
- a) The price of products on the top shelf

- b) The average price of a product in a specific state
- c) The consistent price at which a product is sold nationwide
- d) The discounted price offered during sales
- Answer: c) The consistent price at which a product is sold nationwide
4. Why is it essential to collaborate closely with wholesalers when determining pricing in regulated markets?
- a) To ensure bulk purchases
- b) To align with national shelf pricing
- c) To get feedback on product quality
- d) To understand customer preferences
- Answer: b) To align with national shelf pricing
5. Written Response: Explain the primary difference between on-premise and off-premise channels and their significance in FOB pricing.
- Answer: On-premise channels refer to establishments where products are consumed within the premises, such as bars and restaurants. They offer unique experiences and can directly market products to patrons. Off-premise channels, on the other hand, are retailers like liquor stores that sell products for consumption elsewhere. In terms of FOB pricing, understanding the dynamics of each channel is crucial as they have different margin expectations and market dynamics. Recognizing these differences helps in formulating an effective pricing strategy that aligns with market demands.

Chapter 5.1 – Article 5:
1. True or False: Supplier margins primarily consider the cost of marketing and promotional activities.
- Answer: False
2. Which of the following is NOT a factor considered under cost considerations for FOB pricing?
- a) Product Costs
- b) Marketing and Promotional Expenses
- c) Wholesaler Margins
- d) Carrying/Storage Costs
- Answer: c) Wholesaler Margins
3. True or False: Depreciation associated with carrying/storage costs is typically calculated as 5% of the cost.
- Answer: False
4. Why is it essential to provide flexibility in margins to wholesalers?
- a) To ensure bulk purchases
- b) To allow them to make quick pricing decisions
- c) To get feedback on product quality
- d) To understand customer preferences

- Answer: b) To allow them to make quick pricing decisions
5. Written Response: Explain the significance of blended margins in determining the profitability of a product.
- Answer: Blended margins are crucial in determining the profitability of a product as they help strike a balance between the supplier's costs and the wholesaler's margin expectations. Achieving the right equilibrium ensures that both the supplier and the wholesaler can maintain a sustainable business model, covering their respective costs and facilitating growth.

Chapter 5.2
Chapter 5.2 – Article 1:
1. True or False: Depletion Allowances primarily focus on building relationships with wholesalers and have minimal impact on pricing strategies.
- Answer: False
2. Which of the following best describes the primary advantage of Depletion Allowances?
- a) Enhancing product quality
- b) Facilitating market research
- c) Offering pricing flexibility and competitive advantage
- d) Expanding production capabilities
- Answer: c) Offering pricing flexibility and competitive advantage
3. In the context of the alcohol industry, why is it essential to be aware of legal parameters and state variances when using DAs?
- a) To ensure product quality
- b) To align with state compliance regulations and legal stipulations
- c) To enhance marketing strategies
- d) To collaborate with competitors
- Answer: b) To align with state compliance regulations and legal stipulations
4. Written Response: Explain how Depletion Allowances can support the growth and expansion of a business in the alcohol industry.
5. Which of the following is NOT a benefit of Depletion Allowances?
- a) Gaining a competitive advantage
- b) Building strong relationships with wholesalers
- c) Reducing production costs
- d) Optimizing margins
- Answer: c) Reducing production costs

Chapter 5.2 – Article 2:

1. What is the primary purpose of Depletion Allowances (DAs) in the alcohol industry?

Answer: The primary purpose of Depletion Allowances (DAs) in the alcohol industry is to allow suppliers or producers to support specific price points for their products while still maintaining healthy margins for themselves and their wholesale partners. DAs serve as a financial tool to bridge the gap between desired pricing and required margins, ensuring profitability for all parties involved.

2. Which system is involved in the mechanisms of DAs that allows wholesalers to generate a chargeback to the supplier?

Answer: The system involved in the mechanisms of DAs that allows wholesalers to generate a chargeback to the supplier is the billback system. When the wholesaler sells the product at a price that doesn't align with the margin they need, they can generate a chargeback to the supplier, reflecting the difference between the actual cost of the product to the wholesaler and the desired pricing point.

3. Calculate the net cost to the wholesaler if the COGs is $150 per case and the Depletion Allowance is $10.

Formula: Net Cost to Wholesaler = COGs - Depletion Allowance

Calculation: Net Cost to Wholesaler = $150 - $10 = $140 per case.

Answer: The net cost to the wholesaler would be $140 per case.

4. If a wholesaler sells a product to a customer at $28 per 750ml and the net cost to the wholesaler is $21 per 750ml, what is the wholesaler's margin?

Formula: Wholesaler Margin = (Selling Price to customer – Net cost to wholesaler) / selling price to customer

Calculation: Wholesaler Margin = ($28 - $21) / $28 = $7 / $28 = 0.25 or 25%

Answer: The wholesaler's margin would be 25%.

5. For a retailer, if the retail price of a product is $35 and the wholesale price is $27, what is the retailer's margin?

Formula: Retailer Margin = (Retail Price – Wholesale Price) / Retail Price * 100

Calculation: Retailer Margin = ($35 - $27) / $35 * 100 = $8 / $35 * 100 = 22.86%

Answer: The retailer's margin would be approximately 22.86%.

6. Why is it essential for suppliers to consider specific pricing strategies, market dynamics, and customer demands when utilizing DAs?

Answer: It's essential for suppliers to consider specific pricing strategies, market dynamics, and customer demands when utilizing DAs to ensure they effectively support desired price points and maintain healthy margins. By analyzing target markets, understanding price sensitivity, and aligning the pricing structure with customer expectations, suppliers can strategically implement DAs to drive sales, increase market share, and enhance profitability. This approach ensures that DAs are used effectively to meet the unique demands of each market or customer segment.

7. What is the difference between "mark up" and "margin" as mentioned in the article regarding retailer pricing?

Answer: "Mark up" refers to the percentage added to the cost price to determine the selling price. It represents the difference between the cost of a product and its selling price. On the other hand, "margin" represents the percentage difference between the selling price and the profit. In the context of the article, a 25% "mark up" means that the selling price is 25% above the cost price, while a 20% "margin" means that the profit constitutes 20% of the selling price.

Chapter 5.2 – Article 3:

Review Questions:

1. Multiple Choice: Which of the following best describes the primary purpose of Depletion Allowances (DAs)?
- a) To increase the production cost for suppliers.
- b) To maintain healthy margins for wholesalers while offering competitive pricing.
- c) To reduce the sales volume for sales teams.
- d) To decrease brand visibility in the market.

Answer: b) To maintain healthy margins for wholesalers while offering competitive pricing.

2. True/False: Suppliers use DAs primarily to decrease their brand proliferation and market ingress.

Answer: False.

3. Fill in the Blank: Sales teams benefit from DAs by gaining _____, which helps in driving sales momentum and showcasing product value propositions effectively.

Answer: pricing malleability

4. Multiple Choice: Beyond financial metrics, DAs play a crucial role in:
- a) Reducing the negotiation prowess of sales teams.
- b) Amplifying the negotiation prowess of sales teams.
- c) Decreasing brand adoption.
- d) Limiting market expansion.

Answer: b) Amplifying the negotiation prowess of sales teams.

5. True/False: A transparent and collaborative approach to DAs can hinder the formation of synergistic partnerships and reduce profitability.

Answer: False.

Chapter 5.2 – Article 4:
1.   Multiple Choice: Which of the following is NOT a step towards strategic DA implementation?
a. Understanding market dynamics
b. Assessing product performance
c. Ignoring competitor pricing strategies
d. Collaborating with wholesalers
Answer: c. Ignoring competitor pricing strategies
2.   True/False: Regularly monitoring the performance of your products and evaluating the impact of DAs on profitability is unnecessary.
Answer: False
3.   Fill in the Blank: A Depletion Allowance is a mechanism that allows _____ or _____ to support specific price points for their products.
Answer: suppliers, producers
4.   Written: Explain the importance of collaborating with wholesalers when implementing Depletion Allowances.
Answer: Collaboration with wholesalers is key to the successful implementation of DAs. Engaging in open discussions helps understand their margin requirements, pricing strategies, and market positioning. Working together ensures a mutually beneficial approach that supports their pricing objectives while maintaining supplier profitability. Strong partnerships with wholesalers gain their support and commitment to selling products effectively.
5.   Multiple Choice: What should suppliers focus on when assessing product performance for DA implementation?
a. Products with declining sales
b. Products that have the potential for higher sales growth
c. Products with the least market potential
d. Products that are least popular among consumers
Answer: b. Products that have the potential for higher sales growth
Chapter 5.2 – Article 5:
1.   Multiple Choice: Which of the following is NOT a benefit of Depletion Allowances?
a. Ensuring pricing flexibility
b. Adapting to market dynamics
c. Ignoring market trends
d. Maintaining desired margins
Answer: c. Ignoring market trends
2.   True/False: Depletion Allowances can only be used as a short-term strategy.
Answer: False

3. Fill in the Blank: DAs enable suppliers to control and maintain _____ by adjusting the net cost of goods sold.
Answer: singular desired margins
4. Written: Explain the role of Depletion Allowances in balancing wholesaler margins and supplier profitability.
Answer: Depletion Allowances support wholesalers in achieving their margin targets, fostering strong partnerships. Concurrently, suppliers can bolster these margins without jeopardizing their profitability, ensuring a win-win situation for both parties.
5. Multiple Choice: What is the primary purpose of Depletion Allowances in the context of the alcoholic beverage industry?
a. To increase product inventory
b. To ignore market trends
c. To maintain desired margins for long-term profitability
d. To reduce collaboration with wholesalers
Answer: c. To maintain desired margins for long-term profitability.

Chapter 5.3
Chapter 5.3 – Article 1:
1. Multiple Choice: Which of the following is NOT a benefit of using SPAs in the alcoholic beverage industry? a. Tailored pricing based on volume b. Temporary promotional pricing during holidays c. Fixed pricing for all customer segments d. Geographically based pricing adjustments Answer: c. Fixed pricing for all customer segments
2. Fill in the Blank: SPAs allow suppliers to offer tiered pricing based on the _____ of purchase orders. Answer: volume
3. True/False: SPAs are primarily used to increase the price of products in response to high demand. Answer: False
4. Written: Explain the significance of loyalty programs and special incentives within the context of SPAs. Answer: Loyalty programs and special incentives within SPAs are designed to reward higher volume purchasing and foster stronger relationships between suppliers and wholesalers. These programs may offer additional discounts, exclusive offers, or access to limited edition products. By providing customized incentives, suppliers can motivate wholesalers to maintain long-term partnerships and actively promote their products.
5. Multiple Choice: What is the primary purpose of geographically based pricing in SPAs? a. To account for differences in shipping costs b. To adjust pricing based on regional market demand and local competition c. To offer the same price across all regions d. To prioritize sales in

regions with the highest population Answer: b. To adjust pricing based on regional market demand and local competition.

Chapter 5.3 – Article 2:
1. What is the primary purpose of defining the scope and duration in an SPA?
a. To determine the products' color and design.
b. To set the agreement's temporal span and identify the products or categories encompassed.
c. To decide the marketing strategy for the products.
d. To choose the suppliers for the products.
Answer: b. To set the agreement's temporal span and identify the products or categories encompassed.
2. In the Percentage Discounts structure, the Discounted Price is calculated as _____.
Answer: Discounted Price = Regular Price - (Regular Price * Discount Percentage)
3. Lift analysis is used to measure the impact of advertisements on brand awareness. True or False?
Answer: False
4. Explain the significance of monitoring and evaluation in the context of SPAs and how they can influence future pricing decisions.
Answer: Regular monitoring and evaluation are crucial to the success of an SPA. Using key performance indicators (KPIs) such as sales, margins, and market share helps track the performance of the agreement. Analyzing this data assesses the SPA's effectiveness, allowing for necessary adjustments to pricing, incentives, or terms to optimize results.
5. Which of the following is NOT a common pricing structure used in SPAs?
a. Percentage Discounts
b. Fixed Pricing Tiers
c. Seasonal Packaging
d. Volume Commitments and Minimum Purchase Requirements.
 Answer: c. Seasonal Packaging

Chapter 5.3 – Article 2.5 – Lift Analysis:
Review Questions:
1. What is the primary purpose of lift analysis in pricing strategies?
• Answer: Lift analysis is used to measure the impact of discounts or promotions on sales and determine the additional sales volume needed

to offset the discount and maintain the same profit level or achieve a desired profit increase.

2. In the context of a discount percentage, if the regular profit per unit is $5 and a 20% discount is applied, what would be the profit per unit with the discount?

Answer: $4

3. For a quantity-based free goods deal, if a supplier offers 2 free cases for every purchase of 20 cases and normally sells 50 cases at a profit of $15 per case, what is the profit per case with the free goods promotion?

Answer: $13.63 per case

4. True or False: In lift analysis, the break-even volume on profit is calculated by dividing the total profit from the baseline sale by the profit per unit with the discount.

Answer: True

5. In a scenario where a wholesaler purchases 60 cases, qualifying for 6 free cases, and the supplier's profit per case with the free goods promotion is $13.63, what would be the supplier's total profit for 66 cases?

Answer: $899.58

Chapter 5.3 – Article 3:

1. Why is clear and open communication essential in SPA pricing?

Answer: It ensures both parties have a mutual understanding, addresses concerns promptly, and avoids misunderstandings or conflicts.

2. True or False: Sharing market insights with collaborators is not beneficial in SPA pricing.

Answer: False

3. What is the primary purpose of regular performance reviews in SPA pricing?

Answer: To evaluate the effectiveness of the SPA, assess its impact on sales, margins, and market share, and identify areas for improvement.

4. Why is adaptability and flexibility important in SPA pricing?

Answer: To accommodate changing market dynamics, customer preferences, and business circumstances, ensuring the SPA's continued relevance and effectiveness.

5. Fill in the blank: _____ is the foundation of successful SPA pricing relationships.

Answer: Trust

Chapter 5.3 – Article 4:

1. What are the two main types of incentives mentioned in the article?

Answer: Financial and non-financial.

2. True/False: Promotional programs are solely about advertising campaigns.
Answer: False.
3. Fill in the blank: Performance-based incentive structures are tied to measurable _____ or key performance indicators (KPIs).
Answer: Sales targets.
4. Which of the following is NOT a benefit of co-marketing as mentioned in the article?
a) Enhanced product visibility
b) Access to new products
c) Joint promotional campaigns
d) Leveraging each other's strengths
Answer: b) Access to new products.
5. Why is it essential to continuously monitor the effectiveness of incentive and promotional programs?
Answer: To assess their impact on sales, market penetration, and customer engagement and make necessary adjustments for optimization.

Chapter 5.3 – Article 5:
1. True/False: Collaboration in SPAs primarily involves transparent communication and joint business planning.
• Answer: True.
2. Which of the following is NOT a performance metric for evaluating SPAs? a) Sales volume b) Market share c) Number of training sessions d) Promotional effectiveness
• Answer: c) Number of training sessions.
3. Fill in the blank: Regular _____ sessions can significantly enhance product knowledge and selling skills of wholesalers.
• Answer: Training.
4. Why is adaptability crucial in the execution of SPAs?
• Answer: Because market dynamics are ever-evolving, necessitating periodic adjustments to SPA strategies to remain relevant and effective.
5. Which of the following best describes the role of feedback in SPAs? a) To refine strategies b) To increase sales volume c) To set new targets d) To reduce costs
• Answer: a) To refine strategies.

Chapter 6
Chapter 6 – Article 1:
1. The primary revenue stream for producers in the alcohol industry is the sale of products to end consumers.

- Answer: False. The primary revenue stream for producers is the sale of their products to wholesalers.
2. What is a common revenue model for wholesalers in the alcohol industry?
- A) Subscription-based model
- B) Cost-plus model
- C) Flat-rate model
- D) Commission-based model
- Answer: B) Cost-plus model
3. When planning for capital expenditures, alcohol businesses must ensure that investments are _____, feasible, and aligned with long-term business goals.
- Answer: Timely
4. Why is it important for alcohol businesses to include both measurable outcomes and intangible factors in ROI considerations?
- Answer: It is important to include both measurable outcomes and intangible factors in ROI considerations because while measurable outcomes provide quantifiable evidence of success, intangible factors like company culture and integrity can have a significant impact on long-term business sustainability and employee performance.
5. Match the following components of financial planning with their correct descriptions.
- A) Forecasting Sales
- B) Allocating Resources
- C) Risk Management
- D) Capital Expenditure Planning
- 1. Involves anticipating future sales using historical data and market analysis.
- 2. Ensures resources are distributed effectively for various business needs.
- 3. Acts as a financial cushion against market fluctuations and regulatory changes.
- 4. Provides a strategic framework for investments in business growth and infrastructure.
- Answers:
- A) 1. Involves anticipating future sales using historical data and market analysis.
- B) 2. Ensures resources are distributed effectively for various business needs.
- C) 3. Acts as a financial cushion against market fluctuations and regulatory changes.

- D) 4. Provides a strategic framework for investments in business growth and infrastructure.

Chapter 6 – Article 2:
1. True/False: Variable costs in the alcohol industry remain constant regardless of how much is produced.
- Answer: False. Variable costs change based on the production volume.
2. Fill in the Blank: The formula for calculating total cost is Total Cost = Variable Cost + _____.
- Answer: Fixed Cost.
3. Multiple Choice: What is the benefit of leveraging relationships with suppliers?
- A) To receive moral support
- B) To gain better pricing and favorable payment terms
- C) To increase the cost of goods
- D) To create more paperwork
- Answer: B) To gain better pricing and favorable payment terms.
4. Short Answer: Explain how bulk purchasing can affect cost control in the alcohol industry.
- Answer: Bulk purchasing can lead to cost savings by reducing the price per unit through economies of scale. This can happen because suppliers often offer discounts for large orders, which can lower the overall cost of materials and increase the margin on products sold.
5. Calculation: If a company decides to offer a 10% discount on a product that originally costs $15 to produce and is sold for $30, what is the new discounted margin percentage?
- Answer: Discounted Price = $30 - ($30 * 10%) = $27 Discounted Margin = ($27 - $15) / $27 x 100% = 44.44%

Chapter 6 – Article3:
1. Seasonal demand spikes in the alcohol industry can lead to consistent cash inflows throughout the year.
- Answer: False. Seasonal demand spikes can lead to irregular cash inflows, not consistent ones.
2. In the alcohol industry, the time lag between production and sales for beverages requiring aging is a significant challenge to _____ management.
- Answer: Cash flow
3. Which of the following is NOT a strategy for managing cash flow in the alcohol industry? A) Forecasting future sales and cash requirements B) Diversifying revenue streams through on-premise sales and events C)

Ignoring payment terms with suppliers and customers D) Negotiating favorable payment terms with suppliers and customers
*   Answer: C) Ignoring payment terms with suppliers and customers
4. Match the following financing options with their correct sources:
*   Line of Credit
*   Business Credit Card
*   Factoring or Invoice Financing
Sources:
A) Traditional banks or credit unions
B) Most major banks
C) Factoring companies or online platforms like BlueVine
*   Answers:
*   Line of Credit - A) Traditional banks or credit unions
*   Business Credit Card - B) Most major banks
*   Factoring or Invoice Financing - C) Factoring companies or online platforms like BlueVine
5. What does working capital represent in a business, and why is it particularly important in the alcohol industry?
*   Answer: Working capital represents the difference between a company's current assets and current liabilities. It is a key indicator of a company's short-term financial health. In the alcohol industry, it is particularly important because inventory, which is a large part of current assets, can significantly affect liquidity and the ability to meet short-term obligations. Efficient working capital management ensures that funds are not unnecessarily tied up in stock, which is crucial for maintaining financial stability in an industry with unique production cycles and regulatory challenges.

Chapter 6 – Article 4:
1. In the alcohol industry, the return on long-term investments such as aged products can be realized shortly after production.
Answer: False. In the alcohol industry, especially for products that require aging, the return might not be realized for several years, necessitating a long-term view of ROI.
2. What is a significant factor to consider when calculating ROI in the alcohol industry?
*   The color of the packaging
*   Immediate sales after product launch
*   Regulatory and compliance costs
*   The CEO's personal taste preferences
Answer: C. Regulatory and compliance costs.

3. When optimizing ROI, having a _____ can help mitigate market volatility and provide steadier returns.

Answer: Diversified portfolio.

4. Explain why it is important to use data analytics in marketing strategies within the alcohol industry.

Answer: Using data analytics in marketing strategies ensures that the marketing investments are targeted and effective, leading to better returns on marketing investments. It allows companies to make informed decisions based on consumer behavior, market trends, and the performance of past marketing initiatives.

5. Discuss the importance of evaluating both ROI and other financial metrics, such as profit margin analysis and debt ratios, in understanding the financial performance of a company in the alcohol industry.

Answer: Evaluating ROI provides a snapshot of the effectiveness of specific investments or strategies. However, to get a holistic view of a company's financial health, other financial metrics must also be considered. Profit margin analysis helps understand the profitability of different products or segments, which is crucial for targeting growth in profit dollars. Liquidity ratios indicate the company's ability to meet short-term obligations, which is essential for maintaining operations. Debt ratios provide insight into the company's financial leverage and its ability to meet long-term obligations, which affects its financial stability and growth prospects. Together, these metrics tell a comprehensive story of a company's financial performance and strategic direction.

Chapter 6 – Article 5:

1. Fill in the blank: In the context of financial management in the alcohol industry, _____ technology ensures transparency and traceability in supply chain transactions.

Answer: Blockchain

2. Multiple choice: What type of loans are linked to a company's sustainability performance? A) Commercial Loans B) Sustainability-Linked Loans (SLLs) C) Green Loans D) Peer-to-Peer Loans

Answer: B) Sustainability-Linked Loans (SLLs)

3. True/False: Direct-to-Consumer (DTC) sales do not affect cash flow management strategies in the alcohol industry.

Answer: False

4. Fill in the blank: The course "_____" by Coursera is recommended for professional development in financial management within the alcohol industry.

Answer: Financial Management Capstone

5. Multiple choice: Which of the following is a risk associated with the global nature of the alcohol industry? A) Currency Fluctuations B) Fixed pricing strategies C) Localized marketing campaigns D) Domestic supply chain management
Answer: A) Currency Fluctuations

Chapter 7
Chapter 7 – Article 1:
1. The Three-Tier Alcohol System in the U.S. simplifies the supply chain for alcohol distribution.
*   Answer: False.
2. What can cause delays in the alcohol supply chain?
*   A) Global shipping congestion
*   B) Customs clearance backlogs
*   C) Unforeseen weather events
*   D) All of the above
*   Answer: D) All of the above.
3. Robust forecasting in the alcohol industry should include analyzing _____ data, seasonal trends, and market shifts.
*   Answer: Historical sales.
4. What is a key strategy for managing supply sources in the alcohol industry?
*   A) Relying on a single supplier
*   B) Diversifying suppliers across different regions
*   C) Ordering only as needed
*   D) Ignoring supplier quality standards
*   Answer: B) Diversifying suppliers across different regions.
5. Overstocking in the alcohol industry can lead to tied-up capital and potential spoilage of products.
*   Answer: True.

Chapter 7 – Article 2:
1. The Three-Tier Alcohol System was established to promote monopolies in the alcohol industry.
*   Answer: False. The Three-Tier Alcohol System was established to prevent monopolies, promote accountability, and ensure product quality.
2. What is the primary role of the Alcohol and Tobacco Tax and Trade Bureau (TTB) in the U.S. alcoholic beverage industry?
*   A) Overseeing production, labeling, advertising, and import/export of alcoholic beverages.
*   B) Directly selling alcoholic beverages to consumers.

- C) Producing alcoholic beverages.
- Answer: A) Overseeing production, labeling, advertising, and import/export of alcoholic beverages.
3. Each state in the U.S. has its own _____ regulatory body and set of rules for alcohol distribution.
- Answer: Alcohol
4. Temperature control during transportation is only a recommendation and not a regulatory requirement for certain alcoholic beverages.
- Answer: False. Temperature control during transportation is a regulatory requirement for certain alcoholic beverages like wines and craft beers to maintain their quality.
5. How can businesses turn regulatory compliance into a competitive advantage in the alcohol industry?
- A) By ignoring state-specific mandates.
- B) By embracing compliance and positioning themselves as trustworthy industry leaders.
- C) By focusing solely on federal regulations.
- Answer: B) By embracing compliance and positioning themselves as trustworthy industry leaders.

Chapter 7 – Article 3:
1. In the Three-Tier Alcohol System, inventory management primarily focuses on ensuring products are available at the right place and time.
- Answer: True.
2. What is a significant risk associated with Direct Import (DI) in inventory management?
- A) Reduced product variety
- B) Shorter lead times
- C) Longer lead times and potential for overstock
- D) Lower warehousing costs
- Answer: C) Longer lead times and potential for overstock.
3. Advanced inventory management systems, like _____, provide real-time visibility into stock levels and demand trends.
- Answer: Blueridge software.
4. What is a key benefit of stateside ordering in inventory management?
- A) Lower FOB costs
- B) Longer lead times
- C) Quicker access to products
- D) Higher pricing benefits
- Answer: C) Quicker access to products.
5. Collaborative inventory management in the Three-Tier System does not significantly impact the efficiency of the supply chain.
- Answer: False.

Chapter 7 – Article 4:
1. In the Three-Tier Alcohol System, the relationship between suppliers and wholesalers is primarily transactional, not based on partnership.
- Answer: False
2. What is a key benefit of maintaining a harmonious supplier-wholesaler relationship?
- A) Increased regulatory risks
- B) Consistent product quality
- C) Reduced communication needs
- D) Simplified contract terms
- Answer: B) Consistent product quality
3. Transparent communication in supplier relationships helps to foster

   _____.
- Answer: Trust
4. What role does technology play in supplier-wholesaler relationships?
- A) Reducing the need for personal communication
- B) Streamlining communication and enhancing collaboration
- C) Making contracts obsolete
- D) Increasing dependency on manual processes
- Answer: B) Streamlining communication and enhancing collaboration
5. A Californian winery improved its relationship with a glass bottle supplier by severing ties and finding a new supplier.
- Answer: False

Chapter 7 – Article 5:
1. The craft brewery in Oregon expanded its reach nationally to overcome distribution challenges.
- Answer: False. The brewery focused on deepening its roots locally.
2. What solution did the New York-based wine importer implement to navigate regulatory challenges?
- A) Expanded their physical distribution network
- B) Invested in a regulatory tech platform
- C) Reduced the number of products imported
- Answer: B) Invested in a regulatory tech platform
3. Investing in _____ is essential in today's Three-Tier Alcohol System for real-time tracking, demand forecasting, and regulatory compliance.
- Answer: Supply chain software or Digital transformation
4. What was the outcome of the Californian winery's implementation of a Direct-to-Consumer (DTC) channel?
- A) Decrease in overall sales
- B) 70% increase in sales
- C) No significant change in sales

- Answer: B) 70% increase in sales
5. Continuous education and training are unnecessary in the Three-Tier System as long as the business is established.
- Answer: False. Regular training, attending industry seminars, and staying updated are crucial for staying at the forefront of industry knowledge.

Chapter 8
Chapter 8 – Article 1:
1. California's preference for agave spirits significantly influences the distribution strategies of alcohol suppliers in the region.
- Answer: True.
2. When market conditions change, suppliers must adapt their strategies. This adaptation is crucial for maintaining:
- A) Product quality.
- B) Fruitful partnerships with distributors.
- C) The same distribution channels.
- D) Fixed pricing strategies.
- Answer: B) Fruitful partnerships with distributors.
3. In the alcohol industry, _____ offers a vast digital marketplace, while traditional retail provides a personal touch and in-store experiences.
- Answer: E-commerce.
4. Timeless strategies for selecting the most suitable distribution channels include:
- A) Ignoring market research.
- B) Focusing solely on brand identity.
- C) Conducting thorough market research and analyzing consumer demographics.
- D) Relying only on past successes.
- Answer: C) Conducting thorough market research and analyzing consumer demographics.
5. Building robust and transparent relationships with distributors is not essential for securing shelf space and market support.
- Answer: False.
Chapter 8 – Article 2:
1. What is the primary focus of distributor-supplier relationships in the alcohol industry?
- A) Transactional exchanges
- B) Building brand awareness
- C) Establishing shared success and growth

- D) Competitive positioning
- Answer: C) Establishing shared success and growth
2. Distributors in the alcohol industry are primarily interested in products, not the brands behind them.
- Answer: False. Modern distributors seek brands that add value to their portfolio and contribute to their growth.
3. When establishing partnerships with distributors, it is important for suppliers to have a clear understanding of their _____, _____, and _____.
- Answer: Brand identity, target consumers, and sales objectives
4. What role do market insights play in distributor-supplier relationships?
- A) They are irrelevant in modern distribution strategies.
- B) They help in understanding market trends and consumer behaviors.
- C) They are only used for financial forecasting.
- D) They are exclusively for tracking competitor activities.
- Answer: B) They help in understanding market trends and consumer behaviors.
5. Setting realistic goals and expectations with distributors is not necessary for the success of alcohol distribution.
- Answer: False. Setting realistic goals and expectations is crucial for the success of alcohol distribution and strengthens the distributor-supplier partnership.

Chapter 8 – Article 3:
1. True/False: DTC sales in the alcohol industry allow suppliers to bypass traditional distribution channels and directly reach consumers.
Answer: True
2. Multiple Choice: Which of the following online retailers is mentioned in the article as a partner for suppliers to access a broader audience? A) Amazon B) eBay C) wine.com D) Etsy
Answer: C) wine.com
3. Fill in the Blank: In order to successfully integrate DTC channels with existing distribution models, suppliers must view DTC sales as a _____ extension of their overall distribution strategy.
Answer: Complementary
4. True/False: One of the challenges of DTC sales is complying with various state laws, shipping regulations, and age verification measures.
Answer: True
5. Multiple Choice: What is a key benefit of Direct-to-Consumer sales for suppliers? A) Reduced marketing costs B) Access to consumer data and preferences C) Longer shipping times D) Higher production costs
Answer: B) Access to consumer data and preferences

6. Fill in the Blank: To enhance the appeal of DTC purchasing, suppliers can offer exclusive _____ or cover shipping costs.
Answer: Discounts
7. True/False: Investing in compelling branding and storytelling on DTC platforms is not essential for creating a memorable brand experience.
Answer: False
8. Multiple Choice: What is the role of SEO marketing in the context of DTC sales? A) To reduce product prices B) To ensure compliance and optimize online visibility C) To increase production speed D) To design product packaging
Answer: B) To ensure compliance and optimize online visibility

Chapter 9
Chapter 9 – Article 1:
1. True or False: Incentives are only effective for established brands in the adult beverage industry.
(False)
2. Multiple Choice: What is the primary goal of POD incentives? A. Increase overall sales volume B. Expand the number of outlets offering the product C. Focus on individual account performance
(Answer: B)
3. Fill in the Blank: Account-based incentives are designed to foster _____ with key accounts.
(long-term relationships)
4. True or False: Volume incentives are most effective for brands in the early stages of their life cycle.
(False)
5. Multiple Choice: What is a key factor in choosing the right incentive approach? A. The color of the product packaging B. The brand's stage of growth and market dynamics C. The CEO's personal preference
(Answer: B)
Chapter 9 – Article 2:
1. True/False: Volume-based incentives are primarily focused on acquiring new accounts rather than increasing sales volumes.
Answer: False. Volume-based incentives are focused on achieving overall sales targets and encouraging sales representatives to drive higher sales volumes.
2. Multiple Choice: What is the primary goal of New Account Incentives in the adult beverage industry?
• A) To reduce product prices

- B) To acquire new accounts and expand market reach
- C) To increase the number of products per account
- D) To enhance the quality of the products

Answer: B) To acquire new accounts and expand market reach

3. Fill in the Blank: POD Incentives are designed to increase the number of _____ or points of distribution within a territory, thereby improving brand visibility and accessibility.

Answer: Placements

4. True/False: Targeted Placement Incentives, such as securing premium shelf positions, are easy to track and manage without dedicated personnel in the market.

Answer: False. Targeted Placement Incentives require dedicated personnel in the market to manage effectively and support sales representatives.

5. Multiple Choice: Which of the following is a key consideration when designing effective incentive programs?
- A) Focusing solely on short-term sales
- B) Ignoring market dynamics and consumer preferences
- C) Aligning incentives with fiscal timelines and market dynamics
- D) Avoiding budget allocation for incentives

Answer: C) Aligning incentives with fiscal timelines and market dynamics

Chapter 9 – Article 3:

1. True or False: Sampling initiatives and the use of Point-of-Sale (POS) materials are essential strategies for creating brand awareness and driving product trial in incentive programs.
- Answer: True

2. Multiple Choice: When implementing incentive programs, what is crucial for tracking the progress and performance of the programs?
- A) Regular team meetings
- B) Real-time data tracking using technology solutions
- C) Annual performance reviews
- D) Customer feedback surveys
- Answer: B) Real-time data tracking using technology solutions

3. Fill in the Blank: Effective communication during the incentive period should be positive and brief to keep participants engaged and motivated.
- Answer: positive, brief

4. True or False: Hiring the right personnel for the market, such as regional managers, state managers, and brand ambassadors, is not as important as the incentive program itself.
- Answer: False

5. Multiple Choice: What is a key role of regional managers in implementing and executing incentive programs?
- A) Handling customer complaints

- B) Translating national strategies into actionable regional plans
- C) Directly selling products to end consumers
- D) Designing the incentive programs
- Answer: B) Translating national strategies into actionable regional plans

Chapter 10
Chapter 10 – Article 1:
1. True or False: The ancient Egyptians considered beer a sacred drink, used only in religious ceremonies.
Answer: False. Ancient Egyptians didn't just consider beer a sacred drink; it was a daily staple, used in religious ceremonies and also in daily life.
2. Multiple Choice: Which era is known for the monastic legacy in beer and spirit production?
- A) Ancient Greece
- B) The Middle Ages
- C) Modern-Day
- D) Age of Exploration
Answer: B) The Middle Ages. This era saw monasteries at the forefront of beer and spirit production in Europe.
3. Fill in the Blank: The British-influenced drink developed to combat malaria in India was _____.
Answer: gin and tonic. The gin and tonic mix was developed to combat malaria.
4. True or False: Today's adult beverage industry is characterized by a shift towards high-alcohol content and traditional flavors.
Answer: False. The contemporary industry emphasizes artisanal production, unique flavors, and also shows a growing demand for sustainable, organic, and low-alcohol or alcohol-free beverages.
5. Multiple Choice: Which platform is mentioned as a tool for understanding current market trends in the adult beverage industry?
- A) Facebook
- B) SipSource
- C) YouTube
- D) TikTok
Answer: B) SipSource. SipSource is mentioned as a platform that offers deep insights into prevailing trends and future trajectories in the adult beverage industry.
Chapter 10 – Article 2:
1. True or False: The health and wellness movement has led to a decrease in demand for low-alcohol and organic beverages.

Answer: False. The health and wellness movement has actually led to an increase in demand for these types of beverages.
2. Multiple Choice: What does the Shanken newsletter primarily provide insights into?
   - A) Health and Wellness Trends
   - B) Premiumization and Craft Movement
   - C) Technological Advancements
   - D) Global Flavors

Answer: B) Premiumization and Craft Movement.
3. Fill in the Blank: Environmental consciousness in the adult beverage industry is often demonstrated through _____ and water conservation in production.

Answer: eco-friendly packaging. This trend reflects a growing consumer preference for sustainability.
4. True or False: Cultural influences and global flavors have little impact on the U.S. adult beverage industry.

Answer: False. Cultural influences and global flavors significantly impact the industry, introducing diverse tastes and preferences.
5. Multiple Choice: Which of the following has accelerated the shift towards e-commerce in the adult beverage industry?
   - A) Health and Wellness Movement
   - B) The Pandemic
   - C) Premiumization
   - D) Technological Advancements

Answer: B) The Pandemic. The pandemic has significantly accelerated the trend towards online sales and direct-to-consumer channels.
Chapter 10 – Article 3:
1. True or False: Innovation in the adult beverage industry is limited to introducing new flavors.

Answer: False. Innovation encompasses a range of aspects including new flavors, sustainable practices, and leveraging technology.
2. Multiple Choice: Which platform offers detailed analytics on consumer preferences in the adult beverage industry?
   - A) Shanken
   - B) Nielsen
   - C) SipSource

Answer: B) Nielsen.
3. Fill in the Blank: In the NPD process, _____ involves evaluating the feasibility of a product idea.

Answer: Concept Testing.
4. True or False: Collaborative innovation is restricted to partnerships within the same industry.

Answer: False. Collaborative innovation can involve partnerships with entities outside the industry like tech startups or research institutions.

5. Multiple Choice: What is a key challenge in innovation for the adult beverage industry?
- A) Flavor development
- B) Regulatory hurdles
- C) Bottle design
- D) Marketing strategies

Answer: B) Regulatory hurdles.

Chapter 10 – Article 4:

1. True or False: Blockchain technology in the alcohol industry is primarily used for enhancing digital payment systems.

Answer: False. It's mainly used for ensuring product authenticity and traceability.

2. Multiple Choice: What does Drizly use to provide insights on local market trends?
- A) Blockchain Technology
- B) Data Analytics
- C) AI and ML
- D) Smart Contracts

Answer: B) Data Analytics.

3. Fill in the Blank: _____ uses AI to adapt beer recipes based on consumer feedback.

Answer: IntelligentX.

4. True or False: AI and ML applications in the alcohol industry are limited to product development and consumer interaction.

Answer: False. They also assist in tasks like inventory management and demand forecasting.

5. Multiple Choice: What is a key challenge when implementing technological advancements in the alcohol industry?
- A) Flavor development
- B) Regulatory compliance
- C) Packaging design
- D) Marketing strategies

Answer: B) Regulatory compliance.

Chapter 10 – Article 5:

Review Questions

1. True or False: Arbikie Highland Estate is aiming to become the world's first green hydrogen-powered distillery.
- Answer: True.

2. Multiple Choice: Which brand is known for its 100% recyclable packaging?

- A) Rhinegeist
- B) Allagash
- C) Seedlip
- D) Patagonia Provisions
- Answer: C) Seedlip.
3. Fill in the Blank: Patagonia Provisions has ventured into the beer industry with a focus on _____ farming.
- Answer: Regenerative organic.
4. True or False: The concept of a circular economy in the alcohol beverage industry only focuses on recycling and does not include reuse principles.
- Answer: False.
5. Multiple Choice: What is the primary environmental concern addressed by the use of biodegradable six-pack rings by craft breweries?
- A) Air pollution reduction
- B) Water conservation
- C) Reduction of harm to marine life
- D) Soil health improvement
- Answer: C) Reduction of harm to marine life.

Chapter 10 – Article 6:
1. True or False: The rise in non-alcoholic spirits like Seedlip is primarily due to consumer demand for more flavorful soda and mocktail alternatives.
- Answer: True.
2. Multiple Choice: What is the primary focus of Aplos, a new entrant in the non-alcoholic spirits market?
- A) Hemp-based spirits emphasizing relaxation.
- B) Traditional alcoholic spirits.
- C) High-alcohol content beverages.
- D) Carbonated soft drinks.
- Answer: A) Hemp-based spirits emphasizing relaxation.
3. Fill in the Blank: Wilderton Free, known for its _____, offers non-alcoholic spirits crafted using raw botanicals sourced globally.
- Answer: Bold, flavorful, layered.
4. True or False: Low-alcohol beverages like those from Alpenz are gaining popularity because they offer the same taste and quality as high-alcohol content drinks.
- Answer: True.
5. Multiple Choice: What unique approach is Alpenz known for in their low-alcohol beverage offerings?
- A) Mass-produced, generic flavors.

- B) Unique, high-quality selections like Cap Corse Blanc and Sotolon Selections.
- C) Only non-alcoholic options.
- D) Beverages with artificial flavoring.
- Answer: B) Unique, high-quality selections like Cap Corse Blanc and Sotolon Selections.

Chapter 10 – Article 7:

1. True or False: According to the Distilled Spirits Council of the United States, spirits have surpassed beer in revenue market share as of 2022.
- Answer: True.
2. Multiple Choice: Which American whiskey brand has a significant international presence and recently launched an American single malt whiskey?
- A) Jim Beam
- B) Jack Daniel's
- C) New Amsterdam Vodka
- D) Brooklyn Brewery
- Answer: B) Jack Daniel's.
3. Fill in the Blank: The acquisition of a stake in Brooklyn Brewery by _____ in 2016 raised discussions about the definition of "craft" beer.
- Answer: Kirin.
4. True or False: New Amsterdam Vodka, known for its affordability, is primarily focused on the domestic U.S. market and has not ventured into international markets.
- Answer: False.
5. Multiple Choice: When considering international expansion, U.S. liquor brands need to be particularly mindful of:
- A) Only marketing strategies.
- B) Just supply chain logistics.
- C) Understanding local cultures, tastes, and regulatory environments.
- D) Focusing solely on product quality.
- Answer: C) Understanding local cultures, tastes, and regulatory environments.

Chapter 10 – Article 8:

1. True or False: Virtual Reality (VR) in the adult beverage industry is primarily used for gaming purposes.
- Answer: False. VR is being used for immersive marketing experiences like virtual vineyard tours and tastings.
2. Multiple Choice: What does Augmented Reality (AR) offer in the context of the adult beverage industry?
- A) Only gaming experiences
- B) Enhanced shopping experiences with interactive labels

- C) Traditional marketing methods
- D) Product delivery services
- Answer: B) Enhanced shopping experiences with interactive labels
3. Fill in the Blank: 19 Crimes Wines is known for its innovative use of _____ in their wine labels to provide a unique consumer experience.
- Answer: Augmented Reality (AR)
4. True or False: The demand for personalized beverage experiences is diminishing in today's consumer landscape.
- Answer: False. There's a growing demand for personalized beverage experiences tailored to individual tastes and preferences.
5. Multiple Choice: Which technology is being used by wineries and breweries to offer virtual tours and tastings?
- A) Social Media
- B) Virtual Reality (VR)
- C) E-commerce platforms
- D) Traditional advertising
- Answer: B) Virtual Reality (VR)

Chapter 10 – Article 9:
1. True or False: The demand for sustainable and ethically produced beverages is decreasing in the modern consumer market.
- Answer: False. There is an increasing demand for sustainable and ethically produced beverages.
2. Multiple Choice: What trend has the pandemic catalyzed in the adult beverage industry?
- A) Decrease in online sales
- B) Surge in online sales and home deliveries
- C) Decline in the quality of beverages
- D) Shift towards non-alcoholic beverages only
- Answer: B) Surge in online sales and home deliveries
3. Fill in the Blank: The craft beer market has experienced a slowdown, which could be attributed to market _____ and pandemic challenges.
- Answer: Saturation
4. True or False: In the next 1-5 years, the adult beverage industry is expected to see a decline in e-commerce and digital marketing.
- Answer: False. The industry is expected to see continued growth in e-commerce and digital marketing.
5. Multiple Choice: What innovative concept is predicted for the adult beverage industry in the next 10-15 years?
- A) Traditional brick-and-mortar stores only
- B) Elimination of all digital marketing
- C) Virtual bars in the metaverse

- D) Return to pre-pandemic sales methods
- Answer: C) Virtual bars in the metaverse